Advanced Course in Yogi Philosophy and Oriental Occultism

YOGI RAMACHARAKA

Advanced Course in Yogi Philosophy, Y. Ramacharaka
Jazzybee Verlag Jürgen Beck
86450 Altenmünster, Loschberg 9
Deutschland

ISBN: 9783849676018

www.jazzybee-verlag.de
admin@jazzybee-verlag.de

Cover Design: © sweet_caramel - Fotolia.com

Printed by Createspace, North Charleston, SC, USA

CONTENTS:

PUBLISHER'S NOTICE

The twelve lessons forming this volume were originally issued in the shape of monthly lessons, known as "The Advanced Course in Yogi Philosophy and Oriental Occultism," during a period of twelve months beginning with October 1904, and ending September 1905. These lessons were intended as a continuation of, or sequel to "The Fourteen Lessons in Yogi Philosophy and Oriental Occultism" issued during the previous year.

We have been urged to print these "Advanced Course" lessons in book form, and the present volume is the result. Lessons i to iv, inclusive, consist of an analysis and explanation of the little occult manual known as "Light on the Path," and have been highly praised by lovers of that little book as well as advanced students in occultism. They are said to be superior to anything ever written along these lines. Lessons v to vii, inclusive, treat of the several branches of the Yogi Philosophy indicated by their titles. They contain very much information in a small space. Lessons viii and ix, treat of Dharma, the Yogi philosophy of Ethics or Right Action. They have been favorably received by students of ethics, and teachers of morality of different schools. They afford a common ground upon which the differing schools may meet. Lessons x to xii, inclusive, form a wonderful trio of lessons upon the higher Yogi metaphysical and scientific teachings. Their clearness and comprehensiveness is startling, and the most perplexing metaphysical and scientific questions are answered in the simplest manner by the centuries old, Yogi philosophy expressed in modern terms.

We trust that the "Advanced Course" lessons may prove as popular in book form as in their original shape. The author, as usual, declines to write a Preface for the book, saying that the lessons "should speak for themselves."

Yogi Publication Society.

Chicago, Ill. September 1, 1905.

LESSON I. SOME LIGHT ON THE PATH.

We greet our old students who have returned to us for the Advanced Course. We feel that, hereafter, it will not be necessary to repeat the elementary explanations which formed such an important part of the former class work, and we may be able to go right to the heart of the subject, feeling assured that each student is prepared to receive the same. Many read the former lessons from curiosity—some have become so interested that they wish to go on—others have failed to find the sensational features for which they had hoped, and have dropped from the ranks. It is ever so. Many come, but only a certain percentage are ready to go on. Out of a thousand seeds sown by the farmer, only a hundred manifest life. But the work is intended for that hundred, and they will repay the farmer for his labor. In our seed sowing, it is even more satisfactory, for even the remaining nine hundred will show life at some time in the future. No occult teaching is ever wasted—all bears fruit in its own good time. We welcome the students in the Advanced Course—we congratulate ourselves in having such a large number of interested listeners—and we congratulate the students in having reached the stage in which they feel such an interest in the work, and in being ready to go on.

We will take for the subject of our first lesson the Way of Attainment—The Path. And we know of no better method of directing the student's steps along The Path than to point out to him the unequaled precepts of the little manual "Light on the Path," written down by "M. C." (Mabel Collins, an English woman) at the request of some advanced mind (in or out of the flesh) who inspired it. In our notice in the last installment of the "Fourteen Lessons," we stated that we had in mind a little work which would perhaps make plainer the precepts of "Light on the Path." But, upon second thought, we have thought it preferable to make such writing a part of the Advanced Course, instead of preparing it as a separate book for general distribution and sale. In this way we may speak at greater length, and with less reserve, knowing that the students of the course will understand it far better than would the general public. So, the little book will not be published, and the teaching will be given only in these lessons. We will quote from the little manual, precept after precept, following each with a brief explanation.

In this connection it may be as well to state that "Light on the Path" is, practically, an inspired writing, and is so carefully worded that it is capable of a variety of interpretations—it carries a message adapted to the varying requirements of the several planes and stages of life. The student is able to extract meanings suited to his stage of development. In this respect the work is different from ordinary writing. One must take something to the book, before he is able to obtain something from it. In "The Illumined Way" the work is interpreted, in part, upon the lines of the psychic or astral plane. Our interpretation will be designed to apply to the life of the student entering upon The Path—the beginner. It will endeavor to explain the first several precepts in the light of "Karma Yoga," and will then try to point out the plain meaning of the precepts, pertaining to the higher desires; then passing on to an explanation of the precepts relating to the unfoldment of Spiritual Consciousness, which is indeed the key-note of the little manual. We will endeavor to make a little plainer to the student the hidden meanings of the little book—to put into plain homely English, the thoughts so beautifully expressed in the poetical imagery of the Orient. Our work will not contradict the interpretation given in "The Illumined Way"—it will merely go along side by side with it, on another plane of life. To some, it may seem a presumptuous undertaking to attempt to "interpret" that gem of occult teaching "Light on the Path"—but the undertaking has the approval of some for whose opinions we have respect—and has, what means still more to us—the approval of our Higher Self. Crude though our work may be, it must be intended to reach some—else it would not have been suggested.

"These rules are written for all disciples. Attend you to them."

These rules are indeed written for all disciples, and it will be well for us all to attend to them. For the rules for the guidance of occultists have always been the same, and will always remain the same—in all time—in all countries—and under whatever name the teaching is imparted. For they are based upon the principles of truth, and have been tried, tested and passed upon long ages ago, and have come down to us bearing the marks of the careful handling of the multitudes who have passed on before—our elder brothers in the Spirit—those who once trod the path upon which we are now entering—those who have passed on to heights which we shall one day mount.

These rules are for all followers of The Path—they were written for such, and there are none better. They come to us from those who know.

"Before the eyes can see, they must be incapable of tears. Before the ear can hear, it must have lost its sensitiveness. Before the voice can speak in the presence of the Masters, it must have lost the power to wound. Before the soul can stand in the presence of the Masters its feet must be washed in the blood of the heart."

Before the eyes can see with the clear vision of the Spirit, they must have grown incapable of the tears of wounded pride— unkind criticism—unmerited abuse—unfriendly remarks— slights—sarcasm—the annoyances of everyday life—the failures and disappointments of everyday existence. We do not mean that one should harden his soul against these things—on the contrary "hardening" forms no part of the occult teachings. On the material plane, one is constantly at the mercy of others on the same plane, and the more finely constituted one may be, the more keenly does he feel the pain of life, coming from without. And if he attempts to fight back—to pay off these backbitings and pinpricks in like kind—the more does he become enmeshed in the web of material life. His only chance of escape lies in growing so that he may rise above that plane of existence and dwell in the upper regions of the mind, and Spirit. This does not mean that he should run away from the world—on the contrary, if one attempts to run away from the world before he has learned its lessons, he will be thrust back into it, again and again, until he settles down to perform the task. But, nevertheless, one of spiritual attainment may so live that although he is in the midst of the fight of everyday life— yea, may be even a captain in the struggle—he really lives above it all—sees it for just what it is—sees it as but a childish game of child-like men and women, and although he plays the game well, he still knows it to be but a game, and not the real thing at all. This being the case, he begins by smiling through his tears, when he is knocked down in the rush of the game—then he ceases to weep at all, smiles taking the place of the tears, for, when things are seen in their true relation, one can scarcely repress a smile at himself, and at (or with) others. When one looks around and sees the petty playthings to which men are devoting their lives, believing that these playthings are real, he cannot but smile. And, when one awakens to a realization of the reality of things, his own particular part, which he is compelled to play, must evoke a smile from him. These are not mere dreams and impracticable ideas. If many of you had an idea of how many men, high in the puppet-play of worldly affairs, have really awakened to the truth, it would surprise you. Many of these men play their part well—with energy and apparent ambition—for they realize that there is a purpose behind it all, and that they are necessary parts of the machinery of evolution. But deep within the recesses of their souls, they know it all for what it is. One on The Path must needs be brave, and must acquire a mastery over the emotional nature. This precept does not merely refer to physical tears—for they often spring to the eyes involuntarily, and though we may be smiling at the time. It refers to the feeling that there is anything for us to really cry over. It is the thought back of the tears, rather than the tears themselves.

The lesson to be learned from these rules is that we should rise above the incidents of personality, and strive to realize our individuality. That we should desire to realize the I am consciousness, which is above the annoyances of personality. That we should learn that these things cannot hurt the Real Self—that they will be washed from the sands of time, by the waters of eternity.

Likewise our ear must lose its sensitiveness to the unpleasant incidents of personality, before it can hear the truth clearly, and free from the jarring noises of the outward strife. One must grow to be able to hear these things, and yet smile, secure in the knowledge of the soul and its powers, and its destiny. One must grow to be able to hear the unkind word—the unjust criticism—the spiteful remark—without letting them affect his real self. He must keep such things on the material plane to which they belong, and never allow his soul to descend to where it may be affected by them. One must learn to be able to hear the truths which are sacred to him, spoken of sneeringly and contemptuously by those who do not understand— they cannot be blamed, for they cannot understand. Let the babes prattle, and scold, and laugh—it does them good, and cannot hurt you or the Truth. Let the children play—it is their nature—some day they will (like you) have experienced the growing-pains of spiritual maturity, and will be going through just what you are now. You were once like them—they will be as you in time. Follow the old saying, and let such things "go in one ear, and out of the other"—do not let them reach your real consciousness. Then will the ear hear the things intended for it—it will afford a clear passage for the entrance of the Truth.

Yea, "before the voice can speak in the presence of the Masters, it must have lost its power to wound." The voice that scolds, lies, abuses, complains, and wounds, can never reach the higher planes upon which dwell the advanced intelligences of the race. Before it can speak so as to be heard by those high in the order of life, and spiritual intelligence, it must have long since forgotten how to wound others by unkind words, petty spite, unworthy speech. The advanced man does not hesitate to speak the truth even when it is not pleasant, if it seems right to do so, but he speaks in the tone of a loving brother who does not criticize from the "I am holier than thou" position, but merely feels the other's pain—sees his mistake—and wishes to lend him a helping hand. Such a one has risen above the desire to "talk back"—to "cut" another by unkind and spiteful remarks—to "get even" by saying, in effect, "You're another."

These things must be cast aside like a worn-out cloak—the advanced man needs them not.

"Before the soul can stand in the presence of the Masters, its feet must be washed in the blood of the heart"—this is a "hard saying" to many entering The Path. Many are led astray from the real meaning of this precept by their understanding of the word "heart"—they think it means the love nature. But this is not the meaning—occultism does not teach killing out true love—it teaches that love is one of the greatest privileges of man, and that as he advances his love nature grows until, finally, it includes all life. The "heart" referred to is the emotional nature, and the instincts of the lower and more animal mind. These things seem to be such a part of us, before we develop, that to get rid of them we seem to be literally tearing out our hearts. We part with first one thing and then another, of the old animal nature, with pain and suffering, and our spiritual feet become literally washed in the blood of the heart. Appetites— cravings of the lower nature—desires of the animal part of us—old habits—conventionalities—inherited thought—racial delusions—things in the blood and bone of our nature, must be thrown off, one by one, with much misgivings and doubt at first—and with much pain and heart-bleeding until we reach a position from which we can see what it all means. Not only the desires of the lower self are to be torn out, but we must, of necessity, part with many things which have always seemed dear and sacred to us, but which appear as but childish imaginings in the pure light which is beginning to be poured out from our Spiritual Mind. But even though we see these things for what they are, still it pains us to part from them, and we cry aloud, and our heart bleeds. Then we often come to a parting of the ways—a place where we are forced to part mental company with those who are dear to us, leaving them to travel their own road while we take step upon a new and (to us) an untried path of thought. All this means pain. And then the horror of mental and spiritual loneliness which comes over one soon after he has taken the first few steps on The Path—that first initiation which has tried the souls of many who read these words—that frightful feeling of being alone—with no one near who can understand and appreciate your feelings. And then, the sense of seeing the great problems of life, while others do not recognize the existence of any unsolved problem, and who accordingly go on their way, dancing, fighting, quarreling, and showing all the signs of spiritual blindness, while you were compelled to stand alone and bear the awful sight. Then, indeed, does the blood of your heart gush forth. And then, the consciousness of the world's pain and your failure to understand its meaning— your feeling of impotence when you tried to find a remedy for it. All this causes your heart to bleed. And all these things come from your spiritual awakening—the man of the material plane has felt none of these things—has seen them not. Then when the feet of the soul have been bathed in the blood of the heart, the eye begins to see the spiritual truths—the ear begins to hear them—the tongue begins to be able to speak them to others, and to converse with those who have advanced along The Path. And the soul is able to stand erect and gaze into the face of other advanced souls, for it has begun to understand the mysteries of life—the meaning of it all—has been able to grasp something of the Great Plan—has been able to feel the consciousness of its own existence—has been able to say: "I am" with meaning—has found itself—has conquered pain by rising above it. Take these thoughts with you into the Silence, and let the truth sink into your mind, that it may take root, grow, blossom, and bear fruit.

"1. Kill out ambition.

"2. Kill out desire of life.

"3. Kill out desire of comfort.

"4. Work as those work who are ambitious. Respect life as those who desire it. Be happy as those are who live for happiness."

Much of the occult truth is written in the form of paradox— showing both sides of the shield. This is in accordance with nature's plan. All statements of truth are but partial statements— there are two good sides to every argument—any bit of truth is but a half-truth, hunt diligently enough and you will find the opposite half—everything "is and it isn't"—any full statement of truth must of necessity be paradoxical. This because our finite point-of-view enables us to see but one side of a subject at a time. From the point of view of the infinite, all sides are seen at the same time—all points of a globe being visible to the infinite seer, who is also able to see through the globe as well as around it.

The above mentioned four precepts are illustrations of this law of paradox. They are generally dismissed as non-understandable by the average person who reads them. And yet they are quite reasonable and absolutely true. Let us consider them.

The key to the understanding of these (and all) truths, lies in the ability to distinguish between the "relative" or lower, point of view, and the "absolute" or higher, one. Remember this well, for it will help you to see into many a dark corner—to make easy many a hard saying. Let us apply the test to these four precepts.

We are told to: "Kill out ambition." The average man recoils from this statement, and cries out that such a course would render man a spiritless and worthless creature, for ambition seems to be at the bottom of all of man's accomplishments. Then, as he throws down the book, he sees, in the fourth precept: "Work as those who are ambitious"—and, unless he sees with the eyes of the Spiritual Mind, he becomes more confused than ever. But the two things are possible—yes, are absolutely feasible as well as proper. The "ambition" alluded to is that emotion which urges a man to attain from vainglorious, selfish motives, and which impels him to crush all in his path, and to drive to the wall all with whom he comes in contact. Such ambition is but the counterfeit of real ambition, and is as abnormal as is the morbid appetites which counterfeit and assume the guise of hunger and thirst—the ridiculous customs of decorating the persons with barbarous ornamentations, which counterfeits the natural instinct of putting on some slight covering as protection from the weather—the absurd custom of burdening oneself and others with the maintenance of palatial mansions, which counterfeits man's natural desire for a home-spot and shelter—the licentious and erotic practices of many men and women, which are but counterfeits of the natural sexual instincts of normal man and woman, the object of which is, primarily, the preservation of the race. The "ambitious" man becomes insane for success, because the instinct has become perverted and abnormal. He imagines that the things for which he is striving will bring him happiness, but he is disappointed—they turn to ashes like Dead Sea fruit— because they are not the source of permanent happiness. He ties himself to the things he creates, and becomes their slave rather than their master. He regards money not as a means of securing necessities and nourishment (mental and physical) for himself and others, but as a thing valuable of itself—he has the spirit of the miser. Or, he may seek power for selfish reasons—to gratify his vanity—to show the world that he is mightier than his fellow men—to stand above the crowd. All poor, petty, childish ambitions, unworthy of a real Man, and which must be outgrown before the man may progress—but perhaps the very lessons he is receiving are just the ones needed for his awakening. In short, the man of the abnormal ambition works for things for the sake of selfish reward, and is inevitably disappointed, for he is pinning his hopes on things which fail him in the hour of need—is leaning on a broken reed.

Now let us look upon the other side of the shield. The fourth precept contains these words : "Work as those work who are ambitious." There it is. One who works this way may appear to the world as the typical ambitious man, but the resemblance is merely outward. The "ambitious" man is the abnormal thing. The Man who works for work's sake—in obedience to the desire to work—the craving to create—because he gives full expression to the creative part of his nature—is the real thing. And the latter is able to do better work—more lasting work— than the first mentioned man. And, then, besides, he gains happiness from his work—he feels the joy which comes from doing—he lets the creative impulse of the All Life flow through him, and he does great things—he accomplishes, and is happy in his work and through his work. And so long as he keeps true to his ideals he will be safe and secure in that joy, and will be doing well his share in the world's work. But, as he mounts the ladder of Success, he is subjected to terrible temptations, and often allows the abnormal ambition to take possession of him, the result being that in his next incarnation he will have to learn his lesson all over again, and again until he has mastered it.

Every man has his work in the world to do, and he should do it the best he knows how—should do it cheerfully—should do it intelligently. And he should let have full expression that instinct which impels him to do things right—better than they have been done before (not that he may triumph over others, but because the world needs things done better).

True occultism does not teach that man should sit around doing nothing but meditating, with his gaze fastened upon his umbilicus, as is the custom with some of the ignorant Hindu fakirs and devotees, who ape the terms and language of the Yogi teachers, and prostitute their teachings. On the contrary, it teaches that it is man's duty and glorious privilege to participate in the world's work, and that he who is able to do something a little better than it has ever been done before is blessed, and a benefactor to the race. It recognizes the Divine urge to create, which is found in all men and women, and believes in giving it the fullest expression. It teaches that no life is fully rounded out and complete, unless some useful work is a part of it. It believes that intelligent work helps toward spiritual unfoldment, and is in fact necessary to it. It does not teach the beauty of unintelligent drudgery—for there is no beauty in such work— but it teaches that in the humblest task may be found interest to the one who looks for it, and that such a one always finds a better way of doing the thing, and thus adds something to the world's store of knowledge. It teaches the real ambition—that love of work for work's sake—rather than that work which is performed for the world's counterfeit reward. Therefore when the precept says: "Kill out Ambition ... Work as those work who are ambitious," you will understand it. This life is possible to those who understand "Karma Yoga," one of the great branches of the Yogi Philosophy, upon which it may be our privilege to write at some future time. Read over these words, until you fully grasp their meaning—until you feel them as well as see them. The gist of these teachings upon the subject of Ambition, may be summed up by saying: Kill out the relative Ambition, which causes you to tie yourself to the objects and rewards of your work, and which yields nothing but disappointment and repressed growth—but develop and express fully the absolute Ambition, which causes you to work for work's sake—for the joy which comes to the worker—from the desire to express the Divine instinct to create—and which causes you to do the thing you have to do, the best you know how—better than it has ever been done, if possible—and which enables you to work in harmony and unison with the Divine work which is constantly going on, instead of in harmony and discord. Let the Divine energy work through you, and express itself fully in your work. Open yourself to it, and you will taste of the joy which comes from work of this kind—this is the true ambition—the other is but a miserable counterfeit which retards the growth of the soul.

"Kill out desire of life," says the second precept—but the fourth precept answers back: "Respect life as those who desire it." This is another truth expressed in paradox. One must eradicate from the mind the idea that physical life is everything. Such an idea prevents one from recognizing the fuller life of the soul, and makes this particular life in the body the whole thing, instead of merely a grain of sand on the shores of the everlasting sea. One must grow to feel that he will always be alive, whether he is in the body or out of it, and that this particular physical "life" is merely a thing to be used by the Real Self, which cannot die. Therefore kill out that desire of life which causes you to fear death, and which makes you attach undue importance to the mere bodily existence, to the impairment of the broader life and consciousness. Pluck from your mind that idea that when the body dies, you die—for you live on, as much alive as you are this moment, possibly still more alive. See physical life for what it is, and be not deceived. Cease to look upon "death" with horror, whether it may come to you or to some loved one. Death is just as natural as life (in this stage of development) and as much to be happy about. It is hard to get rid of the old horror of physical dissolution, and one has many hard battles before he is able to cast off the worn-out delusion, which has clung to the race in spite of its constantly sounded belief in a future life. The churches teach of "the life beyond" to which all the faithful should look forward to, but the same "faithful" shiver and shudder at the thought of death, and clothe themselves in black when a friend dies, instead of strewing flowers around and rejoicing that the friend is "in a better land" (to use the cant phrase, which is so glibly used on such occasions, but which comforteth not). One must grow into a positive "feeling" or consciousness, of life everlasting, before he is able to cast off this old fear, and no creed, or expressed belief, will serve the purpose, until this state of consciousness is reached. To the one who "feels" in his consciousness this fact of the survival of individuality, and the continuance of life beyond the grave, death loses its terror, and the grave its horror, and the "desire of life" (relative) is indeed killed out, because the knowledge of life (absolute) has taken its place.

But we must not forget the reverse side of the shield. Read again the fourth precept: "Respect life as those who desire it." This does not mean alone the life of others, but has reference to your own physical life as well. For in your letting-go of the old idea of the relative importance of the life in the body, you must avoid going to the other extreme of neglect of the physical body. The body is yours in pursuance of the Divine plan, and is in fact the Temple of the Spirit. If it were not good for you to have a body, rest assured you would not have it. It is needed by you in this stage of development, and you would be unable to do your work of spiritual unfoldment without it.

Therefore, do not be led into the folly of despising the body, or physical life, as a thing unworthy of you. They are most worthy of you, at this stage, and you may make great things possible through them. To despise them is like refusing to use the ladder which will enable you to reach the heights. You should, indeed, "respect life as those who desire it," and you should respect the body as do those who think that the body is the self. The body should be recognized as the instrument of the soul and Spirit, and should be kept as clean, healthy and strong as may be. And every means should be used to prolong the "life" in the body which has been given you. It should be respected and well-used. Do not sit and pine over your confinement in this life—you will never have another chance to live out just the experiences you are getting now—make the best of it. Your "life" is a glorious thing, and you should live always in the "Now" stage, extracting to the full the joy which should come with each moment of life to the advanced man. "Life, life, more life" has cried out some writer, and he was right. Live out each moment of your life, in a normal, healthy, clean way, always knowing it for what it is, and worrying not about the past or future. You are in eternity now as much as you ever will be—so why not make the most of it. It is always "Now" in life—and the supply of "Nows" never fails.

If you ask us for a summing-up of this idea of this non-desiring of life, and its opposite side of respecting it as if you really did desire it, we will say: The desire referred to is the relative desire, which springs from the mistaken idea that physical life is the only life. The absolute desire of life, arises from the knowledge of what the whole life of man is, and what this brief physical life is—therefore while the advanced man does not desire it in the old way, he does not despise it, and really desires it because it forms a part of his whole life, and he does not wish to miss, or part with, any part of that which the Divine Plan has decreed shall be his. The advanced man neither fears death, nor seeks it— he fears neither death nor life—he desires neither (relatively) and yet he desires both, from the absolute sense. Such a man or woman is invincible—neither life nor death have any terrors for such a one. When this consciousness is once reached, the person is filled with such power that its radiance is felt by the world in which he moves. Remember these words: Fear neither death, nor life. Neither fear death, nor seek it. When you have attained this stage, then indeed will you know what life is— what death is—for both are manifestations of life.

The third precept, tells us to "Kill out desire of comfort"—but the fourth adds: "Be happy as those are who live for happiness." This teaching is also paradoxical, and follows the same line as the ones just spoken of. Its apparent contradiction arises from the two view-points, i. e. the relative and the absolute. Apply this solvent to all apparently contradictory occult teaching, and you will be able to separate each part so that you may carefully examine it. Let us apply it to this case.

"Kill out desire of comfort." At first this would seem to advocate extreme asceticism, but this is not the real meaning. Much that is called asceticism is really a running away from things which we may think are too pleasant. There seems to be an idea in the minds of many people of all shades of religious belief, that because a thing produces pleasure it must necessarily be "bad." Some writer has made one of his characters say: "It is so sad—it seems as if all the pleasant things in life are wicked." There seems to be a current belief that God takes pleasure in seeing people unhappy and doing unpleasant things, and accordingly many so-called "religious" people have frowned upon the normal pleasures of life, and have acted as if a smile was offensive to Deity. This is all a mistake. All normal pleasures are given to Man to use—but none of them must be allowed to use Man. Man must always be the master, and not the slave, in his relation to the pleasures of life. In certain forms of occult training the student is instructed in the cultivation of the Will, and some of the exercises prescribed for him consist of the doing of disagreeable and unpleasant things. But this discipline is merely to strengthen the Will of the student, and not because there is any special merit in the disagreeable task, or any special virtue in the self-denial attendant upon the doing without certain pleasant accustomed things. The whole idea consists in the exercising of the Will to resist; do without; and to do things; contrary to the usual custom and habits of the individual, which course, if practiced, will invariably result in a strengthening of the Will. It operates upon the principle of exercising a muscle by calling it into play. These exercises and practices are good, and we may have occasion to refer to them in some of our lessons. The fast-days and penance prescribed by the Catholic church have merit in the manner above indicated, outside of any particular religious significance.

But, to get back to our subject, this precept is not intended to preach asceticism. Occultism does not insist upon that. It does teach, however, that one should not allow himself to be tied to the pleasures and comforts of life to such an extent that he will cease to advance and develop his higher nature. Man may be ruined by too much luxury, and many cases are known where the higher influences at work under the Law took away from a man those things which hindered his growth, and placed him in a position in which he was forced to live normally, and thereby grow and unfold. Occultism preaches the "Simple Life." It teaches that when a man has too many things he is apt to let the things own him, instead of his owning the things. He becomes a slave rather than a master. "Kill out desire of comfort" does not mean that one should sleep on rough boards, as a special virtue pleasing to Deity, or that one should eat dry crusts in the hopes of obtaining Divine favor—neither of these things will have any such effect—Deity may not be bribed and is not specially pleased at the spectacle of one of his children making a fool of himself. But the precept does impress upon us that we should not be tied to any ideas of comfort, and that we should not imagine that true happiness can arise from any such cause. Enjoy the normal and rational pleasures of life, but always retain your mastery over them, and never allow them to run away with you. And, always remember that true happiness comes from within, and that these luxuries and "comforts" are not necessities of the real man, and are merely things to be used for what they are worth. These creature comforts and luxuries are merely incidents of the physical plane, and do not touch the Real Self. The advanced man uses all these things, as instruments, tools (or even toys if it is found necessary to join in the game-life of others), but he always knows them for what they are and is never deceived. The idea that they are necessary for his happiness would seem absurd to him. And, as a man advances spiritually, his tastes are apt to become simpler. He may like well-made things of good quality, best suited for their purpose, but he does not want so many of them, and ostentation and display become very foreign to his tastes and inclinations. He does not necessarily have to "kill out" the last mentioned tastes—they are very apt to leave him of themselves, finding his mental quarters not suited to their accommodation.

Remember, also, that the fourth precept instructs you to "Be happy as those are who live for happiness." This does away with the long-face and dreary atmosphere idea. It says "be happy" (not "make believe you are happy") as happy as those who live for the so-called happiness coming from the things of the physical plane. That is the sane teaching. Be happy—so live that you may obtain a healthy, normal happiness out of every hour of your life. The occultist is not a miserable, sour-visaged, gloomy man, common beliefs to the contrary notwithstanding. His life and understanding lifts him above the worries and fears of the race, and his knowledge of his destiny is most inspiring. He is able to rise above the storm, and, riding safely on the crest of the wave—yielding to every motion of the swell—he escapes being submerged. When things become too unpleasant to be borne on the relative plane, he simply rises into the higher regions of his mind where all is serene and calm, and he gains a peace that will abide with him when he again sinks to meet the trials and burdens of the day. The occultist is the happiest of men, for he has ceased to fear—he knows that there is nothing to be afraid of. And he has outgrown many of the superstitions of the race, which keep many people in torment. He has left Hate and Malice behind him, and has allowed Love to take their vacant places, and he must, necessarily, be happier by reason of the change. He has outgrown the idea of an angry Deity laying traps in which to enmesh him—he has long since learned to smile at the childish tale of the devil with cloven hoofs and horns, breathing fire and brimstone, and keeping a bottomless pit into which one will be plunged if he should happen to forget to say his prayers, or if he should happen to smile at God's beautiful earth, some fine Sunday, instead of drowsing away an hour listening to some long-drawn-out theological sermon. He has learned that he is a Child of God, destined for great things, and that Deity is as a loving Father (yes, and Mother) rather than as a cruel taskmaster. He realizes that he has arrived at the age of maturity, and that his destiny rests to some extent upon himself. The occultist is necessarily an optimist—he sees that all things are working together for good—that life is on the path of attainment—and that Love is over, above, and in all. These things the occultist learns as he progresses—and he is Happy. Happier than "those who live for happiness."

"Seek in the heart the source of evil, and expunge it. It lives fruitfully in the heart of the devoted disciple, as well as in the heart of the man of desire. Only the strong can kill it out. The weak must wait for its growth, its fruition, its death. And it is a plant that lives and increases throughout the ages. It flowers when the man has accumulated unto himself innumerable existences. He who will enter upon the path of power must tear this thing out of his heart. And then the heart will bleed, and the whole life of the man seem to be utterly dissolved. This ordeal must be endured; it may come at the first step of the perilous ladder which leads to the path of life; it may not come until the last. But, O disciple, remember that it has to be endured, and fasten the energies of your soul upon the task. Live neither in the present nor the future, but in the eternal. This giant weed cannot flower there; this blot upon existence is wiped out by the very atmosphere of eternal thought."

The above admonition is a summing up of the first three precepts, as explained by the fourth one. It bids the student seek out in his heart the relative idea of life and cast it from him. This relative idea of life carries with it the selfish part of our nature—that part of us which causes us to regard ourselves as better than our brother—as separate from our fellow-beings—as having no connection with all of life. It is the idea of the lower part of our mind—our merely refined animalism. Those who have carefully studied our former course will understand that this part of our mind is the brute side of us—the side of us which is the seat of the appetites, passions, desires of a low order, and emotions of the lower plane. These things are not evil of themselves, but they belong to the lower stages of life— the animal stage—the stage from which we have passed (or are now passing) to the stage of the Man existence. But these tendencies were long ages in forming, and are deeply imbedded in our nature, and it requires the most heroic efforts to dislodge them—and the only way to dislodge them is to replace them by higher mental states. Right here, let us call your attention to a well established principle of occult training, and yet one that is seldom mentioned in teachings on the subject. We refer to the fact that a bad habit of thought or action is more easily eradicated by supplanting it with a good habit—one that is directly opposed to the habit of which one desires to get rid. To tear out a bad habit by the roots, requires almost superhuman strength of will, but to crowd it out by nursing a good habit in its place, is far more easier and seems to be nature's plan.

The good habit will gradually crowd the bad one until it cannot exist, and then after a final struggle for life, it will expire. This is the easiest way to "kill out" undesirable habits and traits.

Returning to the subject of the relative qualities of the mind, we would say that selfishness; all the animal desires, including sexual desires on the physical plane (there is much more in sex than physical plane manifestations); all passions, such as hatred, envy, malice, jealousy, desire for revenge, self-glorification, and self-exaltation; are also a part of it. Low pride is one of its most subtle and dangerous manifestations, and one which returns again, and again, after we think we have cast it off—each return being in a more subtle form—physical pride, being succeeded by the pride of the intellect—pride in psychic attainments— pride in spiritual development and growth—pride in moral worth, chastity and character—the "I am holier than thou" pride—and so on. Again and again does pride, the tempter, come to bother us. Its existence is based upon the delusion of separateness, which leads us to imagine that we have no connection with other manifestations of life, and which causes us to feel a spirit of antagonism and unworthy rivalry toward our fellow beings, instead of recognizing the fact that we are all parts of the One Life—some far back struggling in the mire of the lower stages of the road—others traveling along the same stage of the journey as ourselves—others still further advanced—but all on the way—all being bits of the same great Life. Beware of Pride—this most subtle enemy of advancement—and supplant it with the thought that we are all of the same origin—having the same destiny before us—having the same road to travel— brothers and sisters all—all children of God—all little scholars in Life's great Kindergarten. Let us also realize that while each must stand alone before he is able to pass the test of initiation— yet are we all interdependent, and the pain of one is the pain of all—the sin of one is the sin of all—that we are all parts of a race working toward race improvement and growth—and that love and the feeling of brotherhood is the only sane view of the question.

The brute instincts are still with us, constantly forcing themselves into our field of thought. Occultists learn to curb and control these lower instincts, subordinating them to the higher mental ideals which unfold into the field of consciousness. Do not be discouraged if you still find that you have much of the animal within your nature—we all have—the only difference is that some of us have learned to control the brute, and to keep him in leash and subordinate and obedient to the higher parts of our nature, while others allow the beast to rule them, and they shiver and turn pale when he shows his teeth, not seeming to realize that a firm demeanor and a calm mind will cause the beast to retreat to his corner and allow himself to be kept behind bars. If you find constant manifestations of the beast within you, struggling to be free and to assert his old power, do not be disturbed. This is no sign of weakness, but is really an indication that your spiritual growth has begun. For whereas you now recognize the brute, and feel ashamed, you formerly did not realize his presence—were not aware of his existence, for you were the brute himself. It is only because you are trying to divorce yourself from him, that you feel ashamed of his presence. You cannot see him until you begin to be "different" from him. Learn to be a tamer of wild beasts, for you have a whole menagerie within you. The lion; the tiger; the hyena; the ape; the pig; the peacock, and all the rest are there, constantly showing forth some of their characteristics. Do not fear them—smile at them when they show themselves—for you are stronger than they, and can bring them to subjection—and their appearance is useful to you in the way of instructing you as to their existence. They are an amusing lot, when you have reached the stage where you are able to practically stand aside and see them perform their tricks, and go through their antics. You then feel strongly that they are not you, but something apart from you—something from which you are becoming rapidly divorced. Do not worry about the beasts—for you are the master.

While the above quotation from "Light on the Path" includes all of the foregoing manifestations of the lower nature, it seems to dwell especially upon that delusion of the lower self—that dream of separateness—that exhibition of what has been called "the working fiction of the universe," which causes us to imagine ourselves things apart from the rest—something better, holier, and superior to the rest of our kind. This manifests in the emotion of Pride—the peacock part of our mental menagerie. As we have said, this is one of the most dangerous of our lower qualities, because it is so subtle and persistent. You will note that the writer speaks of it as living "fruitfully in the heart of the devoted disciple, as well as in the heart of the man of desire." This may seem strange to you, but it is the experience of every advanced occultist that, long after he had thought he had left Pride behind him, he would be startled at it appearing in a new phase—the pride of psychic power—the pride of intellect— the pride of spiritual growth. And then he would have all his work to do over again. Let us state right here that there is a kind of pride which is not a manifestation of the lower self—it may be called the absolute form of pride, if you will. We allude to that pride in things as a whole—a pride that the whole is so great and grand and wonderful, and that we are parts of that whole—that the intellect we manifest is part of that universal mind—that the spiritual growth we have attained is a bit of the great possibilities of the race, and that much more is ahead for all the race. But the danger line is reached when we begin to shut out some others from that universal pride—the moment that we leave out one other manifestation of life (no matter how lowly) from our universal pride, then we make it a selfish pride. The moment we erect a fence with anyone on the outside, then are we indulging in selfish pride. For there is no outside, at the last. We are all inside—there is no place outside of the All. When you feel a pride with all living things—with all of life—with all of being—then you are not selfish. But the moment you place yourself apart in a class—whether that class be composed of but yourself, or of yourself and all of mankind, except one individual—then you are yielding to a subtle form of selfishness. The last man must not be left out—cannot be left out. You are possessed of no quality or attainment that is not the property of the race—something that may be attained by all in time. All that you think is superiority is merely a little more age—a little more experience on this plane of existence. Your pride is the foolish infantile pride of the child who has just passed out of "the baby class" in the primary school and looks condescendingly upon the new flock of little ones who are just entering the class from which he has just passed. To the eyes of those in higher classes, the second grade scholar is a subject for a kindly, pitying smile—but the little fellow does not know that—he feels "big," and gives the peacock quality full sway. Now, before we leave this illustration, let us say that the little fellow is justified in feeling proud of having accomplished his advancement—it is a worthy feeling—the peacock part comes in only when he looks down upon those below him. This is the substance of the folly of Pride—this feeling of superiority toward those still in the lower grade. A feeling of joy from work attained—heights scaled—is not unworthy. But let us beware of the attendant feeling of superiority toward those who are still climbing—there lies the sting of Pride. Extract the sting, and your wasp is harmless.

If you feel tempted toward self-glorification, sometimes, just remember that as compared to some of the intelligences, who have long since passed through your present stage of development, you are no more than is the intelligence of a black beetle as compared with your own intellect—that, to the eyes of some of the greatly developed souls, the everyday life of even the highest of our race on earth to-day is but as are to us the antics and gambols; fights and tumbles; of a lot of Newfoundland puppies whose eyes have been opened but a few days—just remember this, we say, and you will get a better idea of just what place you fill in the scale of intelligence. But this does not mean self-debasement, either. Not at all. As low comparatively, as we may be, we are still well on the way of advancement, and great things are before us—we cannot be robbed of a single bit of life—we cannot be denied our heritage—we are going on, and on, and on, to greater and still greater heights. But, impress this upon your soul—not only are you going there, but all of mankind besides—yes, even that last man. Do not forget this. On the plane of the eternal, there cannot be such a thing as selfish pride—understanding has forever wiped it out—"this giant weed cannot flower there; this blot upon existence is wiped out by the very atmosphere of eternal thought."

We must carry over to the next lesson the remainder of our comments on the above quotation.

LESSON II. MORE LIGHT ON THE PATH.

Before passing to the consideration of the next precept, we must again call your attention to the quotation from "Light on the Path" which we had before us at the close of the last lesson, but which we were compelled to carry over to this lesson, because of lack of space. In the quotation referred to appears the sentence: "Live neither in the present nor the future, but in the eternal." This sentence has perplexed many students, in view of the fact that the teachings have impressed upon them the importance of living in the Now, and of looking forward to the future as the field for further development. And this sentence seems to run contrary to the previous teachings. But it is all a matter of absolute and relative point of view, again.

Let us see if we can make it plain to you. To live in the present, regarding it as something different from the future—or to live (in imagination) in the future, in the sense that it is considered as a separate thing from the present—is an error, springing from the relative view of life. It is the old mistake which causes us to separate time from eternity. The absolute view of the matter shows us that time and eternity are one—that we are in eternity right now, as much as we ever shall be. It does away with the error that a broad line is drawn between this time of mortal life and the "eternity" into which we enter after we have passed out of the body—it shows us that here—right here in the flesh—we are in eternity. It reveals to us that this life is but an infinitesimal part of the great life—that it is merely sunrise in the great day of consciousness—and that to live as if this petty period of life were all is the veriest folly of ignorant mankind. But right here, do not fall into the error of going to the other extreme and ignoring and despising the present life in your desire to "live in the future"—remember the paradox that is to be found in all statements of the truth—the reverse side of the shield. To despise the present life is as ridiculous as to live as if it were all the life there is. To follow this course is to commit the folly of "living in the future," against which the little manual cautions us. This life (small and insignificant though it may be as compared to the great life) is most important to us—it is a stage in our development that is needed by us, and we must not shirk it or despise it. We are just where we are, because it is the very best place for us at this stage of our development, and we cannot afford to spend this life in merely dreaming of the future, for we have tasks to perform—lessons to learn—and we will never be able to advance until we master our present grade duties. This present life is not all—but it is part of all—remember this.

These difficulties of the distinction between the present and future vanish when we regard them from the absolute view-point. The moment that we become fully conscious that the eternal is the only real thing—and that Now is all of eternity that we are able to grasp with our consciousness—that it is always Now with us, and always will be Now—when we realize this, then do the relative terms "present" and "future" lose their former meanings to us, and time and eternity; yesterday, today, tomorrow; and forever and forever; are seen to be but slightly different manifestations of the great eternal Now, in which we live at each moment of our existence. This living in the eternal makes us enjoy every moment of our present life—allows us to look forward to the future without fear—causes us to feel the consciousness of what real life is—helps us to realize the I Am consciousness—allows us to perceive things in their right relations—in short, gives to life a reality that it otherwise lacks, and causes the old relative views to drop from us like the withered leaves from the rose. As the writer of "Light on the Path" so beautifully says: "This giant weed cannot flourish there; this blot upon existence is wiped out by the very atmosphere of eternal thought."

5. Kill out all sense of separateness.

6. Kill out desire for sensation.

7. Kill out the hunger for growth.

8. Yet stand alone and isolated, because nothing that is embodied, nothing that is conscious of separation, nothing that is out of the eternal can aid you.

Learn from sensation, and observe it; because only so can you commence the science of self-knowledge, and plant your foot on the first step of the ladder. Grow as the flower grows, unconsciously, but eagerly anxious to open its soul to the air. So must you press forward to open your soul to the eternal. But it must be the eternal that draws forth your strength and beauty, not desire of growth. For, in the one case, you develop in the luxuriance of purity; in the other, you harden by the forcible passion for personal stature. Here again are we confronted with a set of paradoxical precepts, the first three of which tell us to kill out certain things, and the fourth of which then proceeds to tell us (apparently) to do the very things which we have just been advised not to do. This is another example of the Divine Paradox which underlies all occult teachings—the two sides of the shield. Read what we have said on this subject, on pages 16–17, Lesson 1. What we have said there applies to nearly all of the precepts of "Light on the Path."

In the fifth precept we are told to "Kill out all sense of separateness." The eighth precept gives us the reverse side of the shield : "Yet stand alone and isolated, because nothing that is embodied, nothing that is conscious of separation, nothing that is out of the eternal, can aid you." Here we have two vital truths imparted to us—and yet the two are but different sides of the same truth. Let us consider it.

The sense of separateness that causes us to feel as if we were made of different material from our fellow men and women— that makes us feel self-righteous—that makes us thank God that we are different from, and better than, other men—is error, and arises from the relative point of view. The advanced occultist knows that we are all parts of the One Life—varying only as we have unfolded so as to allow the higher parts of our nature to manifest through us. The lowly brother is but as we were once, and he will some day occupy the same position that we now do. And both he and we will surely mount to still greater heights—and if he learns his lessons better than do we, he may outstrip us in development. And besides this, we are bound up with the lives of every other man and woman. We participate in the conditions which contribute to their sin and shame. We allow to exist in our civilization conditions and environments which contribute largely to crime and misery. Every mouthful we eat—every garment we wear—every dollar we earn—has had some connection with other people, and their lives and ours are intermingled—we touch all mankind at thousands of points. The law of cause and effect makes close companions of persons apparently as far apart as the poles. What we call sin is often the result of ignorance and misdirected energy—if we were in exactly the same position as those who do wrong—with the same temperament, training, environment, and opportunity—would we do so very much better than they? All life is on the Path—we are all advancing slowly—often slipping back two feet for every three we advance, but still registering a net advance of one foot. And all are really trying to do the best they can, although often the appearances are very much against them. None of us are so very good or perfect—then why should we be so ready to condemn. Let us lend a helping hand whenever we can, but let us not say, "I am holier than thou." Let us remember the precept of the great Master who warned us to cast the first stone only when we were free from sin ourselves. Let us avoid the sense of separateness in the relative sense, for it is a snare and a delusion, and the parent of nearly all error.

But now for the other side of the shield. Let us learn to stand alone—we must learn this lesson in order to advance. Our life is our own—we must live it ourselves. No one else may live it for us—and we may live the life of no one else. Each must stand squarely upon his own feet. Each is accountable for his own acts. Each must reap that which he has sown. Each must suffer or enjoy according to his own acts. Man is responsible only to himself and the Eternal. Nothing outside of the Eternal and himself can aid him. Each soul must work out its own destiny, and no other soul may do the work of another. Each soul contains within it the light of the Spirit, which will give it all the help it requires, and each soul must learn to look within for that help. The lesson of Courage and Self-Reliance must be learned by the growing soul. It must learn that while nothing from without can help it, it is equally true that nothing from without can harm it. The Ego is proof against all harm and hurt, once it realizes the fact. It is indestructible, and eternal. Water cannot drown it—fire cannot burn it—it cannot be destroyed—it is and always will be. It should learn to be able to stand erect—upon its own feet. If it needs the assurance of the presence of an unfailing helper—one that is possessed of unlimited power and wisdom—let it look to the Eternal—all that it needs is there.

The sixth precept tells us to "Kill out desire for sensation." And the eighth tells us to "Learn from sensation, and observe it, because only so can you commence the science of self-knowledge, and plant your foot upon the first step of the ladder." Another paradox. Let us try to find the key.

The warning in the sixth precept bids us to let drop the desire for sense gratification. The pleasures of the senses belong to the relative plane. We begin by enjoying that which appeals to the grosser senses, and from that we gradually work up the enjoyment of that which comes through higher senses. We outgrow certain forms of sense gratification. We pass from sensuality to sensuousness, in its lower and higher degrees.

There is a constant evolution in sense gratification in man. The things we enjoyed yesterday, seem crude and gross to us to-day, and so it will always be, as we pass onward and upward in the scale of life. We must cease to be tied to the gratification of the senses—the soul has higher pleasures awaiting it. The pleasures of the senses are all right in their place—they have their offices to perform in the evolution of the soul—but the soul must beware of allowing itself to be tied to them, as its progress will be retarded if it does so—useless baggage must be cast aside as the soul mounts the upward path—light marching order is the proper thing. The ties which bind you to sense gratification must be boldly cut, that you may go on your way. Therefore "Kill out desire for sensation." Remember, the precept does not say that you should kill out sensation—only the desire for sensation.

Neither desire sensation, nor run away from it as an evil thing.

Turn sensation to good account, by studying it, and learning its lessons, that you may see it for what it is really worth, and thus be able to drop it from you.

As the eighth precept tells you: "Learn from sensation, and observe it; because only so can you commence the science of self-knowledge, and plant your foot upon the first step of the ladder."

This does not mean that you should yield to sense-gratification in order to learn its lessons—the advanced soul should have passed beyond this stage. Sensations may be studied as if from the outside, and it is not necessary to indulge a sense in order to learn the lesson it has to teach you. The real meaning of this last precept is that when we find that we experience certain sense feelings—sensations—we should weigh, measure, gauge and test them, instead of viewing them with horror. These things are a part of us—they come from the Instinctive Mind, and are our heritage from our previous lowly states of existence. They are not bad in themselves, but are simply unworthy of us in our present stage of development. They are the shadows of our former selves—the reflection of things which were proper and natural in us in our more animal states, but which we are now outgrowing. You may learn great lessons by noting the symptoms of these dying sense-manifestations, and thereby will be enabled to cast them away from you sooner than if you allow yourself to fear them as the manifestations of an evil entity outside of yourself—the temptings of a personal Devil. In time you will outgrow these things, their places being filled with something better and more worthy. But in the meantime, view them as you would the instinctive desire to perform some trick of childhood, which while once natural is now unnatural and undesirable. Many grown persons have had much trouble in getting rid of the old baby trick of sucking the thumb, or twisting a lock of hair between the fingers, which while considered as quite "cute" in the baby days, nevertheless brought upon the growing child many reproaches and punishments, and in after years, often required the exercise of the will of the adult to cast it aside as an undesirable thing. Let us so view these symptoms of the baby-days of our soul-life, and let us get rid of them by understanding them, their nature, history, and meaning, instead of fearing them as the "work of the Devil." There is no Devil but Ignorance and Fear.

The seventh precept tells us to "Kill out desire for growth," and yet the eighth advises us to grow—"Grow as the flower grows, unconsciously, but eagerly anxious to open its soul to the air. So must you press forward to open your soul to the eternal. But it must be the eternal that draws forth your strength and beauty, not desire of growth. For in the one case you develop in the luxuriance of purity; in the other, you harden by the forcible passion for personal stature."

The writer of the above words has made so plain the meaning of this two-fold statement of truth, that very little comment upon the same is needed, even for those just entering upon the Path. The distinction between the "desire for growth," and the unfoldment that comes to the advancing soul lies in the motive.

"Desire for growth," in the relative sense, means desire for growth for self-glorification—a subtle form of vanity—and a refined form of selfish ambition. And this desire, as applied to spiritual, tends toward what occultists know as "black magic," which consists of a desire for spiritual power to use for selfish ends, or even for the mere sense of power that such development brings. The student of occultism cannot be warned too often against such desires and practices—it is the dark side of the picture, and those who pursue the descending path meet with a terrible punishment by reason of their own acts, and are often compelled to labor for ages before they find their way back to the Path upon which the sun of the Spirit shines brightly.

The natural growth of the soul—that growth which is compared to that of the flower—gradual and unconscious, but yet eager in the sense of opening up one's soul to the beneficent rays of the great Central Sun of Life—the growth which consists in "letting" rather than forcing, is the growth to be desired. This growth comes to us each day, if we but open ourselves to it. Let the soul unfold, and the Spirit will gradually manifest itself to your consciousness. Many students torment themselves, and their teachers, by their eager questionings, "what shall I do?" The only answer is "stand aside from your labored efforts, and just let yourself grow." And you will grow in this way. Every day will add to your experience—every year will find you further along the path. You may think that you are making no progress—but just compare yourself to the self of a year ago, and you will notice the improvement. Go on, living your life, the best you know how—doing the work before you in the manner that seems best for you, day-by-day—worrying not about your future life—living in the great and glorious Now—and allowing the Spirit to work through you in confidence and faith and love. And, dear student, all will be well with you. You are on the right road—keep to the middle of it—enjoy the scenery as you pass along—enjoy the refreshing breezes—enjoy the night as well as the day—it is all good—and you are making progress without feeling the strain of the journey. The man who counts the mile-stones and worries about how much farther he has to go, and how slow he is moving, makes his journey doubly tiresome, and loses all the beauty of the roadside. Instead of thinking about what he is seeing, he is thinking merely of miles, miles, miles, and many more miles ahead. Which is the course of wisdom?

9. Desire only that which is within you.

10. Desire only that which is beyond you.

11. Desire only that which is unattainable.

12. For within you is the light of the world, the only light that can be shed upon the Path.

If you are unable to perceive it within you, it is useless to look for it elsewhere. It is beyond you; because, when you reach it, you have lost yourself. It is unattainable, because it forever recedes. You will enter the light, but you will never touch the flame. These four precepts form another of the many paradoxes contained in the wonderful little manual upon which we are commenting. To those who have not found its key, these four precepts seem strangely contradictory and "wild." To be told to desire a thing that is within you—and yet beyond you—and which is unattainable, seems ridiculous to the average man on the street. But, when one has the key, the teachings seem very plain and beautiful. The four precepts refer to the unfoldment of Spiritual Consciousness—Illumination—which we attempted to faintly describe in our first series of lessons (The Fourteen Lessons). This is the first great attainment before us on the path.

It means everything to the occultist at this stage of the journey, for it takes him from the plane of mere "belief" or intellectual acquiescence, on to the plane where he knows that he is. It does not endow him permanently with universal knowledge, but it gives him that consciousness of real spiritual existence, compared to which every other experience and knowledge sinks into nothing. It brings one face-to-face (perhaps only for a moment) with the Real Self, and the great Reality of which that Self is but a part. This state of consciousness is the great prize which is awaiting the efforts of the race to free itself, and it is a reward worth many lives of unfoldment to attain.

"Desire only that which is within you"—for the Spirit is the only reality, and it is within each of us. As the text says: "For within you is the light of the world, the only light that can be shed upon the Path. If you are unable to perceive it within you, it is useless to look for it elsewhere." Why do not these anxious seekers after truth, take this advice and look within themselves for that which they seek, instead of running hither and thither, after teachers, prophets, seers, and leaders—exhausting first one strange teaching, and then another. All this is useful— because it teaches us that that which we seek is not to be found in this way. And you will never find what you seek, in such ways. You may get a hint here, or a suggestion there—but the real thing is right within yourself waiting patiently for that hour when you will look within for it, confidently, hopefully, and lovingly. Oh, listen to the voice of the soul—look for the light of the Spirit. You have them both within you—why seek further for that which can never reach you from the outside.

"Desire only that which is beyond you." "It is beyond you; because when you reach it, you have lost yourself." It is always just beyond you, and when you become one with it, the old relative self has faded away, and a greater, grander you has replaced it. Man must lose himself to find Himself. In this sense, the great thing to be desired is beyond the to-day "you," although it is within you—it is really Yourself, as you will be.

Can we make this plainer? The child longs for manhood—it is beyond him, and yet the child is the embryo man, and the elements of manhood are within him, awaiting the hour of development. But when that child attains manhood, the child is gone—he has lost himself, and a larger self has taken its place. So that the thing for which the child longs, really causes him to lose his (child) self in its attainment. The butterfly is within the caterpillar—but it is also beyond him—and when he gains it he is no longer a caterpillar but a butterfly. These are crude illustrations, but perhaps they may help you to understand the matter more clearly.

"Desire only that which is unattainable." This sounds discouraging, but, when understood, it really gives renewed energy. The text goes on: "It is unattainable, because it forever recedes. You may enter the light, but you will never touch the flame." As the soul gains in spiritual consciousness, it becomes greater and grander, but it is traveling but the first steps in the real journey—but that journey is becoming more and more pleasant. As we climb the mountain side of Attainment, the view becomes grander at each step. But the mountain top, which seemed so near at the beginning of the journey, seems constantly to recede as one climbs. And yet there is no disappointment, for every step of the way is now accompanied with the keenest pleasure. It is ever so in soul-unfoldment. As step after step is taken, greater heights appear to the view, emerging from the clouds which have surrounded them. There are undreamt of heights. You may, and will, gain the highest point now visible to you (be your attainment ever so great at this moment) but when you get there you will find that there is as much before you as you have left behind—far more in fact. But all this does not disappoint you, when you once grasp its significance. As you enter the great light you become conscious of gradually nearing the great center of Light—but although you are fairly bathed in the glorious effulgence, you have not touched the flame—and never will, as Man. But what of that—why fret because you cannot see the end—if end there be. You are destined to become something so much greater and grander than you are to-day, that your wildest imaginings cannot give you the faintest idea of it. And, still beyond that state, there are other states, and others, and others and others. Rejoice in the light, but sigh not because you are told that you will never touch the flame—you do not begin to realize what the bright light is—the flame is beyond your comprehension.

13. Desire power ardently.

14. Desire peace fervently.

15. Desire possessions above all.

16. But those possessions must belong to the pure soul only, and be possessed therefore by all pure souls equally, and thus be the especial property of the whole only when united.

Hunger for such possessions as can be held by the pure soul, that you may accumulate wealth for that united spirit of life which is your only true self. The peace you shall desire is that sacred peace which nothing can disturb, and in which the soul grows as does the holy flower upon the still lagoons. And that power which the disciple shall covet is that which shall make him appear as nothing in the eyes of men. 17. Seek out the way. 18. Seek the way by retreating within. 19. Seek the way advancing boldly without. Here is another example of the relative and the absolute.

"Desire power ardently." And yet power, selfish power, is the greatest curse of the man who possess it. The power of the Spirit, which is "the power which the disciples shall covet," may indeed make him "appear as nothing in the eyes of men" who are striving after material power. For it is the conscious power of which the average man knows nothing—of which he is unable to form a mental image. And he is very apt to regard as a fool the man who possesses it, or who is reaching out for it. The power which is applied to unselfish uses is incomprehensible to the average man who seeks for worldly power—and yet that worldly power, and all that it is capable of accomplishing, will crumble before the flame of time, as a sheet of tissue before the match, and will be in ashes in the twinkling of an eye, while the real power of spiritual attainment grows stronger and mightier as the ages roll by. The one is the substance—the other the shadow—and yet the world reverses their position because of its imperfect vision. Do not make the mistake of translating this sixteenth precept as meaning that the student should seek to "appear as nothing in the eyes of men." This is not the meaning— the student should avoid seeking to "appear" as anything in the eyes of man, whether that anything be everything or nothing. Let the appearances go—they belong to the world of shadows and the true student has naught to do with them. Let the world attend to its own "appearances"—let it amuse itself with its childish toys, and soap bubbles. Do not seek to "appear"— let the world attend to that, it will amuse the world, and will not hurt you. We say this because some have translated this precept as if it were an incentive to assumed humility which is akin to the "humbleness" of Uriah Heep. As if to "appear" as nothing were some particular virtue! The precept really means to point out the only power worth seeking, and at the same time to show the student how lightly the world is apt to regard such power as compared to what it calls "power," but which worldly power is but as the power of the lunatic who, sitting on a soap-box throne, with a pasteboard crown and a toy sceptre, imagines that he is Lord of All. Let the world amuse itself—it concerns you not—seek ye the real power of the Spirit, no matter how you "appear" to men.

"Desire peace fervently." But that peace is the peace which comes from within, and which you may enjoy even though you be in the midst of the battle of life—though you be commander-in-chief of the worldly army, or its humblest soldier (all one, at the last). This peace of the awakened and conscious soul is indeed "that sacred peace which nothing can disturb, and in which the soul grows as does the holy flower upon the still lagoons." This peace comes only to one who has awakened to the consciousness of his real spiritual existence. This state once attained enables a man to set aside a part of his nature into which he may retire when the troubles and strife of the outer life disturb him, and which immediately surrounds him with a peace "that passeth understanding," because it is beyond the realms of the understanding of the intellect. Such a sanctuary of the soul is a "haven of rest," for the troubled mind, and in which it may seek shelter from the storms which are howling without. When one becomes conscious of what he really is, and is able to see the world of illusions for what they are, he finds this place of peace. And, although, the necessities of his life have placed him in a position in which he must be in the thick of the fight, he really is merely in it, and not of it. For while one part of his nature plays out the part allotted to him, his higher self rises above the tumult, and serenely smiles at it all. Establish for yourself a sanctuary of the soul, in which Silence reigns, and into which your tired soul may creep to rest, and recuperate. It is this peace to which the Yogis refer, when they say: "Peace be with Thee." And may it be with you all! And abide with you.

"Desire possessions above all." This sounds like queer teaching along spiritual lines, but read on. "But those possessions must belong to the pure soul only, and be possessed therefore by all pure souls equally, and thus be the especial property of the whole only when united. Hunger for such possessions as can be held by the pure soul, that you may accumulate wealth for that united spirit of life which is your true self." These possessions, obviously, are not material possessions, but the possessions of the soul. And what is a soul able to possess. Knowledge only, for all else is unreal, and passeth away, Therefore let the soul desire the possession and attainment of the knowledge which it needs—the knowledge of the Spirit. And this best knowledge may be possessed by the pure soul only—the other kind of souls do not care for it. And the pure soul is willing to hold such possessions in common for all other souls who are able to accept a share in it, or to make use of it, and no attempt is made to claim especial property rights in such possessions, and it is recognized as the property of the "united whole." There can be no "corners" in spiritual knowledge, no matter how vigorously some mortals may claim to possess same—there can be no monopoly upon these possessions, for they are free as water to those who are ready and willing to receive them. Although the most valuable of all possessions, they are literally "without money and without price," and woe unto him who attempts to sell the gifts of the Spirit—for he sells that which cannot be delivered except to those who are ready for them, and those who are ready for them have no need to buy—they simply help themselves from the feast. We call your attention to the sentence which says that you should desire to "accumulate wealth for that united spirit of life which is your real self." For when you attain spiritual knowledge you are not merely accumulating for yourself, but for others as well—you are working for the race as well as for yourself. The race is benefited by its individual members attaining spiritual knowledge, and you are making it easier for others of the race—those now living, and those who will come later. You are doing your part to raising the thought of the world. And, as you have enjoyed some of the treasures which have been gathered together by those who have passed on during the ages, so will generations to come be benefited by that which you are accumulating now. We are but atoms in a mighty whole, and the gain of one is the gain of all. Nothing is lost. Therefore "Desire possessions above all."

"Seek out the way." Seek it not by strenuous endeavor, but by opening up yourself to the promptings of the Spirit—by recognizing the hunger of the soul for spiritual bread—the thirst for the draught from the spring of life. Draw knowledge by the Law of Attraction. It will come to you in obedience to that law. It is yours for the asking, and nothing can keep it from you, or you from it. As Emerson says: "The things that are for thee, gravitate to thee. Oh, believe, as thou livest, that every sound that is spoken over the round world which thou oughtest to hear, will vibrate on thine ear. Every proverb, every book, every byword that belongs to thee for aid or comfort, shall surely come home through open or winding passages."

And this will be your test of the truth: When a message comes to you that seems to awaken a memory of an almost forgotten truth, then that truth is yours—it may not be all of that truth, but as much as you feel is true is yours—the rest will come in time. Emerson is said to have been asked to prove certain statements which he had made, in a lecture. He is reported as saying, in reply, "I trust that I shall never utter a statement of the truth which will need to be proved." He was right. Truth is self-evident. When the awakening soul hears a statement of what truth it is ready to receive at that time, it instinctively recognizes it as such. It may not be able to explain it to others, or even to itself. But it knows, it knows. The awakening faculties of the Spiritual Mind perceives truth by methods of their own.

The Spiritual Mind does not run contrary to reason—but it transcends Intellect—it goes beyond, and sees that which the Intellect cannot grasp. In reading, or hearing, statements of what is claimed to be the truth, accept only that which appeals to this higher reason, and lay aside, temporarily, that which does not so appeal to it. In a lecture, or in a book, there may be only one sentence that so appeals to you—accept that, and let the rest go. If that which is passed by be real truth, it will come to you when you are ready for it—it cannot escape you. Be not worried if you cannot understand all you hear or read—pass by that which does not awaken the answering ring of the spiritual keynote within you. This is a safe test, and rule. Apply it to all writings and teachings—our own included. Be not disturbed by the apparently conflicting teachings which you hear and read. Each teacher must teach in his own way, and every teacher will reach some that the others will miss. All teachers have some of the truth—none have all of it. Take your own wherever you find it—and let the rest pass you by. Do not be a bigoted follower of teachers—listen to what they say—but apply the test of your own soul to all of it. Do not be a blind follower. Be an individual. Your soul is as good a judge as any other soul—better, for you, in fact. For it knows what it needs, and is continually reaching out for it. Teachers are useful—books are useful—because they suggest to you—they supply missing links—they give you loose ends of thought, which you may unwind at your leisure—they corroborate that which is lying half-awakened in your mind— they aid in the birth of new thought within your mind. But your own soul must do its own work—is the best judge of what is best for you—is the wisest counsellor—the most skilled teacher. Heed the voice of the Something Within. Trust your own soul, O student. Look within confidently, trustingly, and hopefully. Look within—for there is the spark from the Divine Flame.

"Seek the way by retreating within." We have just spoken of this trust in the Something Within. This precept emphasizes this phase of occult teaching. Learn to retreat within the Silence, and listen to the voice of your soul—it will tell you many great things. In the Silence the Spiritual Mind will unfold and pass on to your consciousness bits of the great truths which lie buried within its recesses. It will pass on to the Intellect certain fragments of truth from its own great storehouse, and the Intellect will afterwards accept them, and reason from the premises thus obtained. Intellect is cold—Spiritual Mind is warm and alive with high feeling. The Spiritual Mind is the source of much that is called "inspiration." Poets, painters, sculptors, writers, preachers, orators, and others have received this inspiration in all times, and do so to-day. This is the source from which the seer obtains his vision—the prophet his foresight. By development of his Spiritual Consciousness, Man may bring himself into a high relationship and contact with this higher part of his nature, and may thus become possessed of a knowledge of which the Intellect has not dared to dream.

When we learn to trust the Spirit, it responds by sending us more frequent flashes of illumination and enlightenment. As one unfolds in Spiritual Consciousness, he relies more upon the Inner Voice, and is more readily able to distinguish it from the impulses from the lower planes of the mind. He learns to follow the guidance of the Spirit, and to allow it to lend him a helping hand. To be "led by the Spirit" is a living and real fact in the lives of all who have reached a certain stage of spiritual development.

"Seek the way by advancing boldly without." Be not afraid. Nothing can harm you. You are a living, eternal soul. Therefore, be bold. Look around you and see what is going on in the world—and learn lessons thereby. See the workings of the great loom of life—watch the shuttles fly—see the cloth of various texture and colors that is being produced. See it all as Life. Be not dismayed. Lessons are lying all around you, awaiting your study and mastery. See life in all its phase—this does not mean that you should take a backward step and try to live over again phases which you have left behind you and with which you are through—but witness them all without horror or disgust. Remember that from the lowly phases, higher phases develop. From the mud of the river the beautiful lotus rears its stalk, and forcing its way through the water reaches the air, and unfolds its beautiful flower. From the mud of the physical, the plant of life passes through the water of the mental plane, on to the air of the spiritual, and there unfolds. Look around you and see what men are doing—what they are saying—what they are thinking—it is all right, in all its phases, for those who are in it. Live your own life—on your own plane of development—but scorn not those who are still on the lower planes. See Life in all its throbbing forms, and realize that you are part of it all. It is all one—and you are part of that one. Feel the swell of the wave beneath you—yield to its motion—you will not be submerged, for you are riding on its crest, and borne on its bosom. Do not fear the outside—even while you retreat within—both are good—each in its place. Let your Inner Sanctuary be your real resting place, but be not afraid to venture without. Your retreat cannot be cut off. See the outer world, knowing that home is always awaiting you. There is no contradiction between the eighteenth and nineteenth precepts.

Let us repeat them, that you may grasp them as but the two sides of the same truth: "Seek the way by retreating within—seek the way by advancing boldly without." Do you not see that they are both needed to form the whole statement of truth?

"Seek it not by any one road." This is a necessary caution. As the writer of the precepts says: "To each temperament there is one road which seems the most desirable." But there is a subtle temptation here—the student is very apt to rest content with that one road which suits his particular temperament, and, accordingly, is likely to shut his eyes to the other roads. He becomes bigoted, narrow, and one-sided. He should explore all the lanes which seem to lead to the truth, gaining a little here and a little there—holding fast to that which appeals to his inner consciousness, and letting the rest go—but condemning not that which he does not see fit to accept. Do not be a partisan—or a bigot—or a sectarian. Because you favor any one form of teaching, do not hastily conclude that all teachings that do not agree with yours must be false. There are many forms of presentation of truth, each suited to the understanding of certain people. Many forms of expression, which at first sight appear contradictory, are afterwards seen to have the same fundamental principle. Much of the apparent difference in teaching may be seen to be merely a matter of the use (or misuse) of words. When we understand each other's words and terms, we often find that we have much in common, and but little apart from each other.

20. Seek it not by any one road.

To each temperament, there is one road which seems the most desirable. But the way is not found by devotion alone, by religious contemplation alone, by ardent progress, by self-sacrificing labor, by studious observation of life. None alone can take the disciple more than one step onwards. All steps are necessary to make up the ladder. The vices of men become steps in the ladder, one by one, as they are surmounted. The virtues of man are steps, indeed, necessary—not by any means to be dispensed with. Yet, though they create a fair atmosphere and a happy future, they are useless if they stand alone. The whole nature of man must be used wisely by the one who desires to enter the way. Each man is to himself absolutely the way, the truth, and life. But he is only so when he grasps his whole individuality firmly, and, by the force of his awakened spiritual will, recognizes this individuality as not himself, but that thing which he has with pain created for his own use, and by means of which he purposes, as his growth slowly develops his intelligence, to reach to the life beyond individuality. When he knows that for this his wonderful complex, separated life exists, then, indeed, and then only, he is upon the way. Seek it by plunging into the mysterious and glorious depths of your own inmost being. Seek it by testing all experience, by utilizing the senses, in order to understand the growth and meaning of individuality, and the beauty and obscurity of those other divine fragments which are struggling side by side with you, and form the race to which you belong. Seek it by study of the laws of being, the laws of nature, the laws of the supernatural; and seek it by making the profound obeisance of the soul to the dim star that burns within. Steadily, as you watch and worship, its light will grow stronger. Then you may know you have found the beginning of the way. And, when you have found the end, its light will suddenly become the infinite light.

The twentieth precept should be read carefully by every student who wishes to live the life of the Spirit, and who desires to advance along the Path. It should be read—re-read—studied. It contains within it much that will not be grasped at the first reading—nor the tenth—nor the one-hundredth. Its meaning will unfold as your experiences renders you ready to receive it. It tells you that your life must not be one-sided—it must be varied.

You must avail yourself of the advantages of the inner life—and yet you must not run away from the world, for it has lessons for you. You are needed by others in the world—others need you—and you must play your part. You cannot run away, even if you want to—so accept the part that is allotted to you, and use your present state as a thing upon which you may mount to greater things. You are a cog in the great machinery of life, and you must do your work. "The whole nature of man must be used wisely by the one who desires to enter the way." This life may be carried into your business, profession or trade—if it cannot be taken with you everywhere, something is wrong with it, or with you. You must not expect the world to understand your view of life. There is no use inflicting your views upon the unready world—milk for babes, and meat for men, remember. The majority of the people around you are like unborn babes, spiritually—and but a very few have even drawn their first baby breath. Do not make the mistake of wearing your heart on your sleeve, for the daws to peck at. Play well your part in the game of life, in which you are forced to join. But though you see it as but the sport of children, do not make yourself a nuisance to the babes—join in as if you enjoyed it—you will learn lessons from it. Do not make the mistake of thinking that you have to go around wearing a "Sunday face"—don't try to pose as one of the "holy" and "too-good-for-life" sort of people. Just be natural—that's all. Don't be afraid to smile or laugh. A sense of humor is one of God's best gifts to man, and prevents him committing many follies. A laugh is often as good as a prayer. Don't take things too seriously—do not let the play of the kindergarten of God seem too real to you. Much of life is really a joke to those who can rise above and view it from there. It is really a play preparing the children of God for the real life.

It is not necessary for us to comment upon the twentieth precept, at length, for that precept is so full and goes so into details, that it covers the ground fully. Study it carefully—it contains a rule of life for students. Its concluding sentences are magnificent—they tell you to open yourself to the unfoldment of your higher self, that by the light which burns within you all may be seen. Listen to its words: "Make the profound obeisance of the soul to the dim star that burns within—steadily as you watch and worship, its light will grow stronger. Then you may know that you have found the beginning of the way—and, when you have found the end, its light will suddenly become the infinite light."

Read, also, the note accompanying this last mentioned precept. All of these teachings lead up to the full dawn of Spiritual Consciousness.

The twenty-first precept bids you "look for the flower to bloom in the silence that follows the storm"—and which blooms only then. The rainbow of Spiritual Consciousness appears only after the fierce storm which has swept you from your feet. It is the divine token of the peace which is coming to you.

Our next lesson will be devoted to the subject of Spiritual Consciousness. In it we will take up the twenty-first precept, and that to which it refers. It is the keystone of this teaching. The other side of the arch must be described, but the keystone must be studied first. Study this second lesson well during the month, that you may understand the one to follow it.

LESSON III. SPIRITUAL CONSCIOUSNESS.

The Twenty-first precept of the first part of "Light on the Path"—the precept that refers directly to the thing that has been led up to by the preceding precepts—tells us to:

21. Look for the flower to bloom in the silence that follows the storm; not till then.

It shall grow, it will shoot up, it will make branches and leaves and form buds, while the storm continues, while the battle lasts. But not till the whole personality of the man is dissolved and melted—not until it is held by the divine fragment which has created it, as a mere subject for grave experiment and experience—not until the whole nature has yielded, and become subject unto its higher self, can the bloom open. Then will come a calm such as comes in a tropical country after the heavy rain, when nature works so swiftly that one may see her action. Such a calm will come to the harassed spirit. And, in the deep silence, the mysterious event will occur which will prove that the way has been found. Call it by what name you will. It is a voice that speaks where there is none to speak, it is a messenger that comes—a messenger without form or substance—or it is the flower of the soul that has opened. It cannot be described by any metaphor. But it can be felt after, looked for, and desired, even amid the raging of the storm. The silence may last a moment of time, or it may last a thousand years. But it will end. Yet you will carry its strength with you. Again and again the battle must be fought and won. It is only for an interval that nature can be still.

The flower that blooms in the silence that follows the storm (and only then and there) is the flower of Spiritual Consciousness, for the production of which the Plant of Life has been striving—that which caused the sprouting of the seed—the putting forth of roots—the pushing of the plant through the soil of the material into the purer region above— the unfolding of leaf after leaf—the discarding of sheath after sheath—until finally the tiny bud of the Spirit was visible, and the real unfoldment began.

This appearance of the bud of Spiritual Consciousness—the first rays of Illumination—mark a most critical period in the evolution of the soul. And, as the little manual states, it occurs only after the storm—only when the silence has succeeded and replaced the rush of the winds—the roar and crash of the thunder—the terrifying incidents of the tempest. In the calm, restful period that follows the storm, great things await the soul. So, remember this, O soul, when you find yourself in the midst of the great storm of spiritual unrest, which is sweeping away all the old landmarks—which is tearing away all that you have been leaning against to support yourself—which causes you to imagine that all is being swept away from you, leaving you alone without comfort, or support. For in that moment of spiritual distress when all is being taken away from you, there is coming to you that peace which passeth all understanding, which will never leave you, and which is well worth the stress of a thousand storms. The time of mere blind belief is passing from you—the time of knowing is at hand.

It is difficult to speak of the higher spiritual experiences in the words of the lower plane. Emerson, who had experienced that consciousness of which we speak, says of it: "Every man's words, who speaks from that life, must sound vain to those who do not dwell in the same thought on their own part. I dare not speak for it. My words do not carry its august sense; they fall short and cold. Only itself can inspire whom it will... Yet I desire even by profane words, if sacred I may not use, to indicate the heaven of this deity, and to report what hints I have collected of the transcendent simplicity and energy of the Highest Law." It is a thing to be felt rather than to be intellectually grasped—and yet the Intellect may partially grasp it, when the illumination of the Spirit has raised it (the Intellect) to higher planes.

Knowing what lies before it, the hand that writes these words trembles over its work. To attempt to put into plain words these experiences of the Higher Life seems futile and foolish—and yet we seem called upon to make the effort. Well, so be it—the task is set before us—we must not shrink from it.

In our "Fourteen Lessons" we have told of the threefold mind of man—the three mental principles—the Instinctive Mind; the Intellect; the Spiritual Mind. We advise that you re-read the lessons bearing upon this subject, paying particular attention to what we have said regarding the Sixth Principle—the Spiritual Mind. This Illumination—this flower that blooms in the silence that follows the storm—comes from that part of your nature.

But, first, let us consider what is meant by "the storm" which precedes the blossoming of the flower.

Man passes through the higher stages of the Instinctive Mind on to the plane of the Intellect. The man on the Instinctive Plane (even in its higher stages where it blends into the lower planes of the Intellect) does not concern himself with the problems of Life—the Riddle of Existence. He does not recognize even that any such problem or riddle exists. He has a comparatively easy time, as his cares are chiefly those connected with the physical plane. So long as his physical wants are satisfied, the rest matters little to him. His is the childhood stage of the race. After a time, he begins to experience troubles on another plane.

His awakened Intellect refuses to allow him to continue to take things for granted. New questions are constantly intruding themselves, calling for answers. He begins to be pestered by the eternal "Why" of his soul. As Tolstoi so forcibly puts it: "As soon as the mental part of a person takes control, new worlds are opened, and desires are multiplied a thousand-fold. They become as numerous as the radii of a circle; and the mind, with care and anxiety, sets itself first to cultivate and then gratify these desires, thinking that happiness is to be found in that way." But no permanent happiness is to be found in this state— something fills the soul with a growing unrest, and beckons it on and on to higher flights. But the Intellect, not being able to conceive of anything higher than itself, resists these urgings as something unworthy—some relic of former superstitions and credulity. And so it goes around and around in its efforts to solve the great problems—striving for that peace and rest which it somehow feels is awaiting it. It little dreams that its only possible release lies in the unfoldment of something higher than itself, which will enable it to be used as a finer instrument.

Many who read these lines will recognize this stage of terrible mental unrest—of spiritual travail—when our Intellect confesses itself unable to solve the great questions pressing upon it for answers. We beat against the bars of our mental cages—or like the squirrel in the wheel, rush rapidly around and around, and yet remain just where we were at the beginning. We are in the midst of the mental storm. The tempest rages around and about us—the winds tear our cloaks from us, leaving us at the mercy of the tempest. We see swept away from our sight all that has seemed so firm, durable and permanent, and upon which we have found much comfort in leaning. All seems lost and we are in despair. Peace and comfort is denied us—the storm drives us hither and thither, and we know not what the end shall be. Our only hope is that reliance and trust in the Unseen Hand which prompted Newman to write those beautiful words, which appeal to thousands far removed from him in interpretation of the Truth, but who are, nevertheless, his brothers in the Spirit, and who therefore recognize his words:

"Lead, kindly light, amid the encircling gloom, Lead thou me on. The night is dark, and I am far from home;

Lead thou me on. Keep thou my feet; I do not ask to see The distant scene; one step enough for me,

Lead thou me on."

In due time there comes—and it always comes in due time—a little gleam of light piercing through the clouds, lighting up to the feet of the storm-beaten wanderer—one step at a time—a new path, upon which he takes a few steps. He soon finds himself in a new country. As a writer has said:

"Soon he becomes conscious that he has entered into a new and unknown land—has crossed the borders of a new country. He finds himself in a strange land—there are no familiar landmarks—he does not recognize the scene. He realizes the great distance between himself and the friends he has left at the foot of the hill. He cries aloud for them to follow him, but they can scarcely hear him, and seem to fear for his safety. They wave their arms, and beckon with their hands for him to return. They fear to follow him, and despair of his safety. But he seems possessed of a new courage, and a strange impulse within him urges him on and on. To what point he is traveling, he knows not—but a fierce joy takes possession of him, and he presses on."

The light pouring forth from the Spiritual Consciousness, leads the traveler along the Path of Attainment—if he has the courage to follow it. The light of the Spirit is always a safe guide, but very few of us have the confidence and trust which will allow us to accept it. The original Quakers knew of this inner light, and trusted it—but their descendants have but a glimmer of what was once a bright light. Its rays may be perceived by all who are ready for it, and who look with hope and confidence to the day when their eyes may view it. For know you, that this inner light is not the special property of the Orientals—far from it. The men of the East have paid more attention to the subject than have those of the West—but this Illumination is the common property of the race, and is before each and every man and woman. Instances of it have been known among all peoples—in all times. And all the records agree in the main, although the interpretations vary widely.

The first indications of the coming of Spiritual Consciousness, is the dawning perception of the reality of the Ego—the awareness of the real existence of the Soul. When one begins to feel that he, himself, is his soul, rather than that he possess a wonderful something called the "soul" of which he really knows nothing—when, we say, he feels that he is a soul, rather than that he has or will have a soul—then that one is nearing the first stages of Spiritual Consciousness, if indeed he is not already within its outer borders.

There are two general stages of this blossoming of the flower, although they generally blend into each other. The first is the full perception of the "I Am" consciousness—the second the Cosmic Knowing. We will try at least clumsily and crudely to give an idea of these two stages, although to those who have experienced neither our words may appear meaningless.

The perception of the "I Am" consciousness may be likened to the bud of the flower—the flower itself being the Cosmic Knowing. Many, who have not as yet experienced this "I Am" consciousness, may think that it is simply the intellectual conception of the self, or perhaps the faith or belief in the reality of the soul which they may possess by reason of their religious training. But it is a far different thing. It is more than a mere intellectual conception, or a mere blind belief upon the word or authority of another—more indeed than even the belief in the Divine promise of immortality. It is a consciousness—a knowing—that one is a soul; an awareness that one is a spiritual being—an immortal. Here, dear friends, we are compelled to pause for lack of words adequate to describe the mental state. The race, having had no such experiences, have coined no words for it. The Sanscrit contains words which have been injected into the language by the ancient Yogis, and which may be at least intellectually comprehended by the educated Hindu, but our Western tongues contain no words whereby we may convey the meaning. We can only try to give you the idea by crude illustration. No one can describe Love, Sympathy, or any other emotion to a race which had never experienced the sensation. They are things which must be felt. And so it is with the "I Am" consciousness. It comes to a soul which has unfolded sufficiently to admit of the rays of knowledge from the Spiritual Mind, and then that soul simply knows—that's all. It has the actual spiritual knowledge that it is an entity— immortal—but it cannot explain it to others, nor can it, as a rule, even intellectually explain it to itself. It simply knows. And that knowing is not a matter of opinion, or reasoning, or faith, or hope, or blind belief. It is a consciousness—and like any other form of consciousness, it is most difficult to explain to one who has never experienced it. Imagine what it would be to explain light to a man born blind—sugar to one who had never tasted a sweet thing—cold to one who dwelt in a tropical country and who had never experienced the sensation. We simply cannot explain to those who have not experienced them our spiritual experiences—a fact that is well known to those who have at some time in their lives had what are generally known as "religious" experiences. We know of a case in which this consciousness came to a man who lived in a community in which there seems to have been no one in a like stage of development. He was a business man of no mean ability, and his associations had been along entirely different lines. He felt the flood of light beating into his mind—the certainty of his spiritual existence impressed upon his consciousness—and he became very much disturbed and worried. He thought it must be a sign of approaching insanity, and he hoped it would pass off, although it gave him the greatest happiness. But it did not pass off, and he went so far as to make arrangements to transfer his business interests, fearing that he was becoming mentally unbalanced, for he had never heard of a similar case. However, one day he picked up a book, in which the writer gave utterances to words which could come only from one who had had a like experience. The man recognized the common language (although another would not) and throwing his hands above his head, he cried aloud: "Thank God, here's another crazy man."

This awareness of the "I Am" has come to many more people than is generally imagined, but those who have this consciousness, as a rule, say nothing about it, for fear that their friends, relatives and neighbors would consider them abnormal and mentally unsound. And, indeed, it is not always wise to relate these experiences to others, for those who have not reached the same plane cannot understand, and seeing in another a thing of which they can have no comprehension, are apt to consider him irrational. It is a strange thing—an amusing thing—that in a world made up of people who claim to believe that each man is (or "has" as the term goes) an immortal soul, one who claims to really know this to be a fact is regarded as abnormal. The belief of the race is only skin-deep—the people are as much afraid of death, or more so, than the man who believes that death ends all. They reject all evidences of other planes of existence, considering those who teach of and believe in them as being either imposters or lunatics. They live and act as if this earth-life were all, in spite of all their claims and expressed beliefs. They half-believe certain teachings, but have no real knowledge, and deny that anyone else may possess that which they themselves lack.

But to the one into whose field of consciousness have come some rays of the truth from the Spiritual Mind, these things are no longer mere beliefs—they are realities, and although such a one may apparently conform to the beliefs of the world around him, he becomes a different being. Others notice a something different about him, keep he ever so quiet. They cannot explain just what it is, but they feel something. It must not be imagined that this budding consciousness springs fullgrown into a man's mind at once. It has done so in some cases, it is true, but in the majority of instances, it is a matter of slow growth, but the man is never just the same after the growth commences. He apparently may lose his full consciousness of the truth, but it will come back to him again and again, and all the time it is working gradually to make over that man's nature, and his changed mental attitude manifests itself in his actions. He becomes more cheerful and happy. Things that worry his neighbors seem to have but little effect upon him. He finds it hard to manifest a respectable amount of regret and grief over things that bear heavily upon those around him. He is apt to be regarded as unfeeling and heartless, notwithstanding his heart may be full of Love and Kindness. His mental attitude is changed—his viewpoint has shifted. He finds himself ceasing to fear, and those around him are apt to consider him reckless or thoughtless. Time has less meaning to him, for the idea of eternity has come to him. Distance ceases to appal him, for is not all space his? Such a one had better keep quiet, or he will be sure to be considered a "queer fish," and people may tap their foreheads significantly when speaking of him (behind his back).

There is another peculiarity about this phase of Spiritual Consciousness, and that is that one who has it will recognize its language in the writings of others. He may pick up the works of some of the ancient writers, or even some of the modern ones, and where others see only beautiful language, he will listen to a heart-to-heart talk from his brother-in-thought. Some writers, having but a slight degree of spiritual insight will fall into a "mood" in which the Spiritual Mind deftly passes on its words to the lower mental principle, and the result is that the spiritual meaning is readily grasped by those ready for it, even though the writer may not fully understand what he has written. When Spirit speaks, Spirit hears.

Let those who read these words, if they have had this consciousness in a greater or lesser degree, take courage. Let not your loneliness oppress or depress you. There are thousands who are your brothers and sisters in this great understanding, and their thought will seek yours and both will be benefited. Keep quiet to those around you, if you see fit, but open up yourself to the sympathy and help that will surely come to you along the channels of the thought currents. Your thought will attract to you the similar thought of others of the same consciousness, and theirs will attract yours. In books, writings, pictures, you will find words which are written for you and your kind. Read over the old books, and see how different they appear to you, now that you understand. Read the Bible; read Shakespeare; read the poets and the philosophers; and see how soon you will recognize that the writers are your brothers. The dark corners and hard sayings will become plain to you now. You need not be alone—you are one of a great and growing family.

But, on the other hand, avoid being possessed of an inflated idea of your own development. You are but on the threshold, and the great hall of the Occult is before you, and in that hall there are many degrees, and an initiation must be met and passed before you may go on.

Before we pass to the next stage of the growth of the flower, it may be interesting to our readers to listen to a description of a peculiar experience related by that great modern writer, Rudyard Kipling—he who understands much more than he tells his English and American readers—in his story of East Indian life, entitled "Kim." Many read what he has said and can "see nothing in it," but those who have had glimpses of this Spiritual Consciousness will readily understand it. Here it is:

"'Now am I alone—all alone,' he thought. 'In all India is no one else so alone as I! If I die to-day, who shall bring the news—and to whom? If I live and God is good, there will be a price upon my head, for I am a Son of the Charm—I, Kim.'

"A very few white people, but many Asiatics, can throw themselves into amazement, as it were, by repeating their own names over and over again to themselves, letting the mind go free upon speculation as to what is called personal identity. …

"'Who is Kim—Kim—Kim?'

"He squatted in a corner of the clanging waiting room, rapt from all other thoughts; hands folded in lap, and pupils contracted to pin points. In a moment—in another half-second—he felt that he would arrive at the solution of the tremendous puzzle; but here, as always happens, his mind dropped away from those heights with the rush of a wounded bird, and passing his hand before his eyes, he shook his head.

"A long-haired Hindu bairagi (holy man) who had just bought a ticket, halted before him at that moment and stared intently. "'I also have lost it,' he said sadly. 'It is one of the gates of the Way, but to me it has been shut many years.' "'What is thy talk?' said Kim, abashed. "'Thou wast wondering, there in thy spirit, what manner of thing thy soul might be. … I know. Who should know but I?'" (Kim, by Rudyard Kipling. Pages 295–96. Doubleday, Page & Co., New York.)

Tennyson, the poet, according to the testimony of intimate friends, at times produced an ecstatic mood and a mild degree of spiritual illumination by a similar process to that followed by "Kim." He would repeat his first name, over and over, meditating on his real identity, and he stated that at such times he would become perfectly aware of immortality and the reality of his existence as a living soul, independent of the body.

Personally we do not favor this method of "breaking into the Kingdom," but prefer that the unfolding Spiritual Mind should gradually throw its light into the field of consciousness. This we consider the better way, although many Yogi teachers think otherwise, and instruct their students in exercises calculated to cause this consciousness to unfold. It is simply a difference of opinion as to methods, and we have no desire to urge our ideas upon our students, if they prefer the other method.

One of the most rational and reasonable of these Yogi exercises for aiding the unfoldment is given in the next several paragraphs.

Exercise.

Place your body in a relaxed, reclining position. Breathe rhythmically, and meditate upon the Real Self, thinking of yourself as an entity independent of the body, although inhabiting it and being able to leave it at will. Think of yourself, not as the body, but as a soul. Think of your body as but a shell, useful and comfortable, but merely an instrument for the convenience of the real You. Think of yourself as an independent being, using the body freely and to the best advantage, and having full control and mastery over it. While meditating, ignore the body entirely, and you will find that you will often become almost unconscious of it. You may even experience the sensation of being out of the body, and of returning to it when through with the exercise. (Rhythmic breathing is described in our little book, "Science of Breath.")

Mantram and Meditation. In connection with the above Yogi exercise, the student may, if he desire, use the following Mantram and Meditation:

"I am. I assert the reality of my existence—not merely my physical existence, which is but temporal and relative—but my real existence in the Spirit, which is eternal and absolute. I assert the reality of the Ego— my Soul—My-self. The real 'I' is the Spirit principle, which is manifesting in body and mind, the highest expression of which I am conscious being Myself—my Soul. This 'I' cannot die nor become annihilated. It may change the form of its expression, or the vehicle of its manifestation, but it is always the same 'I'—a bit of the Universal Spirit—a drop from the great ocean of Spirit—a spiritual atom manifesting in my present consciousness, working toward perfect unfoldment. I am my Soul— my Soul is I—all the rest is but transitory and changeable. I Am—I Am—I Am." Repeat the words "I Am" a number of times.

The student should endeavor to give a few minutes each day to silent meditation, finding as quiet a place as possible, and then lying or sitting in an easy position, relaxing every muscle of the body and calming the mind. Then when the proper conditions are observed, he will experience that peculiar sensation of calmness and quiet which indicate the condition known as "entering the Silence." Then he should repeat the above Mantram, or some similar one (there is no special virtue in the mere words), and should meditate along the lines indicated. The Mantram "I am," if clearly understood and impressed upon the mind, will give to the student an air of quiet dignity and calm manifestation of power, which will be apparent to those with whom he comes in contact. It will surround him with a thought aura of strength and power. It will enable him to cast off fear and to look the world of men and women calmly in the eyes, knowing that he is an eternal soul, and that naught can really harm him. Even the more simple stages of this consciousness will lift one above the petty cares, worries, hates, fears, and jealousies of the lower mental states, and will cause one to be a man or woman "of the Spirit," in truth. Such people have a helpful effect upon those with whom they come in contact, as there is an undefinable aura surrounding them which causes others to recognize that they are worthy of confidence and respect.

These meditations and exercises will often aid one materially in developing a consciousness of the reality of the soul. The sense of immortality will come gradually as the consciousness unfolds. But the student must not allow himself to live too much in "the upper regions," or to despise his body or the world and people around him. This is known as "spiritual pride," and will have its downfall. You are here in the world for a purpose, and must get the experiences necessary to fully round you out. You are in exactly the best position for the experiences you need—and you will not be kept there one moment longer than is necessary for your ultimate good. Live, grow, and unfold— living your own life—doing the best you can. "And be Kind."

This "I Am" consciousness, while a great advance over the consciousness common to the race, is still but a preliminary to the Cosmic Knowing which awaits the unfolding soul. It is but the bud which will in time open out and grow into the perfect flower. If it has been difficult to explain in simple words the experiences just touched upon, it may be imagined how we feel about approaching this higher phase. But we will try to do our best, although of necessity our words must be weak and inadequate. To those not ready for the truth what we say must seem like the veriest nonsense, but even these people will remember what we say, and when the time comes may be partially prepared for it. As good old Walt Whitman has said: "My words will itch in your ears till you understand them." This Cosmic Knowing is the full flower which will "bloom in the silence that follows the storm," as the writer, or transcriber, of "Light on the Path" has so beautifully expressed it. It is that which comes as the result of "Illumination."

The occult writers of all times have spoken of this thing, and it has also been partially described by people in all times—of all forms of religious belief. Many have supposed it to have come as the result of the worship of some particular conception of Deity, or as the incident of some particular form of creed. But it is really a thing above creeds or particular conceptions of the Absolute—it is a part of the Divine heritage of the race. Many of the Oriental writers have described this thing in their own words—many of the old Quakers experienced it, and have given it their own names—many Catholic saints describe it in their writings, and even some of the great Protestant leaders and preachers have given bewildered accounts of the great thing that came upon them. Each, as a rule, however, attributed it to some particular thing in their faith. Great poets have felt its influence, and testimony along the same general lines comes to us from many different sources. Some have had it gradually dawn upon them, wax strong, and then fade away, leaving them changed beings, living afterwards in hope of again experiencing the great thing. Others have had it burst upon them suddenly, with an impression that they were submerged in a brilliant light (from whence comes the term "illumination"), which also passed away, leaving them changed beings. The experience seems to come to no two souls in exactly the same way, and yet there is a common point of resemblance between the testimony of all. A Western writer (now passed out of the body) one Dr. Richard Maurice Bucke, of London, Ontario, Canada, having experienced this illumination, and having found that his friend Walt Whitman and other friends had had similar experiences, has gathered the testimony of a number of people whom he believed to have undergone the same unfoldment. He published the result of his research in a very valuable book entitled "Cosmic Consciousness: a Study in the Evolution of the Human Mind" (Innes & Sons, Philadelphia, Penna., U. S. A.), which book was issued in the shape of a limited edition of five hundred copies, and is now, we believe, out of print. It may possibly be found in some of the great libraries in our principal cities, and is well worth a careful reading. The Oriental writings are full of this subject, and Western literature is beginning to show signs of its recognition.

In nearly all the Western writings, however, what is described are but typical incidents of spontaneous flashes of this great consciousness. Occultists of great degree of advancement are able to produce this state at will, and certain most highly advanced souls in the flesh, who are not before the public as teachers or writers, are believed to dwell in this consciousness almost continually, their work for the world being done through others (less highly developed), whom they inspire with fragments of their great wisdom.

In a general way, the experience may be described as an actual realization of the Oneness of all, and of one's connection with that One. The atom of light helping to compose the ray, realizes for an instant its connection with the Central Sun— the drop in the ocean realizes for a moment its relation to the Ocean of Spirit. The Hindus have spoken of the more intense manifestations of this breaking in upon the consciousness of the light from the Spiritual Mind, as the "Brahmic Splendor."

The prevailing emotion during this experience is a feeling of intense joy—something far above any other joy that has ever been felt—a sensation of Absolute Joy, if the term may be permitted. And the memory of this great Joy—the reflection from its light—lingers with the soul forever after. Those who have once experienced this thing, are ever after more cheerful, and happy, and seem to have a hidden and secret fount of joy from which they may drink with the soul thirsts. The intense joy fades away gradually, but something is left behind to comfort and cheer. This feeling of Joy is so strong that it can ever after be thought of with the keenest delight—its very recollection will cause the blood to tingle and the heart to throb whenever the mind reverts to the experience.

Then there is experienced an intellectual illumination, or a pouring in of "knowing," impossible to describe. The soul becomes conscious that it possess in itself absolute knowledge—knowledge of all things—the "why and wherefore" of everything is recognized as being contained within itself. The sensation cannot be described, even faintly. It is so far above anything that the human mind has ever experienced that there is simply no words with which to tell that which has been felt and known. Everything seems made plain—it is not a sense of an increased ability to reason, deduce, classify, or determine— the soul simply knows. The feeling may last but a fraction of a second of time—one loses all sense of time and space during the experience—but the subsequent intense feeling of regret over the great thing that has slipped away from the consciousness can scarcely be imagined by one who has not experienced it. The only thing that enables the mind to bear the loss is the certainty that some time—some where—the experience will be repeated, and that certainty makes existence "worth while."

It is a foretaste of what is before the soul.

One of the principal things indelibly impressed upon the mind by this glimpse of the higher consciousness is the knowledge—the certainty—that Life pervades everything— that the Universe is filled with life, and is not a dead thing. Life and Intelligence is seen to fill everything. Eternal Life is sensed. Infinity is grasped. And the words "Eternal" and "Infinite," ever after have distinct and real meanings when thought of, although the meaning cannot be explained to others.

Another sensation is that of perfect Love for all of Life— this feeling also transcends any feeling of love ever before experienced. The feeling of Fearlessness possesses one during the experience—perhaps it would be better to say that one is not conscious of Fear—there seems to be no reason for it, and it slips away from one. One does not even think of Fear during the experience, and only realizes that he was entirely free from it when he afterwards recalls some of his sensations. The feeling of knowledge, certainty, trust and confidence that possesses one, leaves no room for Fear.

Another sensation is that that something which we might style "the consciousness of Sin" has slipped from one. The conception of "Goodness" of the entire Universe takes its place. By "goodness" we do not mean the goodness of one thing as compared to another, but a sense of absolute Goodness.

As we have said, this experience when it has once come to the soul, leaves it as a changed entity. The man is never the same man afterward. Although the keen recollection wears off, gradually, there remains a certain memory which afterward proves a source of comfort and strength to him, especially when he feels weak of faith and faint of heart—when he is shaken like a reed by the winds of conflicting opinions and speculations of the Intellect. The memory of the experience is a source of renewed strength—a haven of refuge to which the weary soul flies for shelter from the outside world, which understands it not.

Let us conclude this feeble attempt to describe that which may not be described, by repeating our own words, spoken to you in the Third of the Fourteen Lessons:

From the writings of the ancient philosophers of all races; from the songs of the great poets of all peoples; from the preachings of the prophets of all religions and times; we can gather traces of this illumination which has come to Man—this unfoldment of the Spiritual Consciousness. One has told of it in one way, the other in another form—but all tell practically the same story. All who have experienced this illumination, even in a faint degree, recognize the like experience in the tale, the song, the preaching of another, though centuries roll between them. It is the song of the Soul, which once heard is never forgotten. Though it be sounded by the crude instrument of the semi-barbarous races, or by the finished instrument of the talented musician of to-day, its strains are plainly recognized. From old Egypt comes the song—from India in all ages—from Ancient Greece and Rome—from the early Christian saint— from the Quaker Friend—from the Catholic monasteries—from the Mohammedan mosque—from the Chinese philosopher— from the legends of the American Indian hero-prophet—it is always the same strain, and it is swelling louder and louder, as many more are taking it up and adding their voices or the sound of their instruments to the grand chorus.

May this great joy of Illumination be yours, dear students. And it will be yours when the proper time comes. When it comes be not dismayed—when it leaves you mourn not its loss, for it will come again. Live on, reaching ever upward toward your Real Self and opening up yourself to its influence.

Be always willing to listen to the Voice of the Silence—willing always to respond to the touch of the Unseen Hand. Do not fear, for you have within you always the Real Self, which is a spark from the Divine Flame—it will be as a lamp to your feet, to point out the way.

We would call the attention of the student to what the "Light on the Path" says about the blossoming of the flower. It tells us that while the storm continues—while the battle lasts—the plant will grow; shoot up; will make branches and leaves; will form buds (note what we have said about the budding stage which precedes the full bloom), but that the bloom cannot open until the "whole personality of the man is dissolved and melted—not until it is held by the divine fragment which has created it, as a mere subject for grave experiment and experience—not until the whole nature has yielded, and become subject unto its higher self."

The "whole personality" referred to is the lower part of the soul—its lower principles. Not until the lower nature is brought under the mastery of the highest that has unfolded in one, can this longed for event occur. So long as the lower part of one's nature is allowed to rule and master him, he shuts out the divine light. Only when he asserts the real "I" does he become ready for further unfoldment. We have told you what the bloom or bud is—the "I Am" consciousness. When you have fully grasped this, and realize what you are, and have made that highest (as yet) consciousness the master of your lower principles, then are you ready for the bloom to open.

Listen to these beautiful words, from the text: "Then will come a calm such as comes in a tropical country after the heavy rain, when nature works so swiftly that one may see her action. Such a calm will come to the harassed spirit. And, in the deep silence, the mysterious event will occur which will prove that the way has been found." We have tried to tell you what is that mysterious event. We trust that we have at least made possible a clearer conception of it on your part.

The writer of the little manual evidently shared the difficulty that confronts everyone who attempts to describe the great experience. She goes on to say: "Call it by whatever name you will, it is a voice that speaks where there is none to speak; it is a messenger that comes—a messenger without form or substance—or it is the flower of the soul that has opened. It cannot be described by any metaphor. But it can be felt after, looked for, and desired, even amid the raging of the storm."

She goes on then to speak of the duration of "the silence that follows the storm," in which occurs the "mysterious event." She says: "The silence may last a moment of time, or it may last a thousand years. But it will end. Yet you will carry its strength with you. Again and again must the battle be fought and won. It is only for an interval that nature can be still."

In this last paragraph, the text evidently refers to the partial or temporary Illumination to which we have referred in this lesson. The time when the Spiritual Consciousness will become permanent—when the Brahmic Splendor remains with the soul continuously, is far beyond us—those who enjoy that state are now beings far beyond us in the spiritual scale. And yet they were once are as we—we shall some day be as they now are.

These flashes of Illumination come to the advanced student as he progresses along the Path. And although they leave him, he carries their strength with him.

We would also call the attention of the student to the foot note accompanying this last precept, as it contains a wonderful occult truth in the shape of a promise. This promise has cheered thousands along The Path—has nerved them for further efforts—has given them renewed ardor and courage. Listen to it: "Know, O disciple! that those who have passed through the silence, and felt its peace, and retained its strength, they long that you shall pass through it also. Therefore, in the Hall of Learning, when he is capable of entering there, the disciple will always find his master."

The last foot note in Part I, of "Light on the Path" (the one that concludes that part of the little manual), should be read carefully by the student, as it contains important information. We think it better to insert it here, lest it may be overlooked. We trust that we have enabled you to understand it a little more clearly than before. When one has the key he is able to open the many doors in the Hall of Learning, and gaze upon its wonderful contents, even though he may not as yet be privileged to enter. Here is the foot note referred to:

Note.—Those that ask shall have. But, though the ordinary man asks perpetually, his voice is not heard. For he asks with his mind only, and the voice of the mind is only heard on that plane on which the mind acts. Therefore, not until the first twenty-one rules are past, do I say those that ask shall have.

To read in the occult sense, is to read with the eyes of the spirit. To ask, is to feel the hunger within—the yearning of spiritual aspiration. To be able to read, means having obtained the power in a small degree of gratifying that hunger. When the disciple is ready to learn, then he is accepted, acknowledged, recognized. It must be so; for he has lit his lamp, and it cannot be hidden. But to learn is impossible until the first great battle has been won. The mind may recognize truth, but the spirit cannot receive it. Once having passed through the storm, and attained the peace, it is then always possible to learn, even though the disciple waver, hesitate and turn aside. The voice of the silence remains within him; and though he leave the path utterly, yet one day it will resound, and render him asunder, and separate his passions from his divine possibilities. Then, with pain and desperate cries from the deserted lower self, he will return.

Therefore, I say, Peace be with you. "My peace I give unto you" can only be said by the Master to the beloved disciples who are as himself. There are some, even among those who are ignorant of the Eastern wisdom, to whom this can be said; and to whom it can daily be said with more completeness.

This concludes our consideration of the first part of "Light on the Path." The second part lies before us. It may be objected to that the second part refers to the experience of the student, after he has passed through the silence which followed the storm, and that it concerns not the student who has not as yet reached that stage. To this we answer, that the experiences of the privileged student have very close correspondences in the experiences of the student who has not yet attained. The Path is a spiral, and although the traveler along it constantly mounts higher, yet he goes around and around, a single turn of the spiral above the place where he walked a little while back. Therefore these experiences have correspondences on the higher and lower levels of the spiral. We feel impressed to continue this consideration of this wonderful little manual, and we feel that the student on the lower levels may receive encouragement, benefit and understanding from the same. The second part of the manual contains great truths, which may profit us all. Let us face them.

Many of our students have asked them for some of the Yogi exercises for developing this Spiritual Illumination. Answering this, we say that the best Yogi authorities do not encourage many of the practices indulged in by the less enlightened of their brethren. They believe that such practices are more or less abnormal, and instead of producing the real illumination desired, simply help to bring on a psychic condition which is but a reflection of the desired state—a moon instead of the Sun. And such psychic states do not aid in spiritual unfoldment, although they undoubtedly do produce an ecstatic condition, pleasing for the moment—a psychic intoxication, if we are permitted to use the term.

Meditation along the lines of thought touched upon in this lesson, or similar writings, is of course of benefit, and many Yogi students accompany this with rhythmic breathing which has a tranquilizing effect. But at the best, these things merely prepare the ground for the growth of the plant from which the blossom springs. The plant itself comes when its time is ripe, and cannot be forced unduly. Let us prepare the best conditions for its growth and welfare. Give it welcome when it comes—and until that time let us live up to the highest within us. The fact that you (the student) are attracted toward these subjects, is a sign that you are unfolding spiritually. Otherwise they would not attract you. If these words find a response in your soul, be assured that your own is coming to you, and that you are well along The Path. Look for the light, for it will come—be worthy of its coming.

In conclusion, listen to these words of Edward Carpenter:

"O, let not the flame die out! Cherished age after age in its dark caverns, in its holy temples cherished. Fed by pure ministers of love— let not the flame die out."

LESSON IV. THE VOICE OF THE SILENCE.

Part II of "Light on the Path" opens with the following statement:

Out of the silence that is peace, a resonant voice shall arise. And this voice will say: It is not well, thou has reaped, now thou must sow. And, knowing this voice to be the silence itself, thou wilt obey.

The resonant voice that proceeds from "out of the silence that is peace" is the voice of Spirit forcing its way into the field of consciousness. The voice is not as plain as when heard at the moment of illumination, for the ear is filled with the vibrations of the lower planes, and cannot sense so clearly the high vibrations proceeding from the upper regions of the mind. But the voice is insistent, and if listened to will make itself heard. It will not be confused with the thought-waves with which the ether is filled, for when one thinks of the spiritual plane he is lifted upward mentally, and the lower vibrations cannot reach him so plainly. He soon learns to distinguish the clear pure voice of Spirit from the grosser thought-waves that are beating upon him. The voice of Spirit always has an "upward" tendency, and its influence is always toward higher things.

"And this voice will say: It is not well; thou hast reaped, now thou must sow." This passage pictures the longing which possesses the true occultist, who has experienced the higher consciousness, and which impels him to carry out in actual life the truth which he has received—to manifest in action and association with the world, the thought which has come to him in the silence. The soul may wait in solitude until the truth comes to it— but the truth, when once received and given a lodgment in the heart, fills the soul with a divine unrest, and causes it to go forth into the world and live the life of the Spirit among and with men, instead of apart and away from them. The man to whom spiritual illumination has come—even in its lightest form—is a changed being. He radiates thought of a different character from that emanating from the minds of those around him. He has different ideals and consequently different thoughts. And his thought-waves have an effect upon the great body of thought-waves of the world. They leaven the mass— they are like the stream of pure water pouring into the muddy pond, which pure stream gradually clears the entire pond. His thoughts and presence are needed in the world's work, and so the Spiritual Mind sends him an impulse to go forth and live the life—to live it among men and women, and not apart from them. It says to him: "Thou hast reaped, now thou must sow." "And knowing this voice to be the silence itself," he obeys. There are three great stages in the spiritual and mental life of the race, and as the babe before birth goes through all the physical changes, shapes and forms that the race has passed through during long ages of evolution, so does the growing man go through the stages of the mental and spiritual evolution of the race. But the individual goes through only such changes as lead up to the stage of evolution he has reached at full maturity. He may reach only Stage i, if he is a Stage i individual. If he is a Stage ii individual he passes through Stage i and then on to Stage ii. If he is a Stage iii soul, he passes through Stage i, and then Stage ii (as rapidly as may be) and then unfolds into the Stage iii consciousness. Let us consider these three stages. Stage i is that plane of life in which the Instinctive Mind is in control, the Intellect not being sufficiently developed to assert itself fully and the Spiritual Mind being scarcely recognized. In this stage live the primitive races—and the young child. Those dwelling in it have but little concern for aught but that which pertains to the physical life. Their thoughts are mainly those relating to food, shelter, and the gratification of the physical senses. There exists among these people a certain freedom, democracy, and a lack of the "I am holier than thou" or "better than thou" feeling, which renders their life freer and easier, and happier, than that of those in the next highest stage. They know little or nothing about "sin," and generally follow their desires without question. They have a sort of instinctive belief in a higher power, but do not trouble themselves much about it, nor do they imagine that certain ceremonies or observances are pleasing to Deity, and that failure to perform are apt to arouse his wrath. They do not worry much about their chances of "salvation," and are disposed instinctively to realize that the Power that takes care of them Here, will take care of them There. Stage ii commences when the Intellect begins to assume control. Man then begins to awaken to a sense of "good and evil" He recognizes a mysterious something coming from a still higher part of his mind, which makes him feel ashamed of doing certain selfish things, and which causes him to experience a feeling of peace and satisfaction when he has done certain (comparatively) unselfish things. But the Intellect does not stop with this. It begins to invent "good" things, and "bad" things. Priests and prophets arise who say that certain

things (usually the giving of a part of one's goods to the temple) are "good" and pleasing to Deity; and that certain other things (for instance, the refusal to attend the temple, or to contribute to its support) are "bad" and certain to be punished by Deity. These priests and prophets invent heavens suited to the desires of their followers, and hells filled with the particular things that their people fear. Things are separated into "good" and "bad," the "bad" list seeming to be the larger. Most of the pleasant things of life are placed in the "bad" list for no other reason than that they are pleasant. In the same way the "good" list includes the majority of unpleasant things, the prevailing idea being that Deity delights in seeing his children doing things unpleasant to them, and waxes wroth if they chance to indulge in a pleasant act. Creeds and sects are devised, and dire punishment is meted to those who do not accept the former and join the latter. The idea seems to be that those who do not agree with one's particular conception of Deity are "against God," or "God's enemies," and must and will be punished by him.

People often prefer to relieve God of the task of punishing these unbelievers, and proceed to do it themselves.

People in this stage of spiritual development are usually quite strenuous. They declare certain days to be "holy" (as if all days were not so) and insist that certain places are holier than others. They claim that certain peoples and races are "chosen" and favored, and that the rest are hated by Deity. They insist that only a handful of men are to be "saved," and that the majority of God's children are destined to everlasting damnation and punishment. Hell is very hot when seen from the viewpoint of Stage ii. Hate, arising from the feeling of self-righteousness, is a marked characteristic of this stage—sects are formed, and hate and jealousy are manifested between them. Fear reigns, and the Divine Love is almost lost sight of. The Brotherhood of Man is but a name in this stage—all the brotherly feeling that is to be seen is confined to the people belonging to some particular sect. The outsiders are not "brothers," but "heathen," "pagans," "unbelievers," "dissenters," "heretics," etc. The sense of the Oneness of All, which is instinctively felt in Stage i (and both seen and felt in Stage iii), is apparently neither seen or felt in Stage ii. In this stage separateness seems to be the keynote. As the race passes still further along in this stage, and Intellect further unfolds, the reasoning faculties cause it to discard many superstitions and foolish notions that had at one time seemed sacred and the truth itself. Sheath after sheath is discarded as outworn and no longer necessary, and usually a period of disbelief and skepticism sets in. The old things have been thrown aside, but nothing seems to have come to take their place. But after this phase, the Spiritual Mind seems to concentrate its effort to force into the field of consciousness the internal evidence of the truth—of real religion—of the teachings of Spirit. And Man gradually passes into Stage iii.

Stage iii people see good in everyone—in all things—in every place. Some things are seen to be more highly developed than others, but all are seen to form a part of the great plan. The developed soul parts with certain things from lack of desire, casting them off as worn out tools or clothing. But it sees that to others these same things are the best they have, and are far better than some other things which these undeveloped people had parted company with still farther back. It sees that all of life is on the Path—some a little farther advanced than others, but all journeying in the same direction. It sees all learning their lessons and profiting by their mistakes. It sees manifestations of both "good" and "bad" (relative terms) in each man and woman, but prefers to look for the "good" in the sinner, rather than for the "bad" in the saint. It sees in "sin" principally mistakes, misdirected energy, and undeveloped mind.

The Stage iii soul sees good in all forms of religions—so much so that it finds it hard to follow the narrow creeds of any particular one. It sees the Absolute worshiped and recognized in all the conceptions of Deity that have ever originated in the human mind, from the stone idol to the highest conception of Deity known to any of "the churches," the difference being solely in the spiritual growth of the different worshipers. As man grows, his conception of Deity advances—a man's idea of God is merely himself magnified. The God of the advanced man does not appeal to the savage, any more than does the God of the savage attract the advanced man. Each is doing the best he can, and is setting up a conception corresponding to his particular stage of growth. A writer has aptly expressed this thought in these words: "A man's god is himself at his best, and his devil is himself at his worst." But devils pass away from Man as his conception of Deity enlarges.

But the great distinguishing thought of the Stage iii man is his consciousness of the Oneness of All. He sees, and feels, that all the world is alive and full of intelligence in varying degrees of manifestation. He feels himself a part of that great life. He feels his identity with all of Life. He feels in touch with all of nature—in all its forms. In all forms of life he sees something of himself, and recognizes that each particular form of life has its correspondence in something within himself. This does not mean that he is blood-thirsty like the tiger; vain like the peacock; venomous like the serpent. But, still he feels that all the attributes of these animals are within himself—mastered and governed by his higher self—but still there. And consequently he can feel for these animals, or for those of his race in which the animal characteristics are still in evidence. He pities them, but does not hate his brother however much that brother's traits may seem undesirable and hurtful to him. And he feels within himself all the attributes of the higher life as well as the lower, and he realizes that he is unfolding and growing into these higher forms, and that some day he will be like them.

He feels the great throbbing life of which he is a part—and he feels it to be his life. The sense of separateness is slipping from him. He feels the security that comes from this consciousness of his identity with the All Life, and consequently he cannot Fear. He faces to-day and to-morrow without fear, and marches forward toward the Divine Adventure with joy in his heart. He feels at home, for is not the Universe akin to him—is he not among his own?

Such a consciousness divests one of Fear, and Hate, and Condemnation. It teaches one to be kind. It makes one realize the Fatherhood of God and the Brotherhood of Man. It substitutes a knowing for a blind belief. It makes man over, and starts him on a new stage of his journey, a changed being.

No wonder that one in this Stage iii is misunderstood by Stage ii people. No wonder that they often consider him to be a Stage i man because he fails to see "evil" in what seems so to them. No wonder that they marvel at his seeing "good" in things that do not appear so to them. He is like a stranger in a strange land, and must not complain if he be misjudged and misunderstood. But there are more and more of these people every year—

they are coming in great quantities, and when they reach a sufficient number, this old earth will undergo a peaceful revolution. In that day man no longer will be content to enjoy luxury while his brother starves—he will not be able to oppress and exploit his own kind—he will not be able to endure much that to-day is passed over without thought and feeling by the majority of people. And why will he not be able to do these things? may be asked by some. Simply because the man who has experienced this new consciousness has broken down the old feeling of separateness, and his brother's pain is felt by him—his brother's joy is experienced by him—he is in touch with others.

From whence comes this uneasiness that causes men to erect hospitals, and other charitable institutions—from whence comes this feeling of discomfort at the sight of suffering? From the Spiritual Mind that is causing the feeling of nearness to all of life to awaken in the mind of man, and thus renders it more and more painful for them to see and be aware of the pain of others—because they begin to feel it, and it renders them uncomfortable, and they make at least some effort to relieve it. The world is growing kinder by reason of this dawning consciousness, although it is still in a barbarous state as compared to its future condition when Stage iii becomes more common. The race to-day confronts great changes—the thousand straws floating through the air show from which direction the wind is coming, and whither it is blowing. The breeze is just beginning to be felt—soon it will grow stronger, and then the gale will come which will sweep before it much that man has thought to he built for ages. And after the storm man will build better things—things that will endure. Have you not noticed the signs—have you not felt the breeze? But, mark you this—the final change will come not from Hate, Revenge, or other unworthy motives—it will come as the result of a great and growing Love—a feeling that will convince men that they are akin; that the hurt of one is the hurt of all; that the joy of one is the joy of all—that all are One. Thus will come the dawn of the Golden Age.

We may have appeared to have wandered from our text, but what we have said has a direct bearing upon the question of sowing after the reaping—of giving after the receiving—of working after the acquiring of new strength. The voice out of the silence will indeed say to all of us: Go forth and labor in my vineyard—labor not by strenuous effort, or by an attempt to force the growth of living things—thy work is best done by living—you are needed as leaven to lighten the mass.

Here follows the next command from the little manual:

Thou who are now a disciple, able to stand, able to hear, able to see, able to speak; who hast conquered desire, and attained to self-knowledge; who hast seen thy soul in its bloom, and recognized it, and heard the voice of the silence—go thou to the Hall of Learning, and read what is written there for thee.

Let us also read the note following this command; it is very helpful:

Note.—To be able to stand, is to have confidence; to be able to hear, is to have opened the doors of the soul; to be able to see, is to have obtained perception; to be able to speak, is to have attained the power of helping others; to have conquered desire, is to have learned how to use and control the self; to have attained to self-knowledge, is to have retreated to the inner fortress from whence the personal man can be viewed with impartiality; to have seen thy soul in its bloom, is to have obtained a momentary glimpse in thyself of the transfiguration which shall eventually make thee more than man; to recognize, is to achieve the great task of gazing upon the blazing light without dropping the eyes, and not falling back in terror as though before some ghastly phantom. This happens to some; and so, when the victory is all but won, it is lost. To hear the voice of silence, is to understand that from within comes the only true guidance; to go to the Hall of Learning, is to enter the state in which learning becomes possible. Then will many words be written there for thee, and written in fiery letters for thee easily to read. For, when the disciple is ready, the Master is ready also.

The disciple is spoken of as one able to stand; able to hear; able to see; able to speak. The consciousness of the Real Self enables one to stand firmly upon his feet—causes him to feel the Majesty of Self. It enables him to hear the truth pouring in to him from the thousand channels of life, all claiming kinship with him, and willing and anxious to impart to him knowledge and truth. It enables him to see life as it is, in all its varied forms—to see his relation to the Whole and all of its parts, and to recognize the truth when it presents itself before him—it gives him the clear vision of the Spirit. It enables him to speak so that his words will reach others, even when he is unconscious of the fact—he is possessed of that peace which passeth understanding, and his inward state finds utterance in his everyday speech, and he adds a little to the spiritual knowledge of the world.

The manual tells the student who has conquered desire— that is, who has recognized desire for what it is, who has attained to the knowledge of the Self; who has seen his soul in its bloom, and recognized it, and heard the voice of the silence; to proceed to the Hall of Learning, and read what is written there for him. The little note throws additional light on the passage which it follows. Its description of the sight of "the soul in its bloom" is particularly interesting in view of what we have said in our last lesson—it refers to Illumination, or the dawn of spiritual consciousness—the flower that blooms in the silence that follows the storm. Well does its writer say that it is "to have obtained a momentary glimpse in thyself of the transfiguration which shall eventually make thee more than man; to recognize is to achieve the great task of gazing upon the blazing light without dropping the eyes, and not falling back in terror as though before some ghastly phantom." Well has the writer added that "This happens to some; and so when the victory is all but won, it is lost." But she might have added, that it is only temporarily lost, for the memory will remain, and the soul will never rest satisfied until it regains that which it lost. Some who catch glimpses of their souls, shrink back in fright, and treat the matter as a delusion, or some "wicked thought." It upsets one's preconceived and conventional notions to such a degree, in some instances, that those experiencing it begin to be afraid that they are losing their virtue and goodness, because they cease to condemn and hate "evil" as of yore—they imagine that they are growing "bad," and retreat from the consciousness so far as they are able. They fail to perceive that although one may hate the "bad" things less, he loves the "good" things more than ever—that is the things which are known to be good by the Spiritual Mind, not the manufactured and artificial "good" things that pass current as the real article with the majority of people.

The little note also truthfully tells us that "To hear the voice of the silence is to understand that from within comes the only true guidance." Remember these words—they are golden: "Understand that from within comes the only true guidance." If you can grasp the meaning of these words—and have the courage to trust and believe them, you are well started on the Path. If you will always live true to that little voice within, there will be but little need of teachers and preachers for you.

And if we will but trust that little voice, its tones will become plainer and stronger, and we will hear it on many occasions. But if we turn a deaf ear to it and refuse to heed its warning and guidance, it will gradually grow fainter and fainter, until its voice is no longer distinguishable amidst the roar and bustle of the material world.

The Hall of Learning is the state of consciousness which comes when the Spiritual Mind is allowed to flow freely into the conscious mind. Little by little the student is impressed with the truth, so gradually, often, that he scarcely realizes that it is advancing—but he is continually progressing and unfolding.

The next four precepts are very important. Although intended for quite advanced students, much of their meaning may be grasped by those who have not attained so fully. We will try to make a little plainer these difficult passages.

1. Stand aside in the coming battle; and, though thou fightest, be not thou the warrior. 2. Look for the warrior, and let him fight in thee. 3. Take his orders for battle, and obey them. 4. Obey him, not as though he were a general, but as though he were thyself, and his spoken words were the utterance of thy secret desires; for he is thyself, yet infinitely wiser and stronger than thyself. Look for him, else, in the fever and hurry of the fight, thou mayest pass him; and he will not know thee unless thou knowest him. If thy cry reach his listening ear, then will he fight in thee, and fill the dull void within. And, if this is so, then canst thou go through the fight cool and

unwearied, standing aside, and letting him battle for thee. Then it will be impossible for thee to strike one blow amiss. But if thou look not for him, if thou pass him by, then there is no safeguard for thee. Thy brain will reel, thy heart grow uncertain, and, in the dust of the battle-field, thy sight and senses will fail, and thou wilt not know thy friends from thy enemies. He is thyself; yet thou are but finite, and liable to error. He is eternal, and is sure. He is eternal truth. When once he has entered thee, and become thy warrior, he will never utterly desert thee; and, at the day of the great peace, he will become one with thee.

These four precepts refer to the recognition of the Real Self—Spirit—which is within each soul, and which is constantly struggling to cast from itself (when the time is ripe) each encumbering sheath of the lower self which is hindering and confining it. The precepts bid the soul to look within for the real source of strength—to be guided by it—to allow it to manifest freely through oneself—to be led by Spirit. When one has sufficiently freed oneself from the restrictions and confining bonds of the lower self, and is able to allow Spirit to flow freely and manifest with a minimum degree of resistance, then will Spirit act through him and work for him, and guide him. And even the less advanced soul may obtain the greatest benefit from opening up itself to the inflow of the divine principle, and allowing it to work through it. The man who is led by Spirit— who recognizes the existence of the Real Self, and trusts it— may live in a great measure apart from the turmoil and strife of the outer world. Not that he may withdraw from the world (for that is often cowardice), but he is able to take his place in the great game of Life, and to do his work there and do it well, and yet feel certain that while he is in it he is not of it. He is able practically to stand aside and see himself act. Spirit will guide him through the struggle, and will see that he is nourished and cared for, and will always act for his ultimate good. It will lead him to that which is best for him, and will attract to him that which he needs. Fear and unfaith are the great obstacles to this free working of Spirit, and until they are cast aside Spirit is hampered and hindered in its work. But when they are thrown aside Spirit will be free to do its work.

The first precept: "Stand aside in the coming battle; and though thou fightest, be thou not the warrior," states this truth distinctly. Note that the precept does not tell you to run away from the battle, or to hide yourself, or to seek seclusion. On the contrary, it distinctly assumes that you will fight. But it tells you to "stand aside" (that is for you, in your present consciousness to stand aside) and let the real self fight through you and for you. That is, to allow Spirit to lead you, and for you to be content with its leading.

The second precept is akin to the first. It tells you to "Look for the warrior, and let him fight in thee." Look for him; believe in him; trust in him; recognize him—and let him fight the battle for you.

"Take his orders for battle, and obey them," says the third precept. If he places you in a certain exposed position, where the enemy's fire is concentrated upon you, and your retreat seems to be utterly cut off, fear not but obey orders implicitly, for there is a plan behind the orders, and you will in the end triumph. Question not the orders, nor their result, for they are given by a higher form of intelligence than your present consciousness, and have a distinct (and good) object in view. Spirit is moving for your advancement, and though it brings you temporary pain and suffering, you will be a gainer in the end. And if you once grasp the meaning of it all, you will not feel the suffering and the pain as do others, for they will be seen to be only temporary and fleeting, and unreal, and you will lose sense of them in your knowledge of the greater thing coming to you through and by means of them.

The fourth precept tells you further to "Obey him, not as though he were a general, but as though he were thyself, and his spoken words were the utterance of thy secret desires; for he is thyself, yet infinitely wiser and stronger than thyself." This admonition serves to warn us of the mistake of considering Spirit as an outside entity—a thing apart from ourself—and to remind us that it is our real self—ourself. Wiser and stronger than our present conception and consciousness of self, is Spirit, and we may trust it implicitly.

"Look for him, else, in the fever and hurry of the fight, thou mayest pass him; and he will not know thee unless thou knowest him," continues the precept, and the warning is worthy of note.

In the midst of the fight we are most apt to forget that the Real Self is working through us, and, being excited and inflated by success, we may imagine that we (the conscious self) are doing all the work, and may cease to look for the Spirit, and thus close the channel of communication. "And he will not know thee, unless thou knowest him." Unless you recognize Spirit within, Spirit will not be able to work through you as freely as would otherwise be the case. Unless you recognize the existence of Spirit, you cannot expect it to respond. Spirit's guidance is for those who desire it and look for it.

"If thy cry reach his listening ear, then will he fight in thee, and fill the dull void within." Note the promise, and the statement that Spirit is listening—ever listening—for your call for help. When you become disheartened and discouraged—tired and worn from the fight—wounded and bleeding from the struggle—then cry to Spirit for help, and the listening ear will hear thee and will "fight in thee and fill the dull void within." He who opens himself up to Spirit no longer is conscious of the "dull void within" which has oppressed him for so long. "And if this is so, then canst thou go through the fight and unwearied, standing aside, and letting him battle for thee." You will gain that feeling of calm content, knowing that thy warrior is invincible, and that the battle must be yours in the end. He who is conscious of Spirit working through him has indeed acquired "that peace which passeth understanding."

"Then it will be impossible for thee to strike one blow amiss." True, indeed, for then every act and move is the act and movement of Spirit, and cannot be amiss or wrong. No matter how meaningless or mistaken the act or move may seem to the conscious mind, at the time, later on it will be recognized as having been the very best thing under the circumstances.

"But if thou look not for him, if thou pass him by, then there is no safeguard for thee. Thy brain will reel, thy heart grow uncertain, and, in the dust of the battle-field, thy sight and senses will fail, and thou will not know thy friends from thy enemies." Is not this the experience of all of us before we recognize and trust Spirit's guidance? Have we not gone through these things, and suffered and grieved because we could see no light; no hope? Long have we cried aloud, demanding to know the reason of it all—demanding to be told what was truth; what was right; what was wrong. And no answer has come to us, until we threw off the confining bonds of the lower self, and allowed the pure rays of Spirit to pour into our souls.

"He is thyself; yet thou are but finite, and liable to error. He is eternal, and is sure. He is eternal truth." The distinction between the lower, temporary, consciousness of self, and the reality, is here pointed out. The paradox of the self and the Self is here presented to you. Think well over it, and the truth will gradually reach you—and having reached you will never again depart from you, no matter how dim it may seem at times.

"When once he has entered thee, and become thy warrior, he will never utterly desert thee." Wonderful promise. The consciousness of the existence of the Spirit within you, once obtained, is never entirely lost. Though you may learn to doubt it, as not having come through your ordinary senses, yet will the memory linger with you—and when it is most needed you will be able to recall the experience and again open yourself to the inflow of the divine wisdom and power.

"And, at the day of the great peace, he will become one with thee." In the time when sheath after sheath has been cast off and the flower of Spirit unfolds in full bloom—when man shall become more than man—then will the consciousness of the individual melt into the "knowing" of Spirit, and the soul will be at one with its highest principle. This will not be a surrender of individuality—but, on the contrary will be such an enlargement of individuality and consciousness as can scarcely be imagined by the greatest intellect of to-day. Then the great knowing, power, and joy, of which we have gained a faint glimpse during the flash of illumination, will become a permanent consciousness with us. Then will we pass from the realms of the relative into the regions of the absolute.

We come now to another group of four precepts. Let us consider them.

5. Listen to the song of life. 6. Store in your memory the melody you hear. 7. Learn from it the lesson of harmony. 8. You can stand upright now, firm as a rock amid the turmoil, obeying the warrior who is thyself and thy king. Unconcerned in the battle save to do his bidding, having no longer any care as to the result of the battle—for one thing only is important, that the warrior shall win; and you know he is incapable of defeat—standing thus, cool and awakened, use the hearing you have acquired by pain and by the destruction of pain. Only fragments of the great song come to your ears while yet you are but man. But, if you listen to it, remember it faithfully, so that none which has reached you is lost, and endeavor to learn from it the meaning of the mystery which surrounds you. In time you will need no teacher. For as the individual has voice, so has that in which the individual exists. Life itself has speech and is never silent. And its utterance is not, as you that are deaf may suppose, a cry: it is a song. Learn from it that you are a part of the harmony; learn from it to obey the laws of the harmony. "Listen to the song of life."

The note that is attached to this precept is so beautiful— so full of truth—so instructive—that we can find nothing to add to it, and we insert it in this place as the best possible explanation of the precept to which it is attached:

Note.—Look for it, and listen to it, first in your own heart. At first you may say it is not there; when I search I find only discord. Look deeper. If again you are disappointed, pause, and look deeper again. There is a natural melody, an obscure fount, in every human heart. It may be hidden over and utterly concealed and silenced—but it is there. At the very base of your nature, you will find faith, hope and love. He that chooses evil refuses to look within himself, shuts his ears to the melody of his heart, as he blinds his eyes to the light of his soul. He does this because he finds it easier to live in desires. But underneath all life is the strong current that cannot be checked; the great waters are there in reality. Find them, and you will perceive that none, not the most wretched of creatures, but is a part of it, however he blind himself to the fact, and build up for himself a phantasmal outer form of horror. In that sense it is that I say to you: All those beings among whom you struggle on are fragments of the Divine. And so deceptive is the illusion in which you live, that it is hard to guess where you will first detect the sweet voice in the hearts of others. But know that it is certainly within yourself. Look for it there and, once having heard it, you will more readily recognize it around you.

The sixth precept: "Store in your memory the melody you hear," and the seventh precept: "Learn from it the lesson of harmony," relate to the fifth precept and need no special explanation.

The eighth precept is full of information. It starts with the assurance that you (now being open to the guidance of Spirit) can stand upright, firm as a rock amid the turmoil, obeying the warrior (Spirit), who is spoken of as being "thyself and thy king" (again a reference to the relative and the absolute relation).

It speaks of the soul led by Spirit as being unconcerned in the battle, save to do his (Spirit's) bidding, and "having no longer any care as to the result of the battle" (that is, caring nothing about the apparent result—the temporary defeats, pains, and trying circumstances)—for only one thing is important and that is that Spirit should win, and win it must, for it is invincible, and incapable of defeat. The soul is spoken of as "standing thus, cool and awakened," and using the hearing which it has acquired by pain and by the destruction of pain. This paradox of "pain and the destruction of pain" is interesting. One necessarily learns lessons from pain—many lessons may be learned in no other way—and yet after the true nature of pain is learned and fully impressed upon the mind, then pain no longer is pain—pain is destroyed, and another lesson is learned. And so the voice of the Spirit—the song of life—comes to the hearing which has been awakened both by pain and by the destruction of pain.

"Only fragments of the great song come to your ears while you are but man." For when you reach the stage when you may listen to the grand volume of the divine song, then you are no longer man, but are something far higher in the scale of spiritual evolution and life. But the mere fragments of the song are so far beyond any other human experience that the mere echo is worth living a life to hear. We are further told that "if you listen to it, remember it faithfully, so that none which has reached you is lost, and endeavor to learn from it the meaning of the mystery which surrounds you," the voice of Spirit will beat upon your ears, so that, in spite of the material interferences you will from time to time have borne in upon your consciousness bits of knowledge which will seem to come from another world. Light will be thrown gradually upon the great problems of existence, and veil after veil will be withdrawn.

The precept then gives us the glad tidings that: "In time you will need no teacher. For as the individual has voice, so has that in which the individual exists. Life has speech and is never silent. And it is not, as you that are deaf may suppose, a cry; it is a song. Learn from it that you are a part of the harmony; learn from it to obey the laws of the harmony." In time you will have passed beyond the need of a human teacher, for the light of Spirit will illuminate every object upon which you gaze, and the ears opened by Spirit will hear the lessons coming from every object in nature. In the stone; in the plant; in the mountain; in the tempest; in the sunshine; in the stars; in all things high or low; will you perceive that great throbbing intelligent life of which you are a part—and from them will you hear notes of the great song of life: "All is One; All is One." As the precept tells us, the sound from nature and nature's things, is not a cry, as many have supposed, but a great triumphant song—a song rejoicing in the flow of life of the singer, and vibrating in unison with the Absolute. "Learn from the song that you are a part of the harmony; learn from it to obey the law of the harmony."

The next group of four precepts are along the same lines as those preceding:

9. Regard earnestly all the life that surrounds you. 10. Learn to look intelligently into the hearts of men. 11. Regard most earnestly your own heart. 12. For through your own heart comes the one light which can illuminate life, and make it clear to your eyes. Study the hearts of men, that you may know what is that world in which you live, and of which you will to be a part. Regard the constantly changing and moving life which surrounds you, for it is formed by the hearts of men; and, as you learn to understand their constitution and meaning, you will by degrees be able to read the larger word of life.

The ninth precept: "Regard earnestly all the life that surrounds you," refers to that part of the subject mentioned by us in the preceding paragraph—the knowledge that comes to one by viewing nature by the light of the Spirit.

The tenth precept tells you to "Learn to look intelligently into the hearts of men, that you may understand the world of men, that forms a part of the great world. By knowing men you will be able to help them, and will also learn many lessons that will aid you in your journey along the path. But take notice of what the little accompanying note says regarding this study of men. Here it is:

Note.—From an absolutely impersonal point of view, otherwise your sight is colored. Therefore impersonality must first be understood. Intelligence is impartial; no man is your enemy, no man is your friend. All alike are your teachers. Your enemy becomes a mystery that must be solved, even though it take ages; for man must be understood. Your friend becomes a part of yourself, an extension of yourself, a riddle hard to read. Only one thing is more difficult to know—your own heart. Not until the bonds of personality are loosed, can that profound mystery of self begin to be seen. Not until you stand aside from it, will it in any way reveal itself to your understanding. Then, and not till then, can you grasp and guide it. Then, and not till then, can you use all its powers, and devote them to a worthy service.

The eleventh precept tells you to "Regard most earnestly your own heart." And the twelfth precept goes on to say: "For through your own heart comes the one light which can illuminate life, and make it clear to your eyes." In your own nature you will find all that is in the nature of other men—high and low—pure and foul—it is all there, the foul outlived, perhaps—the pure yet to be lived, perhaps—but all there. And if you would understand men, and their motives, and their doings, and their thoughts, look within, and you will understand other men better. But do not identify yourself with all the thoughts you may find in your heart. View them as would an outsider, look at them as you would upon objects in a case in a museum—useful to study but not to make a part of your life. And, remember this, that none of the things in your heart is good enough to use or master you—although many of them may be used by you to advantage. You are the master, and not the mastered—that is if you are a delivered soul.

The thirteenth precept says that: "Speech comes only with knowledge. Attain to knowledge, and you will attain to speech." The little accompanying note is explanatory (in part) of this precept. We herewith print it:

Note.—It is impossible to help others till you have obtained some certainty of your own. When you have learned the first twenty-one rules, and have entered the Hall of Learning with your powers developed and sense unchained, then you will find there is a fount within you from which speech will arise.

Do not be worried if you anticipate being called upon to impart words of comfort and knowledge to others. You need not prepare yourself. The person will draw forth from you (through Spirit's guidance) just what is best for him or her. Fear not—have faith.

We must come to an end. We have tried to explain, partially, the wonderful teachings of this little manual—"Light on the Path," so that the beginner, perhaps, might be able to grasp the loose end of the teaching, and then gradually unwind the ball at his leisure. The task has grown heavier, and the work less satisfactory, as the precepts passed before us. Words are finite— truth is infinite—and it is hard to even attempt to explain infinite truth in finite words. The thirteenth precept is the last one that we may consider. The remaining ones must be read alone by the student, with the light of the Spirit. They are only for those who have attained spiritual sight, and to such their meaning will be more or less plain, according to the degree of unfoldment which has come to the individual.

We feel that our task has been poorly executed, although many have written us that these lessons have opened their spiritual eyes, and that many things heretofore very dark, are now seen plainly. We trust that this is indeed so, and that many more may obtain help and comfort from our words, although to us it seems that we have written nothing. And yet, we know that if these words had not some task assigned to them—if they were not intended to form a part of the great work, they never would have been written. So we send them forth to go where they will, without a full knowledge on our part of their destination. Perhaps some into whose hands they may fall may understand better than do we why they were written and sent forth. They were produced at the dictates of Spirit—let Spirit attend to the placing of them where they are called for.

In our following lessons we will take up other phases of occultism which may be of interest and profit to our students. But before leaving the beautiful precepts and teachings of "Light on the Path," let us urge upon our students the importance of that little manual. It contains within its pages the greatest amount of high spiritual teaching ever combined into so small a space. Let not the student imagine that he has mastered it, because he seems to understand its general teachings. Let him read it again a little later on, and he will see new beauties in it. We have never met a student—no matter how highly developed— who could not learn something from the little manual. Its teachings are capable of being interpreted in many different ways, for it portrays the experiences of the soul as it journeys along the path. You will remember that the upward ascent is along the spiral path, and the soul goes around and around but ever mounting higher. One may think he grasps the meaning of the first precepts of the little manual, but as he again reaches a certain point, just one round higher, he may again take up the first precepts and find in them new meaning suitable for his newly discovered needs. And so on, and so on. Not only is there spiritual progression along spiral lines extending over ages, but in each life-time there is a spiral path to be mounted, as will be apparent to all of us who will stop to consider the matter. The soul which has not found the entrance to the path, seems to go around and around in a circle, traveling over the same ground, and making no real progress. But once it discovers the little path which enters the circle at one of its points, and takes steps thereon, it finds that while it still goes around and around, it is really traveling the spiral, and is mounting one round higher with each turn. And we know of no little book so helpful on the journey as this little manual—"Light on the Path."

We trust that we may be pardoned for inserting in this lesson the following words from our introduction to the little manual in question. They are as appropriate at the close of this lesson as at the beginning of the little book:

The treatise, "Light on the Path," is a classic among occultists, and is the best guide known for those who have taken the first step on the Path of Attainment. Its writer has veiled the meaning of the rules in the way always customary to mystics, so that to the one who has no grasp on the Truth these pages will probably appear to be a mass of contradictions and practically devoid of sense. But to the one to whom a glimpse of the inner life has been given, these pages will be a treasury of the rarest jewels, and each time he opens it he will see new gems. To many this little book will be the first revelation of that which they have been all their lives blindly seeking. To many it will be the first bit of spiritual bread given to satisfy the hunger of the soul. To many it will be the first cup of water from the spring of life, given to quench the thirst which has consumed them. Those for whom this book is intended will recognize its message, and after reading it they will never be the same as before it came to them. As the poet has said: "Where I pass all my children know me," and so will the Children of the Light recognize this book as for them. As for the others, we can only say that they will in time be ready for this great message. The book is intended to symbolize the successive steps of the neophyte in occultism as he progresses in the lodge work. The rules are practically those which were given to the neophytes in the great lodge of the Brotherhood in ancient Egypt, and which for generations have been taught by guru to chela in India. The peculiarity of the rules herein laid down, is that their inner meaning unfolds as the student progresses on The Path. Some will be able to understand a number of these rules, while others will see but dimly even the first steps. The student, however, will find that when he has firmly planted his foot on one of these steps, he will find the one just ahead becoming dimly illuminated, so as to give him confidence to take the next step. Let none be discouraged; the fact that this book attracts you is the message to you that it is intended for you, and will in time unfold its meaning. Read it over and over often, and you will find veil after veil lifted, though veil upon veil still remains between you and the Absolute.

LESSON V. KARMA YOGA.

The Yogi Philosophy teaches that while there is but one goal for true human endeavor—one end to be sought— still there are different paths to that goal, each path best suited to the particular temperament of the individual. Temperament, of course, is not the result of accident or chance, but is the result of the particular development of the soul in its evolution, and represents the particular line of thought (and resulting action) which has been pursued by the soul in its development. It is a very real thing at each stage of unfoldment, and forms the line of least resistance for the individual. And, so, the Yogis teach that the particular path best adapted to the requirements of the temperament and tastes—that is, to the desires—of each individual soul, is the one for him to follow. They divide the Path of Attainment into three sub-paths leading up to the main road. They call the three paths (1) Raja Yoga, (2) Karma Yoga, (3) Gnani Yoga; each of these forms of Yoga being a path leading to the great road, and each fit to be traveled by those who may prefer it—but all leading to the same place.

Raja Yoga is the path followed by those who feel inclined to develop the powers latent in Man—the gaining of the control of the mental faculties by the Will—the attainment of the mastery of the lower self—the development of the mind, to the end that the soul may be aided in its unfoldment. Karma Yoga is the Yoga of work—the path of action. Gnani Yoga is the Yoga of Wisdom. In addition to the above mentioned three forms of Yoga, there is that which is known as "Bhakti Yogi," or the Yoga of devotion—the path of religious feeling. Some writers treat this path as if it were distinct from the others—a separate path—but we prefer thinking and teaching that it is merely an incident of each of the three paths, as we cannot conceive of any student of Yoga divorcing his work from the love and devotion to the Absolute—to God. We fail to see how one may follow any of the several Yoga paths without being filled with love and reverence for the great centre of all life. In these lessons we will speak of Bhakti Yogi separately, but we wish to be understood that we do not consider it a separate thing, but feel that the student of any, or all, of the forms of Yogi must combine Bhakti Yogi with his favorite form of study.

In this lesson we will take up the branch of the subject known as "Karma Yoga"—the Yoga of action—of work. But we must explain that although the necessities and tendencies of the student may make this path the more attractive to him, still he may take a keen interest in the other forms of Yogi, such as Gnani Yoga, Raja Yoga, etc. And the students of these other branches must not overlook Karma Yoga as being beneath their notice, for it is a matter which concerns their daily life, and in this Western world where nearly all men live a life of action, the student must combine the principles of Karma Yoga with his other studies.

This lesson will be devoted to Karma Yoga. The next lesson will take up the subject of Gnani Yoga. The one following Gnani Yoga will take up that branch of the subject known as Bhakti Yoga. We will not touch upon Raja Yoga in these lessons, as we are now preparing a separate book upon that branch of Yoga.

Before considering Karma Yoga it may be well for us to take a general view of the subject of Yoga. What is the end and aim of the teachings and the practices? What does it all mean? What is Man seeking for in all these endeavors? What does life, and growth, and development, and evolution mean? These are questions that thinking people are constantly asking, and which but few are able to answer even partially.

The Yogi Philosophy teaches that the end of all human endeavor and life is to allow the soul to unfold until it reaches union with Spirit. And as Spirit is the divine part of man—the bit of God-material in him—this union eventually will result in what is known as Union with God—that is the bringing of the individual soul into conscious touch and union with the centre of all life.

Some may think and teach that the end of human life is happiness, and this is true if they mean the real happiness of the soul—the only true happiness. But if they mean the relative and transitory thing usually called "happiness," they quickly find that they are pursuing a "will-o'-the-wisp," that constantly recedes as they approach it. True happiness is not to be found in relative things, for these turn to ashes like Dead Sea fruit, the moment we reach out to grasp them. We may find a certain amount of happiness in the pursuit of things, but when we pluck the fruit it withers. No matter how high may be the thing pursued in the chase for happiness, the result is the same. Relative things cannot help being relative and consequently fade away. They are creatures of time and space and while they serve their purposes they cannot live beyond their time.

They are mortal, and like all mortal things must die. Only the absolute thing remains unchanged, and is deathless.

And all this struggle, and pain, and life, and effort, really is directed toward the unfoldment of the soul that it may recognize its real self. This is what it all means. This is why we pursue first this thing and then that thing, thinking that we need them, only to find out that we need them not. We feel a hunger that cannot be appeased—a thirst that will not be quenched. And we try all the experience of life, sometimes feverishly and eagerly, sometimes listlessly and sluggishly, but find them all to be shadows and unrealities. But the hunger and thirst still remain, and torment us to further efforts. And this will be so always, until we learn that the thing we desire is within us, instead of outside of us—and when we learn this lesson, even faintly, we begin to seek intelligently and are changed beings. This is the meaning of life—of evolution.

The great majority of the race is engaged in this pursuit of happiness in a blind, unconscious fashion. They run hither and thither, trying one thing after another hoping to find that intangible something that they instinctively feel will bring them peace and happiness. And, although meeting with repeated disappointments, they keep up the search with unabated zeal, being impelled thereto by the unfolding soul crying for that which is necessary to it. As the soul awakens and unfolds, through experience after experience, it gradually obtains an intelligent and conscious conception of the true nature of that for which it seeks, and thereafter it follows only the roads which lead to the thing so long sought after, but so recently known to be the sought-after thing.

Many Western seekers after truth have complained that the philosophies of the East were not adapted to the needs and requirements of the Western student, as the conditions of life were so different in the two parts of the world. This objection, if it were sustained, would be positive proof that the teachings of the East were not sound and true, for any true and sound teaching and philosophy must be applicable to all sorts and conditions of men, irrespective of race, climate, country, occupation, surroundings or environment. If the teachings are not fitted for the wants of every soul they are unsound, and must be discarded. Even the lowliest, humblest and vilest of the race must be taken into consideration, or the teachings fall short of being the truth. For even that lowly individual, as well as the most exalted (in the world's estimation) form part of the race, and are under the law and cannot be left out.

The trouble with these objecting Western students is that they have considered the Eastern teachings to be fit only for those who could spend their life in dreaming, meditating, and in seclusion far away from the busy world. But this is a great mistake. It is true that some Eastern students follow this retired life, and obtain great results therefrom—this is their Karma— the result of desire and tendencies acquired in their past lives. But no true Yogi would think of teaching that this plan was the only one—or even the best one for all students. On the contrary, he recognizes that even in the East a life of activity is right and proper for those who are thrown into it, and that to shirk its duties or run away is a violation of the great law. This being so, it follows that the intense activity of the Western races (all of which is in accordance with well established laws, and a distinct and well understood stage of evolution) renders seclusion and retirement literally impossible for thousands of earnest students, who must follow the path or plan called for by their Karma. And they gladly point out to such students the beauties and advantages of that branch of their philosophy known as "Karma Yoga," which we take up in this lesson.

The word "Karma" comes from the Sanscrit word "Kri," meaning "to do"; "to act." "Karma" is more frequently used to designate what may be called the "effect of actions." In our "Fourteen Lessons" we have considered the Eastern teachings of Karma, under the chapter entitled "Spiritual Cause and Effect." In that chapter we gave you a brief description of the law of cause and effect in the spiritual world—how the effects of actions follow actions, just as actions follow thoughts. The real effect of actions is really the effect of thoughts, as actions result from thoughts.

We are what we are today, simply because we have done, or left undone, certain things in our past lives. We have had certain desires, and have acted upon them, and the result is manifested today. We do not mean that we are literally being "punished" because we have done certain things in the past—for punishment (as such) forms no part of the law. But we have desired to do certain things, and have done them so far as we were able, and the inevitable results came in their train. We put our fingers into the fire and we are now nursing the burn—that's all. These things that we did in the past were not necessarily "bad" things. We merely may have become unduly attached to certain things, and our attachment and desires have brought upon us certain effects which effects, while perhaps more or less unpleasant and painful, are good because they teach us that we do not want the thing we had sought, and we will not make the same mistake again. Moreover, once we have had our eyes opened so that we understand the nature of our trouble, the smart of the burns decreases and the hurt fades away.

This spiritual law of cause and effect is known in the East as "Karma." When the Eastern students speak of one's "Karma," they mean that which has come to the person in pursuance of that law, or that which is attached to him by its operations. Everyone has generated Karma, the effects of which are manifesting constantly. There is no reason why we should feel frightened or disturbed at this knowledge. A realization of the truth enables us to live out our Karma with the minimum degree of pain and trouble, and also prevents us from acquiring new undesirable Karma. Our Karma may be pleasant, or unpleasant, according to the causes we have set into operation, or they may be made pleasant or unpleasant by our mental attitude toward them.

The philosopher may transmute "bad" Karma into "good" by refusing to see the "bad" in it, and the ignorant person may find fault with the best of Karma.

Many students of the Eastern philosophies seem to regard this law of Spiritual Cause and Effect—Karma—as a system of punishment decreed, regulated and administered by the spiritual powers that be. This is erroneous. While Karma often does act as a punishment—that is, as an equalizing and deterring factor—yet there is no element of revenge in it—no plan of Divine "getting even." It is simply cause and effect. It is difficult to explain just what we mean, without giving specific examples, which plan is almost impossible in a work of this kind. We may say, however, that one who is possessed with a desire for power, which desire he constantly nourishes and feeds with selfish thoughts, is sure to become involved in a sequence of causes and effects which may cause him the greatest pain and suffering, physical or mental. He may attain his desire, sooner or later, if his desire be sufficiently strong and persistent, but he is very apt to suffer from unsatisfied longings which have been smothered out by the over-ruling passion. He may gain his prize at the cost of all else dear to him. Or, his desire not being so strong as a like desire in some other minds, he may not attain his goal, but will be ground to pieces in the great mental or psychic machinery which he has helped to set into motion, and into which he is irresistibly drawn. When a man has a keen desire for the fruit of some action, he is very likely to start into motion (in connection with others) certain psychic machinery, which either may work to his advantage, or else may grind him to pieces according to the circumstances of the case, his strength of purpose, or his mental powers. Men are often blown up by their own bombs, or consumed in fires of their own starting. They get "mixed into things" and often suffer from that course.

Even those who attain that for which they have been seeking (either in this life or in some future one) may be greatly disappointed and may find life a curse. The autocratic ruler may suffer untold mental agonies, and the multi-millionaire may be more unhappy than the beggar at his gates. But, not only is this so, but those who have entered the race, and have not been able to keep up with the winners, are tossed about, pushed, thrown down and trampled upon, and otherwise hurt, because they have entered the race. They not only suffer from disappointment, but are hurt besides. We recall a man who started to hate certain persons—hated them bitterly—tried to injure them in every possible way. The result was that he entangled himself in the psychic machinery of hate which is in full operation in the world, and before long brought upon himself the hatred and enmity of hundreds of other persons, and was hurt in mind and purse, and suffered great agony and mental torture. Of those whom he had started to hate, he succeeded in hurting only one person, and that person was a man also living on the "hate plane" of thought, who naturally attracted to himself thoughts and actions of like nature. But the lesson was a valuable one to the first mentioned man, for his eyes were opened to the folly and consequences of hate, and thereafter he refused to allow himself to become entangled in its net. Those who play the game of hate must not complain if they are hurt. Those who are entangled in the machinery of greed must not complain if they suffer from some shrewder person on the same plane. Those who pin their lives upon some material object must not wonder if they suffer pain through the person or thing to whom they attach themselves so closely.

"But," one may say, "how am I to escape these things if I am in the active world at all? How may I escape the effects of actions?" The Yogi Philosophy answers: "By taking part in the great game of life—by going through its motions—by doing the best thing possible for you—but all the time remembering that you do not allow yourself to become attached to the fruits of the work. Work for work's sake—do your part in the world gladly, cheerfully, willingly and heartily, but realize that the fruits are as naught in the end, and laugh at the thought that these relative things have any real value to you." To a consideration of this answer, we will devote the remainder of this lesson. We trust that we shall be able to show you that this advice, as impracticable and difficult as it may seem at first sight, is not only practicable to the most strenuous business worker of the lot but is the only true plan of life. This old Eastern Wisdom seems to be particularly adapted to the requirements of the busy Western world at this time, although, on the surface, it may seem to fly in the face of modern progress.

But, at this place, we must remind the student that these teachings will be accepted by only a few of the race. The great majority of people are too much infatuated with the present condition of things—the pulling down, and climbing over the dead bodies of their brothers—the cannibalism and savagery of modern industrial and commercial life—to follow any other course. This being so, they will continue to eat and be eaten— kill and be killed—crush down and be crushed down—hate and be hated. And those who deal out these things to others— and who take a delight in them—bring themselves under the operation of the law of cause and effect to such an extent that they become enmeshed in the machinery, and often get ground up while expecting to aid in the tearing apart of others.

The few who are ready for the teachings, will understand what we mean and will be able to stand aside and see themselves fight and struggle in the rush, while their soul stands apart from the fray. They will live the same life and do the same things as their undeveloped brothers—that is, apparently—but they will know the truth and keep themselves free from being drawn into the machinery, or entangled in the nets.

We are asked frequently, "What would become of things if everyone were to follow your teachings?" We might answer that the whole structure of modern life would fall to pieces, to be succeeded by something infinitely better. But there is no need for this answer, because there is no likelihood of the majority of the race accepting these teachings in the near future. A greater number are accepting them every day, but at the best, those who accept and live them will be but a handful in the crowd of those who live and act. Many years of struggle, and trial— endeavor and experiment—must come before the race, as a whole, is ready to take even the first step toward improvement. We say this, not in sadness, but philosophically, knowing that all the struggle and pain is a necessary part of the evolution of the race. (When we speak of "these teachings" we do not refer to the particular presentation of the truth given through us, but to the various forms of these teachings which are being given through hundreds of teachers of the various schools at this time.)

One of the first things to be learned by the Karma Yogi is that he is a unit in the whole machinery or plan of life. He has his place and must take his part in the work. But, no matter how important his position—or how responsible a place he is called upon to fill—he is but a unit in the plan, and must be willing to be used in accordance with that plan. And however lowly or unimportant he may seem to be, he is still a unit having a purpose and work. Nothing is unimportant, and the most important is still subject to the law underlying the plan. We must all play our parts—play them well—not only because we are working out our own development and evolution, but also because we are being used by the Divine Mind as a pawn, or higher piece, in the great game of life. Not that we are mere automatons—far from that—but that our interests are bound up with that of the race, and we touch all mankind at some point. We must be perfectly willing to be so used, and we will find that the willingness prevents friction and pain. It is difficult to express this point as clearly as we would like to do, but we trust that our meaning will be made clear as we proceed.

Our lives are not merely for the development of our individuality, but we are needed to play upon and be played upon by other individualities, that the entire race be assisted in its upward trend. A certain piece of work may seem to us to be useless as a part of our own development, but that particular bit of work is evidently needed in some part of the great plan and we should perform our part willingly. Every move and position has a meaning, just as a move in a game of chess apparently may be devoid of meaning and purpose, but, later in the game, it will be seen to have been the first move in a great plan. And, so the true Karma Yogi allows himself to be moved by the Spirit without complaint, knowing that all will be well with him, and that the move is needed to effect certain combinations or changes in the great game of life being played by all men. Those who do not understand this secret of the inner workings of the game, generally rebel and set up resistance to these enforced moves, and thereby cause themselves great pain and suffering from the friction—the resistance causes a forcible move—while the awakened soul, seeing things as they are, smiles and allows itself to be moved, and consequently escapes the pain, and generally reaps a positive benefit from the change, although it does not expect such benefit as a reward. It simply recognizes the Master Hand making the move, willingly allows itself to be moved to another square, and used to effect a new combination.

This is not a mere dream of transcendental philosophy. It would surprise many of you to be told that some of the leading figures in every branch of human effort recognize this force behind them, and have learned to trust to it. Let us give you the testimony of a very prominent man—one whose name is known all over the world as a great leader and "master of circumstances." He has no knowledge of the Eastern teachings (or, had not at the time of the following statement), but several years ago he confided the following information to a friend of his, who repeated it to us. This "captain of industry" said: "The public give me credit with being a most strenuous character, and as planning a long way ahead some wonderful combinations and schemes. They are quite wrong. I plan very little ahead, in fact, often see no more than one step at a time, although the general plan seems to be stored away somewhere in my mind. I feel that to a great extent I am merely a pawn in a great game of chess, and am being used by some great power as a means of working some great changes in things and men, although I am ignorant of what these changes are. I do not feel that I am favored by Providence for any special good in me, for, without mock modesty, I may truthfully say that I feel that I do not deserve any special reward, for I am no better or wiser than my fellows. I cannot help feeling, at times, that the things I do are done for some other people, possibly the race, although many of my acts, or rather the results of my acts may seem in the direction of working injury to the public at large. I get no special pleasure from my money, although I feel a keen interest in the game of making it, for the time being, and when a thing is accomplished I feel like flinging it away like a wornout toy. I do not know what it all means, to be sure, but am sure it means something. Some day, perhaps, I may be stripped of my possessions, but I feel that even if that happens I will be given something that will repay me for my apparent loss. I noticed this thing early in life, and I soon learned to be "led" or moved by it whatever it is. When I resisted, I found that I was hurt somehow, but that when I allowed myself to be moved without resistance, I was successful. Sometimes I laugh to see how the public regard my "achievements" when really I have been merely a checker-man or pawn in some great game, the mover of which I do not know, and of whom I have no reason to believe myself a special favorite."

This man, unconsciously, stumbled upon one of the principles of "Karma Yoga"—that principle which is known as "The Secret of Work." He cares little for results—for the fruits of his work—although he feels a keen interest in the game while it is being played. He does not seem to be "attached" to the fruits of his work, although this is not apparent to those who view him from a distance. He feels that he is a cog in the great machinery, and is willing to play his part. Many of the things he does, or apparently does (the doing is really done by many men, whose interests conflicting and agreeing, focus upon him) bear hard upon many of the race, but close observers see that he, and others of his kind, are unconsciously paving the way for the great economic changes that are coming to the race, and which are based upon a dawning consciousness of the Brotherhood of Man. We do not hold out this man as an illustration of a Karma Yogi—he is not that, because he lives the life unconsciously and without understanding, while the Karma Yogi is fully conscious of what it all means and understands the causes behind it. We merely cite this case as an illustration of its common occurrence. Many others in all walks of life are practicing some of the principles of Karma Yoga more or less unconsciously. They speak of taking life "philosophically," by which they mean they are not allowing themselves to become "attached," or to take too seriously the fruits of their labors, attained or anticipated. They work, more or less, from a love of work—"work for work's sake"—they like to be "doing things," and take a pleasure in the game of life, that is, in the game itself rather than in its prizes. They play the game—play it well—play it with a zest—take an interest in its workings and details. But as for the trumpery prizes that are to be awarded to the winners, they want none of them, let those who value those things have them, the real player has outgrown such childishness.

Fame, position, prestige, the world's cheap favors are despised by the strong men—they see them as the baubles that they are. They leave such things for the children. They may allow the prize ribbon to be pinned to their coats, but in their hearts they smile at it. The other players in the game may not detect this inner consciousness, and to all intents and purposes the awakened player may be like those around him—but he knows, and they know not.

"The Secret of Work"—non-attachment—is the keynote of Karma Yoga. Non-attachment does not mean that the student of such should repress all enjoyment. On the contrary, it teaches that this principle, if faithfully followed, will cause one to enjoy everything. Instead of taking away his pleasure, it will multiply it a thousand-fold. The difference lies in the fact that the attached man believes that his happiness depends upon certain things or persons, while the freed man realizes that his happiness comes from within and not from any outside thing, and he, therefore, is able to convert into pleasure-producing things, circumstances which otherwise would cause dissatisfaction and even pain. So long as one is tied or attached to any particular person or thing, so that his happiness seems dependent thereon, he is a slave of that person or thing. But when he frees himself from the entangling influences, he is his own master, and has within himself an unfailing source of happiness. This does not mean that we should not love others—on the contrary we should manifest abundant love, but the love must not be selfish—but we will speak of that phase of the subject a little later on.

To the man living the attached life, the Karma Yoga plan may seem foolish, and likely to result in failure or half-hearted effort. In this view he is wrong. Who is apt to do the best work in a shop, office, or workroom—the man who works merely for his wage, and who keeps his eye on the clock in order that he may not give a minute overtime, or the man who, while looking to his occupation to furnish him with a comfortable livelihood, is so interested and in love with his work that he almost forgets that he is working for money, and during certain hours, but is fairly carried away with his task?

Many such workers exist, and they are practicing a form of Karma Yoga, although they know it not. The best work of the world is produced by men who take an interest in their tasks, and do not go through the motions of work simply to earn their wage. The instinct that causes the artist to paint a great picture—the writer to produce a great book—the musician to compose a great work—will cause a man to make a success of any line of work. It is work for work's sake—work for the joy of the worker. All great work is produced in this way.

To many the mystic is regarded as a visionary person, unfit for the work of the world—a mere dreamer—a weaver of idle speculations. But those who have looked beneath the surface, realize that the "practical mystic" is a man to be reckoned with in any branch of human endeavor. His very non-attachment gives him a strength that the attached man lacks. The mystic is not afraid—he is daring—he knows that his happiness and success depends upon no particular combination, and that he will emerge safe and sound from the most unpromising combination of circumstances. He feels that he is standing on solid rock—that he has the power of the Universe back of him. This gives him a strength and courage unknown to the man who stakes his entire happiness upon the success of some particular thing, and who feels that he is doomed to despair if that thing does not succeed. The unattached man allows the stream of life to play upon him, and through him, and takes a fierce joy in being a part of it all. He goes out into a crowded thoroughfare, and sees the movement of the people, and feels it all to be a part of himself—he feels himself as a part of it all. He is conscious of the activity, growth and motion of the mass of people, and enjoys it all. He is not afraid, for he knows what it all means. He is moved from one sphere of activity to another, and knows it to be the work of the forces behind him, which are friendly to him. He works away, from the very joy of it, and takes the keenest interest in the masterful performance of his task. And, because of this he does the best of work. But for the results of the work—that is, for the reward and praise—he cares nothing. He can turn to another task with equal pleasure, and forget all about the one just completed. He is not attached to it—it has not entangled him in its meshes.

Such a man is sure to draw a proper support from his work—it comes to him as his right. Those who have mastered Karma Yoga, while not caring for the vanities and show of life, nevertheless find themselves supplied with a recompense sufficient to supply their wants and to render them comfortable. Of course their wants are comparatively few—their tastes are always simple, and manifest in the desire for fewer things but better ones—but they draw their means of support to them as the tree or plant draws nourishment from the soil, water and air. They do not pursue wealth any more than they pursue happiness, and yet happiness comes to them unasked, and the means of support are found at their hand. The man who has freed himself from the entanglements of the material life, finds a keen joy in the mere living, that the attached man never finds even in his most successful moments.

Anything, if sought as the expected source of happiness, when finally found is seen to carry in its bosom the sting of pain. But if one ceases to look upon the thing as the source of happiness, and regards it as simply one of the incidents and accompaniments of life, then the poison is neutralized and the sting is blunted. If one looks to Fame as the thing that will bring the long sought for happiness, he will find when he becomes famous that his success has brought with it many painful things that will kill the joy of his attainment. But to the one who is freed and who works for the love of work without allowing himself to be attached, Fame may come as an incident and its pain will not be in evidence.

Many things to which men devote their entire lives bring more pain than happiness. And this simply because men look to the thing for happiness instead of to themselves. The moment one pins his chance of happiness to an outside thing or person, he opens the door to pain and unhappiness. For no outside person or thing can satisfy the longings of the soul, and the disappointment which will come—and which must come, of necessity—from such dependence upon person or thing, causes pain and sorrow instead of the expected happiness.

Even Love, that noble emotion, is the source of pain to the attached person. The Yogi Philosophy preaches the doctrine of Love—more Love—still more Love. And yet it also teaches that when Love is selfish it brings pain in its train. When we say we love a person, we usually mean that we wish that person to love us, and are unhappy if that Love is denied. True love is not like this. Unselfish love flows out toward the loved one, and asks nothing in return. Its joy lies in the happiness of the loved one, rather than in the selfish demand for a return of the love. True love is constantly saying to itself, "Give, give, give," while the selfish, material love is continually demanding of the other person "Give, give, give to me." True love radiates like the sunlight, while selfish love would draw to itself like the whirlpool.

If one loves another in such a way that if the other's love be withdrawn all happiness will fade out of life, then that first person is the slave of circumstances—slave of the other's emotions or passions. He is attached in such a way that he must suffer the pain of disappointment, neglect or change. And he usually has such pain come to him, for such a love, being mortal, must die, and its death will bring great pain and suffering to the one who relies upon it for happiness. The love of the freed and unattached person is different. It is not a lesser lover—it is the greater of the two—but it is not attached to the personality of the other, nor is it dependent upon the manifestation of affection on the part of the other. It is Love—pure Love, and not the passionate, selfish thing that passes current as the real thing, of which it is merely a base counterfeit.

Edward Carpenter says of Love:

"Who loves the mortal creature, ending there, is no more free—he has given himself away to Death.

"For him the slimy black Form lies in wait at every turn, befouling the universe;

"Yet he who loves must love the mortal, and he who would love perfectly must be free:

("Love—glorious though it be—is a disease as long as it destroys or even impairs the freedom of the soul.)

"Therefore if thou wouldst love, withdraw thyself from love—

"Make it thy slave, and all the miracles of nature shall lie in the palm of thy hand."

And again:

"Seek not the end of love in this act or in that act—lest indeed it become the end;

"But seek this act and that act and thousands of acts whose end is love—

"So shalt thou at last create that which thou now desirest;

"And when these are all past and gone there shall remain to thee a great and immortal possession, which no man can take away."

In Lesson i of this course we refer to the first precept of the first part of the manual: "Kill out ambition." And to the fourth precept of the same part: "Work as those work who are ambitious.'" This apparently paradoxical statement of truth, gives the keynote of work without attachment. In the lesson named we have endeavored to give the student a view of the two sides of the shield, and to show him how one may kill out ambition and yet work as those work who are ambitious. We advise the student to re-read that part of the lesson, when he finishes the present one.

The fundamental idea of non-attachment—the secret of work—is to avoid becoming entangled in the unreal things of life—the delusions which fool so many people. Men are so apt to tie themselves to the things they create, or to the things for which they are working. They make themselves slaves instead of masters. They attach themselves to certain desires, and the desires lead them this way and that way, through swamp and over rocky roads, only to leave them worn and weary at the end. These desires come from the undeveloped part of the mind, and while they are perfectly right in their place, they belong to the past of the developed man who has outlived them. He does not fear them, for he sees them as part of himself—he knows their origin and history and recognizes the part they have played in his development, and the development of the race, but he has outgrown them, and allows them to bind him no longer. He refuses to be entangled with them. As Carpenter says:

"Slowly and resolutely—as a fly cleans its legs of the honey in which it has been caught— "So remove thou, if it only be for a time, every particle which sullies the brightness of thy mind: "Return into thyself—content to give, but asking no one, asking nothing; "In the calm light of His splendor who fills all the universe—the imperishable indestructible of ages— "Dwell thou—as thou canst dwell—contented."

The same poet says of desire:

"When thy body—as needs must happen at times—is carried along on the wind of passion, say not thou, 'I desire this or that';

"For the 'I' neither desires nor fears anything, but is free and in everlasting glory, dwelling in heaven and pouring out joy like the sun on all sides.

"Let not that precious thing by any confusion be drawn down and entangled in the world of opposites, and of Death and suffering. "For as a light-house beam sweeps with incredible speed over sea and land, yet the lamp moves not at all.

"So while thy body of desire is (and must be by the law of its nature) incessantly in motion in the world of suffering, the 'I' high up above is fixed in heaven.

"Therefore I say let no confusion cloud thy mind about this matter; "But ever when desire knocks at thy door, "Though thou grant it admission and entreat it hospitably—as in duty bound— "Fence it yet gently off from thy true self, "Lest it should tear and rend thee."

The Karma Yogi recognizes work and life as what they are, and is not deluded by the popular misconceptions of these subjects. He sees the fallacy of the popular idea that work is a curse placed upon mankind. He sees it, instead as one of the great blessings and privileges of the race. He realizes the benefits and happiness that spring from work, when performed free from attachment, and he accordingly makes use of it. When perplexed or disturbed from any cause he finds relief in his work. He finds it a great help in overcoming the temptations of the lower part of his nature, and a wonderful aid in helping him to meet the new problems that are constantly presenting themselves to him. It is natural to man to work. It is a manifestation of the divine creative power manifesting through him. It is the desire for expression and unfoldment. If thy soul recoil from the sight of the vanities of the world— from its hollow ideals and aims—from its cruelty—from its injustice—from its blindness—from the puppet-show play manifest on all sides to one who sees and thinks—rest thyself for a moment, retiring into the silence of the inner chambers of thyself. Do not be discouraged—do not feel like withdrawing from it all—do not cry out in anguish and sorrow. You have a work to do, and no one can do it so well as you. Your life has a meaning—a purpose. So go back again into the midst of the fray. Play well thy part—do the tasks set before you to-day—do the "duties" that seem proper for your doing. It is all a part of your soul development, and the development of the race. Let not the hollowness and worthlessness of it all dishearten and disgust you. It all means something.

But beware of becoming entangled in the fruits of your action—in the desire for reward. Keep your eyes clear and your mind unclouded. Do not think that you may keep out of the fight, but, as the "Light on the Path" says: "And though thou fightest, be not thou the warrior." If thy Karma has set thee in the midst of action—act! It is thy only chance of working out of the conditions that fret and disturb thee. You cannot run away from your Karma—you must exhaust it—work it out. You will be repaid in the end. This question is beautifully treated upon in the great Sanscrit poem, "The Bhagavad-Gita." The Prince Arjuna, complains of being forced in the battle of life, and beseeches Krishna to relieve him of the duty. Krishna tells him his duty, and urges him to perform it. Edwin Arnold has translated this poem into that beautiful English poem "The Song Celestial." Arnold's poem makes Krishna say to Arjuna:

"No man shall escape from act, By shunning action; nay, and none shall come By mere renouncements unto perfectness. Nay, and no jot of time, at any time, Rests any actionless; his nature's law Compels him, even unwilling, into act. (For thought is act in fancy). He who sits Suppressing all the instruments of flesh, Yet in his idle heart thinking on them, Plays the inept and guilty hypocrite: But he who, with strong body serving mind, Gives up his mortal powers to worthy work Not seeking gain, Arjuna! such an one Is honorable. Do thine allotted task! Work is more excellent than idleness; The body's life proceeds not, lacking work. There is a task of holiness to do, Unlike world-binding toil, which bindeth not The faithful soul; such earthly duty do Free from desire, and thou shalt well perform Thy heavenly purpose."

We know of no better words with which to close our lesson than those of Edwin Arnold, in the poem above mentioned. We consider these lines among the most beautiful ever written in the English language. You will do well to commit them to memory:

"Never the spirit was born; the spirit shall cease to be never; Never was time it was not; End and Beginning are dreams! Birthless and deathless and changeless remaineth the spirit for ever; Death hath not touched it at all, dead though the house of it seems!"

If you can but grasp the true spirit of these words of Arnold's, and make them a part of your consciousness, you will need no further instruction in Karma Yoga—you will lead the life instinctively, and will be able to see things as they are, and not as they seem to be when seen through the veil of delusion. Such knowledge will lead you to a realization of the Real Self, and, that once attained, the rest will be made plain.

May these words, and the thought, bring you Peace!

LESSON VI. GNANI YOGA.

Gnani Yoga is known as the "Yoga of Wisdom." The word, "Gnani," is derived from the Sanscrit root-word "Gna," meaning "to know." We prefer the word "Gnani," although the words, "Jnana," "Gnyana," etc., are often used, and have the same meaning.

Gnani Yoga is the path to which student, philosophers— men and women of the intellectual temperament are attracted. Those who are attracted by metaphysical reasoning and speculation, subtle intellectual research, philosophy, science, and similar lines of mental effort, turn naturally to "Gnani Yoga" as it holds out to them a pleasant and agreeable path to that which is dear to their hearts.

But one does not have to be a skilled metaphysician, or a deep student, to avail himself of the lessons of this branch of the Yogi Philosophy. It is open to all of those who wish to know the why and wherefore of life—who are not satisfied with the commonplace and childish explanations of the great problems of existence that are offered to them by the ordinary teachings and creeds—to those who regard the exoteric side of the subject as all very well in its way, but whose natures call out for the hidden knowledge, the esoteric phase of the truth.

The Karma Yogi is continually asking "How?" or "What?" The Gnani Yogi's eternal question is "Why?" And this "Why?" is beginning to unfold in the minds of more people every day. The thirst for real spiritual knowledge is rendering many uncomfortable, and causing them to seek that with which to quench the thirst—the spiritual hunger is demanding nourishing food for the soul.

People are beginning to see the unreality of the material things around them, great as these material things may seem to be. They see that civilization follows civilization—races rise, flourish and fall—people rise from savagery up and on to the heights of material achievement, and then begin to decay. In the ruins found buried beneath the earth's surface may be found traces of former great civilizations, of which history has no record. And one is awed by the thought that the people of those civilizations must have thought themselves at the apex of human achievement and that there was but little left for the generations to come. And yet, they have faded away, leaving not even a trace on the pages of history. The great warriors, statesmen, philosophers and teachers of these civilizations are unknown, and the people themselves are without a name to us. Nothing is left to tell the tale, but a broken column here, or a mutilated statue there. And the thinker sees that this fate must meet all races—all civilizations—even our own. We must pass away—our work will be forgotten—future races, building a civilization upon the ruins of that which is our proudest boast, will wonder who and what we were.

Religions have risen, flourished, dominated millions, and have faded away, borne down by the weight of the superstition and outward forms which man persists in building around the bit of truth which originally caused the religion to spring into existence. It has ever been so, and must be so in the future. We may doubt this fact (so, doubtless, did the people of the vanished civilizations), but it must come. It is mortal—man's work—and the mortal ever must perish and pass away.

Men look around them, and, becoming conscious of the unreality of all that goes to make up mortal life, begin to ponder over the meaning of it all. They ask "Whence come we— whither go we—what is the object of our existence?" They try to solve the riddle of life by countless theories. They discard the dogmas that are handed down to them, only to create fresh dogmas equally unsatisfying. They travel around like a squirrel in a cage, and exhaust themselves on the wheel—but they stop just where they began. They are like a caged bird, that beats itself to death against the confining bars of its prison. They go around and around the circle of intellectual reasoning, only to find themselves travelling over and over the same ground, and making no real progress. They try to explain things, but succeed merely in giving things new names. They climb the mountain of knowledge, and when they reach the top they look around them and see that they merely have reached the top of a small foot-hill, while, far above them, towering higher and higher, rise range after range of the real mountains, the highest peaks of which are hidden among the clouds.

The mistake of the searchers is that they are continually seeking the truth from outside—it is not to be found there, for it is within. It is true that with the inner light every outside thing may be studied to advantage, and bits of truth gathered therefrom. But without this inner light the outer objects will give no real answer, and one may shout aloud to nature and hear only the echo of his own cry. The seekers on the relative plane find only that for which they look. They find that which they expect, for there is more or less truth in the theories favored by them, and accordingly they must find something that will correspond with that bit of truth. But the man who looks for the thing exactly opposed to that sought for by these seekers also will find that for which he looks, for he, likewise, has a bit of the truth, and must find that which corresponds to it. Each realizing that he has found a bit of the truth, but each making the mistake of supposing it to be all of the truth, disputes the claims of the other, and various schools form. Then the schools quarrel over details, and split into sub-schools, and so it goes, and the inquiring student is perplexed more than ever to know just what is the truth.

Let not our students suppose that we are speaking alone of the Western schools of religion and philosophy—the Eastern world is just as bad. In India there are countless sects, schools and cults. Each started with a bit of the truth, but they have added much nonsense to that sacred thing, until the real truth has been lost sight of by the followers, and superstition and idle theories have taken the place of the calm, clear reasoning of the founders. The East and the West stand alike in this respect— but while this is so, there is a small number of men in all parts of the world, who keep alive the lamp of truth—who keep the flame burning by watchful care, and unceasing devotion.

These men refuse to allow any theories of their own, or others, to be mixed up with the truth. They say: "Let us speculate if we see fit—let us listen to the speculations of others—but let us not confound it with the bit of Divine Truth that has been handed down to us. Let us mix no alloy with the pure metal." It is true that India always has been the source and center of great spiritual truths. All great religions have had their real birth in the East. And in India to-day the conditions are more favorable for deep thought and study than is the case in the hustling West. But this does not mean that the masses of the Hindu people are highly developed spiritually. On the contrary, there is no land where the weed of superstition grows more rankly. And the reason of this may be understood, readily, when we consider that the same conditions which are conducive to high metaphysical and spiritual research and study, likewise furnish the best soil in which the weeds of superstition may grow. In the soil of California, fruits and flowers grow in a way unknown to the rest of the United States, but the same soil will grow a rank vegetation of weeds if untended and neglected. In India, if a farming settlement be neglected, in a year or so the jungle has again claimed its former home, and rank vegetation flourishes where the field of the farmer formerly stood.

In the East, the false gods of superstition are found in great number, while in the West the new god (equally false) of Material Wealth occupies the place in the temple. Between Mammon and the false gods of India there is a strong family resemblance.

The Gnani Yogi sees truth in all forms of religion, and in all schools of philosophy, but he recognizes that this truth is but a small part of the great truth. He finds no fault with any religion or school of philosophy—he has no argument with them—the only point he raises is "this is not the Whole Truth." He has no special school or creed, for he recognizes as brothers all thinkers and professors of religion, everywhere, of all shades of opinion. His belief is large enough to take them all in—but he refuses to be bound by the limitations of any of them. The trouble with the conflicting schools and creeds is that they wish to limit God, and to exclude some men. The Gnani Yogi can see no limit to God, and can conceive of no exclusion of any of God's children or creatures.

In this lesson, we will try to give our students a plain idea of the fundamental ideas and teachings of the Gnani Yogis, divested of the conflicting theories of their several schools of followers, each of whom accept the main premise, and then build up certain arguments and conclusions from the same. These fundamental truths are to be found in the esoteric teachings of all religions, among all races, and have been imparted to these religions by the original founders (who obtained them through their Spiritual Minds), through their favored disciples. These teachings become impaired with each generation of followers, until the original truths are almost entirely lost sight of. As an illustration of this fact, read the "Sermon on the Mount," the teachings of which are understood and venerated by occultists and mystics of all schools and countries. Then see how His followers maintain the outward form while stating boldly and unblushingly that Christ's teachings are "not practicable." Unbelievers may deny the truth of Christ's teachings, but it remains for professing Christians to pronounce them "foolish" and not fitted for the use of mankind. And so it is with the mass of the followers of all religions—they maintain the name and outward form, but accept only such of the teachings as fit in with their lives. Instead of making their lives conform to the teachings, they make the teachings conform to their lives. We mention these things, not in the spirit of harsh criticism, but merely as an example of the difference between the esoteric and the exoteric teachings of all religions.

In these fundamental teachings of the Gnani Yogis, there is nothing to conflict with the real teachings—the esoteric teachings—of any religion, and one may retain his connection with any form of religion while accepting these fundamental truths. In fact, such knowledge will enable anyone to see the esoteric side of his own religion, and appreciate the beauties thereof, while his fellow worshippers tie themselves to forms and words. And, likewise, those having no special form of religion will find that these teachings afford to them the spiritual comfort that they have not been able to find elsewhere, and that, when the idea is fully grasped, these teachings are found to be in full accord with reason. And the unbeliever, and materialist, may find in these teachings the spirit of the thing to which he has held. He has been talking about "Nature"—let him consider that to the Gnanis the words "God" and "Nature" have the same sense, and the scales will drop from his eyes.

In this lesson, we will state fundamentals only, and shall not attempt to build up any special theories or philosophy. The material furnished should give one the key to all philosophies, and each student may build up a little philosophy to suit himself, remembering, always, that all such theories are to be used merely as working hypotheses, and not as fundamental truth. With this understanding, we will proceed with our work.

In the consideration of the Riddle of the Universe we of necessity must go back to first principles—to that which underlies everything evident to the senses. The average man dismisses this thought with the remark that "God is back of everything, and we cannot understand God," which is very true. But ask him for his conception of God, and you will find that it varies with each individual. Each has his own idea—or lack of idea—but nearly all will tell you that God is a thing or being outside of Nature, who has somehow started things going, and then left them to run themselves in some mysterious manner.

The average man considers the answer "God did it" as a sufficient explanation of everything, notwithstanding the fact that such a man's idea of "God" is but very little advanced above the idea of Deity entertained by the savage. Unless we understand something about the nature of God, we can not understand anything about the nature of the Universe or of Life. Of course, the finite mind can grasp but little of the Infinite, but still it may grasp a little, through the channel of the Spiritual Mind, and that "little" is what the Gnanis state to be the "truth"—not in the sense that it is "true" simply because it is their belief, but that it is "true" because the knowledge of it may be obtained by any man who will allow the Spiritual Mind to impart its knowledge. The mere presentation of the truth often intuitively carries the evidence of its truth to the minds of those who are ready for it. It may transcend Intellect, but Intellect does not refuse it when the mind has been cleared of the rubbish that has been piled into it.

To the student of Gnani Yoga, the teacher always advises that he go through a course of mental training, discipline and self-examination, with the intent and idea that he shall "lay aside" former prejudices, preconceived opinions, dogmatic teachings, inherited tendencies, unreasoned suggestions poured into his mind in childhood, and similar furniture of the mind. Remember, we say "lay aside," not "discard"—merely "lay aside" to be taken up again and used if need be—but surely laid aside in order that the mind may grasp the new and full presentation of the truth, without interference and obstacle, and without danger of having the truth mixed up with old theories, limitations and misrepresentations. The Gnanis claim that a mind ready for the truth, if cleared in this way, will intuitively recognize the truth when it is presented to them, and will know the true metal from the base, without trouble.

We do not insist upon our students going through this course of preparation, at this time, but merely ask that they "lay aside" prejudice for the moment, and give this presentation a "fair field" for thought. If it does not appeal to you, lay it aside for some future consideration—there is no harm done, and you are not ready for it. If it does appeal to you—if it seems to fill your soul as it never has been filled before—then you are ready for it—the Truth is yours. The Gnani Yogi's conception of Deity is likened by many to a form of Pantheism, but it is much more than Pantheism. Pantheism teaches that God is the sum of all things, seen, felt, heard, tasted, or smelled—in fact, that the Universe as we know it is God. The Gnani Yoga teaching is that this is only a half-truth. It holds that all of the things of which we may become aware are only a infinitesimal part of the real Universe, and that to say that this is God would be like saying that the paring of a finger-nail was The Man. Gnani Yoga teaches not that

The Universe is God, but that God is manifest in all that comprises our Universe, and in a million times more. It claims that the true idea of God is beyond human conception, and that even beings as much more highly advanced than man in the scale of life, as man is higher than the beetle, can form merely a faint idea of his nature. But they claim that man may grow to know, actually, that God is in all Life. The teaching may be summed up, roughly, by the statement that God is present in all Life, manifest or unmanifest, created or not-created, seen or not seen, known or not known. This idea, you will see, is far different from the one that God is merely the sum of things known and seen, and, likewise, is different from the idea that He is a thing apart from his creations. The Gnanis speak not of "creations," for their idea is that all things are "manifestations" of God.

The student, who is accustomed to the ordinary use of the word "God," may have a difficulty in forming a mental conception of the Gnani idea of Deity. He will be apt to carry in his mind the anthropomorphic conception of God—that is, the conception of God as a man, or, at least, as having the form, passions, habits and characteristics of man. This idea of God belongs to the infant stages of the race, and the great thinkers of all religions have long since outgrown this childish idea. Although Deity must possess all the higher attributes generally ascribed to the personal idea of God, yet He must so transcend any such personal idea that no thinking man, having the proper respect for the Source of Being, can continue to maintain the anthropomorphic conception, no matter what his religious belief may be.

And, in view of the conception and mental image ordinarily called forth by the word "God," and the possibility of misunderstanding of our meaning, we think it better to use the term "The Absolute" in speaking of God in this lesson. This course is rendered particularly desirable in view of the fact that Gnani Yoga is more of a philosophy than a religion—more of a study for the higher powers of the mind, than an emotional subject, or one inculcating devotion. When we come to the subject of "Bhakti Yoga," which deals with the worship of God—the religious phase of the Yoga Philosophy, we may appropriately resume the use of the word "God" as applied to Deity, without danger of a misapprehension. So when, in this lesson, we speak of "The Absolute," we are not attempting to set up a new God, but merely are using a general term for the Source of Being, which is sufficiently broad to fit in with the conceptions of Deity held by any and all students, irrespective of their creed, belief, or training—and with the conceptions of the philosophers who prefer to think of a "principle" rather than of Deity. We ask the student to re-read this paragraph, in order that he may clearly understand the reason of the use of the term, in this lesson.

The Gnani Yoga Philosophy starts with the statement: "The Absolute is." It does not pretend to be able to explain to the human intellect, the how, wherefore, and why, of the Absolute. It merely states that it "is." In answer to the question, "How can there be a thing without a cause?" it replies that this understanding of cause and effect belongs to the relative plane of causation, and the Absolute is above the relative plane, as a matter of course. We see that everything around us has a cause, and is itself a cause of succeeding effects. Everything that we see, feel, or hear is a part of the chain of cause and effect. That is, it has a chain of preceding causes running back to—where? and it has a chain of succeeding effects that extends away into the future, ending—where? In each case the answer is

"The Absolute." We may trace the causes of a thing so far back that the reason refuses to act, and we may imagine a train of effects from a cause extending so far into the future that even the imagination refuses to carry the matter along further. The secret is that everything begins and ends in The Absolute. The human intellect is utterly unable to form a clear conception of a thing without a cause, because the Intellect is on the relative plane, and in this world of relativity everything has its cause, and we cannot imagine a thing entirely transcending our sense experience, and, therefore, can conceive of no thing without a cause. The philosophers who claim that everything must have a cause, are met with two propositions, one of which they must accept, and either of which destroys their own theory. They must accept the proposition (1) that there is a first cause, in which case they simply remove the problem back a few steps, and must admit that the First Cause has no cause; or they must admit (2) that the chain of cause and effect is infinite, in which case they are confronted with the difficulty that a beginningless thing can have no cause—that a thing that has no beginning can have no cause—in which case the law of cause and effect is incomplete. In short, the human intellect is utterly incapable of solving the question, and the more it attempts it the more does it become muddled. It is the old question of the child, "Who made the Universe?" the answer being "God." The child then asks, "Then who made God ?" You see, it is merely moving the question back another stage. Even the materialist who says he does not believe in God at all, has to assert that Matter has existed forever, and cannot explain why Matter should have no cause, when all manifestations of it show a chain of cause and effect. (The materialist is merely setting up a conception of one of the manifestations of The Absolute and calls it Matter, while he refuses to accept another manifestation of The Absolute, which men usually call Mind, or Intelligence.)

And, so at the end, the Intellect is forced to admit that there is some thing that has no cause. In other words, it must admit itself beaten, and beaten it must be because it belongs to the relative plane, and cannot conceive of The Absolute.

The Gnanis call The Absolute "The Causeless Cause," and merely assert that it is. The student must grasp this idea of the reality of The Absolute before he proceeds. He need not give it any attributes, or pretend to understand it—he may not even give it a name. But he must admit that there is an absolute Something, be it called God, Mind, Matter, Force, Life, or what not. He must admit and conceive of the absolute Thing, from which all the rest proceeds—or which is manifested in all the rest.

The next step for the student is the assimilation of the fact that all there is, seen or unseen, must be a manifestation or emanation of that Absolute Thing. For there can be nothing outside of The Absolute, or which has not emanated from it. There is no outside. There is nothing outside. Everything must have come from the one source. If The Absolute were to make a thing, it must make it out of itself, at least so far as our Intellect can conceive of the matter. There cannot be two Absolutes— there is room only for One.

We think it well to insert in this place a little poem, the name of the writer of which is unknown to us. It states a great truth in the simplest language.

"Thou great eternal Infinite, the great unbounded Whole, Thy body is the Universe—thy spirit is the soul. If thou dost fill immensity; if thou art all in all; If thou wert here before I was, I am not here at all. How could I live outside of thee? Dost thou fill earth and air? There surely is no place for me outside of everywhere. If thou art God, and thou dost fill immensity of space, Then I'm of God, think as you will, or else I have no place And if I have no place at all, or if I am not here, 'Banished' I surely cannot be, for then I'd be somewhere. Then I must be a part of God, no matter if I'm small; And if I'm not a part of Him; there's no such God at all,"

The third step for the student is the mastery of the mental conception that The Absolute must be possessed of the three attributes, (1) Omnipotence; (2) Omniscience; (3) Omnipresence. The student is not asked to accept this statement blindly. Let him examine it.

(1) Omnipotent means all-mighty, all-powerful. Not that The Absolute is mightier than something else, or all the rest put together, but that it is all-mighty—all-powerful. That it is possessed of all the power there is, and, consequently, that all the power of which we are conscious is a manifestation of The Absolute. There is no room for any other power, and all the power that is manifested, of all kinds and descriptions, must be manifestations of The Absolute. Do not try to evade this question and answer—it must be met. Many persons speak of God being Omnipotent—of an Almighty, all-powerful God, but they have merely the faintest conception of what the word means. And they will "dodge" the truth inevitably springing from the statement of All-power, namely, that all power must be of God. They would attribute to God all the manifestations of power that are pleasing to them, or which are conducive to their welfare, but when it comes to a manifestation of power that hurts them, or seems cruel, they are afraid to attribute it to God, and either ignore the question, or else attribute the undesirable thing to some other power, the "Devil," for instance, failing to see that if God is All-powerful, there can be no other power in the Universe, and that all manifestations of power, good or bad (relative terms), as they may seem to

be, must be from the same source. The trouble with man is that he calls all the things that inure to his material comfort and welfare, "good," and all that interfere with it, "bad." ("Good" weather is weather that is pleasant to man—and "bad" weather is that which is unpleasant to him. If he were out of the body, he would see them both as equally good, for neither would affect him.)

(2) Omnipresent means all-present—everywhere present at the same time. It means The Absolute is present in all space as we know it, and everywhere else without regard to our relative idea of space. It is Everywhere—space has no existence to it— it is Infinite. Here is another thing that the unaided Intellect is unable to grasp—Space. The Intellect cannot conceive of endless space any more than it can of a causeless cause. And yet (poor Intellect) it cannot imagine anything beyond space, or of the end of space. It cannot conceive of a space with an end, or without an end—of time with an end, or without an end. But to get back to our subject. If The Absolute is Omnipresent (and we cannot conceive of it not being), it must be present in all places at all times, in all persons, in all atoms, in matter, mind, and spirit. If it is absent from a single point of space, or without space, then it is not Omnipresent, and the whole statement is false. And if it is present everywhere, there is room for nothing else to be present at any place. And if this be so, everything must be a part of The Absolute, or an emanation of it. Everything must be a part of a Mighty Whole. Many people speak quite glibly of "God being everywhere"—every child is taught this in Christian countries. But how few stop to think of what the words mean—they do not know that they are saying that God is in the low places as well as in the high places—in the "bad" places as well as in the "good" places. They do not know that they are saying that God, being everywhere, everything must contain God—must, indeed, be a part of His manifestation. The words which they use so lightly carry an awful meaning. The student is not asked to accept this statement of Omnipresence without examination. We have no space here to go into the matter in detail, but modern science is filled with theories of there being but one substance, and that substance pervading all space. Just as science holds that there is but one Force, manifesting in different ways, so does it hold that there is but one Substance, appearing in different forms. It is true that science arrives at this conclusion through materialistic reasoning, but the conclusions are practically identical with those of the Gnani Yogis, held by them for many centuries, and obtained by them from teachers still farther back in the world's history. And orthodox religions affirm the same thing with their statements of Omnipotence, and Omnipresence—though they know it not.

(3) Omniscient means all-knowing, all wise. It means that The Absolute is possessed of all knowledge; that it knows everything; that there is nothing that it does not know; that it is the sum total of all the knowledge there is, ever has been or ever will be. If we admit that there is the slightest thing that is not known, or cannot be known, to The Absolute, then we admit that the

word is meaningless. And if The Absolute is possessed of all the knowledge there is, then it can make no mistakes; does not find it necessary to change its mind; cannot think or act except wisely, and therefore, justly. And yet people seem to think that God makes mistakes, or does not know all about things, and they frequently feel called upon to call his attention to matters that He has overlooked, or mistakes he has made, and request him to do better by them in the future. They seem to have an idea that they can flatter God, or fool him. Poor little children! The student may realize the truth of this statement of Omniscience, if he but looks around him and thinks a little. If The Absolute is not possessed of all-knowledge, from whence do we gain knowledge? Surely not from outside of The Absolute. Is it not more likely that the knowledge is always there, and that our acquiring of knowledge is merely the unfolding of our minds sufficiently to absorb it, or to let the Divine Knowledge play upon our minds. At any rate it would seem hopeless to expect knowledge from any other source than from The Absolute, for there is nothing else.

The Gnanis teach that The Absolute is All-powerful; is All-wise; is Everywhere. That it possesses all the power that there is—all the knowledge that there is—and occupies all space, or all that takes the place of space, if such there be, and is in everything, everywhere, at the same time, and in all time.

They teach that The Absolute in its sense of pure-being is incapable of being understood by the human Intellect, at the present time, but that it manifests in three forms, which forms of manifestation may be sensed, studied, and partially understood by the Intellect, even of the man of to-day.

These three forms of manifestation of The Absolute are known as (1) Substance, or Matter; (2) Energy, or Force; (3) Intelligence, or Mind. That which occultists know as Spirit is a transcendent manifestation, and is not included in the three manifestations above mentioned. Some writers treat of Spirit as a highly developed state of Mind, but it is more—it is a portion of The Absolute not manifest to our senses. So for the purpose of this lesson we will consider the three manifestations to be as above stated.

The student's attention is called to the correspondence between the three mentioned manifestations of The Absolute, and the three attributes, mentioned a few pages further back. Thus (1) the attribute of Omnipresence is manifested in Substance, or Matter; (2) the attribute of Omnipotence is manifested in Energy, or Force; (3) the attribute of Omniscience is manifested in Mind, or Intelligence. That is, the manifestations mentioned are a part of the manifestations of the attributes mentioned—a very small manifestation as compared with others on higher planes, but still manifestations for all that.

Do not understand us as saying that this three-fold manifestation of The Absolute is The Absolute itself—they are merely manifestations, or emanations. (It is difficult to select the proper English word, for the best of them is inadequate to express the thought.) The Absolute itself cannot be seen, or thought of clearly by man, and the mind must lay hold of the idea of one or more of the manifestations in order to carry the thought. When we think of The Absolute as Intelligence, we merely think of the manifestation of that name. When we think of it as Force or Energy, or of it as doing something, we merely think of the manifestation of Energy. When we think of it as filling space, we can merely think of Matter in some of its forms, very ethereal forms perhaps, but still the manifestation of Substance or Matter.

The ordinary religious man may find it difficult to conceive of God as manifesting in Substance or Matter; in Force or Energy. He thinks of Him as making, of using, these things, but is not accustomed to regarding Him as in them. The Gnani Yoga will help him to see God on all sides, and in all things. "Lift the stone and thou shalt find me; cleave the wood, and there am I."

And, on the other hand, the materialist will not find it easy to accept these two forms of manifestations as expressions of The Absolute, for that would seem to imply that The Absolute is something akin to the religious man's God, which the materialist has been denying. But Gnani Yoga brings these two brothers together in the truth, and tells them that they have been looking at the same thing from different view-points. The scientist may deny that the manifestation of Mind or Intelligence is a separate manifestation, but that it is merely an incident of matter. The Gnani Yogi sees Intelligence in everything, from the mineral to man—in varying degrees. He realizes that the tiniest cell is possessed of a subconscious intelligence that allows it to perform work that is beyond the intellect of man. The smallest growing thing shows a great intelligence working in and through it, and man will never be able to duplicate its work, notwithstanding his giant intellect. In the growing of the blade of grass, God, or The Absolute, manifests in three forms, i. e., in Substance, or Matter; in Force, or Energy; in Intelligence, or Mind. The scientist may take the elements of the seed from the matter around him, may form it into a seed—may surround it with the proper soil and conditions—may apply to it all the forms of energy or force known to him—but the plant will not grow. It needs the third manifestation—Intelligence, or Mind, and that is beyond the power of man to bestow. Each little cell contains intelligence, or mind, which works along unconscious lines, and builds up the plant. Our bodies are built up in the same way. There is Intelligence in everything—and it all emanates from The Absolute. Does man think that his intellect exhibits, the highest form of intelligence manifested in the universe? Nonsense! He has but to look around him and see the adaptation of means to ends, in order to see how nature dovetails one thing into another. He cannot do these things with his intellect, and yet they were being done ages before he appeared. A greater Intelligence than man's is at work, and the careful student may see signs of it on every hand. The study of the grain of wheat, the examination of the rabbit's eye, will show wonderful design and intelligence. Let the doubter care for a hive of bees, and he will feel as did an acquaintance of ours who was a doubter until he began bee-culture, when his eyes were opened to the wonderful work of "Nature." He said that his thought when gazing at the workings of the hive was: "Nearer, my God, to Thee."

Man is not developing Intelligence—he is merely developing the power to receive and absorb Intelligence and Knowledge from the fountain head. He receives only as much as he is able to hold—God does not try to put a quart of Intelligence in a pint measure. A No. 3 man does not receive a No. 7 amount of knowledge.

And note this coincidence. As the soul develops and unfolds it begins to partake of more of each of the three attributes of The Absolute. It begins to know more—to have more power— to be able to master space and matter. And as the soul unfolds and grows it will continue to partake in an increasing ratio of the three attributes of The Absolute—Omniscience, Omnipotence and Omnipresence.

We will not speak of our attitude toward The Absolute— our duty toward God—in this lesson. This properly comes under the head of "Bhakti Yoga" in our next lesson, and will be touched upon there. In this lesson we have spoken only of the philosophical side of the knowing of God—Gnani Yoga.

Now, right here, we must warn our students against a common mistake of students of the Eastern Philosophies—a mistake not alone common among students, but which also is apparent among some teachers. We allude to the proper conception (or the lack of it) of the relation of the Centre to the Emanation. While Man is of God, he is not God—while he is a manifestation of The Absolute, he is not The Absolute itself. He is but the Finite expression of the Infinite. We hear Hindus, and Western students of the teachings of the East, running about crying aloud, "I am God." They are so overpowered with the sense of the Oneness of All that has burst upon them—are so carried away with the consciousness of their relationship to The Absolute, that they think that they are equal with God, or are God himself. No wonder that the stranger to the teachings is shocked by the apparent impiety, and both his reason and his emotions cause him to recoil from the statement. This is a most subtle, insidious and dangerous perversion of the true teaching, and we warn and caution all students against the same, no matter from how high or apparently authoritative source this false teaching may come. The advanced Hindu teachers do not make this mistake in thought, but some of their followers fall into the error. Some very good Oriental teachers have endeavored to express the Hindu thought in English terms, the result being that the English words not being fitted to express the fine shades of thought possible to the Sanscrit scholar, an entirely wrong idea has been promulgated. Many of the new cults in America and England have fallen into the same error, and their followers horrify and disgust their fellows by their assertions that verily they are God himself. If we are able to set this matter straight, we will feel that these lessons have had a purpose. The real basis of the Gnani Yoga Philosophy of Life is this: All existence, conscious or unconscious, is an emanation of one Being.

Note the word "Emanation"—it gives the key to the problem. Webster defines the word as follows: "Emanate.—To issue forth from a source; to flow out from." The word "Emanation," then, is a thing that "issues forth from a source;" that "flows forth from." Its root is the Latin word Manare, meaning "to flow." And this word gives us as near a correct idea of the thought of the Gnanis as it is possible for us to obtain. Let us take a favorite Gnani illustration—the Sun. The Sun is the Sun itself— the centre—the source of the vibrations that proceed from it, and which vibrations, under certain conditions, manifest in the form of light and heat. Strictly speaking, nothing outside of the Sun is the Sun, and yet each bit of vibration is an emanation from the Sun—a part of the Sun, as it were. And each ray of light or heat which we perceive through our senses is really "Sun," in a way, and yet it is not the source. The ray is the Sun, in this sense, and yet the Sun is not the ray. Do you perceive our idea? In one sense man may be God (as a ray or emanation), but most assuredly God is not man. Man, and all of existence, is of God, but is not God Himself. We trust that the student will go over and over these words, until he gets the thought clearly, as otherwise he will be landed in a morass of error from which he will have much trouble to extract himself later. Many are floundering in this swamp now, and are tired and weary of the struggle.

Some writers have attempted to convey this thought by the illustration of the physical body of Man. They compare each bit of life to a cell of the body, which possesses a certain intelligence, and often independent action. These cells form into cell-groups (See "Hatha Yoga," Chapter xviii., The Little Lives of the Body), having certain centres of energy, but all are dependent upon the brain—the Master. The Central Mind of the man regulates all. These writers have spoken of The Absolute—of God—as corresponding to the Central Mind, controlling and directing and Mastering the individual cells. The illustration, although of necessity more or less imperfect, corresponds sufficiently well with the Gnani idea to mention it here. It may be a help to some student to get the proper mental conception of the idea.

Swedenborg speaks of the individual, or thing, as but a form through which the Universe flows like a stream—this is another expression of the same thought.

J. William Lloyd, in his excellent book, "Dawn Thought" (The Lloyd Group, Westfield, N. J., U. S. A.), says: "When we touch a man's finger-nail we touch him. But it is not the same as touching a nerve. And it is not the same to touch the nerve as to touch the brain. According to the form, the indwelling life and divinity are more or less apparent and revealed. While life and a sort of intelligence are everywhere, they are not the same in degree or expression. They differ in consciousness. Just as in man, while he is one, there is a part where consciousness, intelligence, and volition are especially located, and the other parts differ in their greater or lesser distance from that—in their greater or less resemblance to it—so is the Universal One, there probably, somewhere, is a part which is "God" (better Father, Mother, or Parent) in the peculiar sense—consciousness, life, intelligence, force, in the pure or essence—and other parts may be classified by their greater or less distance from this Center— their greater or less resemblance to it."

We mention these illustrations and views that the student may have different presentations of the same thought, colored by the mentality of their writers. Some will grasp the truth better from one presentation, and others from another. Personally, we favor the illustration of the "Sun"—its centre and its emanations and rays—for we believe that it conveys a closer analogy to the real idea of the Gnanis than does any other. But any illustration that will help the student best is the best one for him. A Hindu teacher once showed his students a fragrant flower, calling their attention to the fact that the flower was throwing off particles of itself constantly, which, when perceived by the sense of smell, caused the sensation of fragrance—and yet while the fragrance was of the rose, a part of itself, the fragrance was not the rose. Of it, but not it.

We find that we have touched merely upon one phase of Gnani Yoga. We will take up some of its other features in subsequent lessons. Our next lesson will be upon Bhakti Yoga— the Yoga of the Love of God —a subject which naturally follows that part of Gnani Yoga which we have touched upon. It will tell of man's real relation to God—will remind that in God doeth man indeed live and move and have his being. The lesson will not be like a conventional sermon, although Bhakti Yoga addresses itself to the heart instead of the intellect. But it is in accord with reason, instead of contrary to it. In the lessons following the next one we will take up the other parts of Gnani Yogi, under appropriate headings. The Yogi Philosophy is suited to all the needs of man—some parts will appeal to each more than certain other parts—but all parts are good and necessary. So, do not neglect any part, simply because some other part appeals to you more. You will get something from each.

In conclusion, we call your attention to the fact that it is a truth that the Universe is not a dead thing—it is alive, pulsating with life, energy and intelligence. It is a living thing, and you are part of it all. You are not The Absolute, but you are an atom comprising one of its rays—its life force is playing through you. You are in touch with the Centre, and the Centre is conscious of you and of its relation to you. While but an atom, you are necessary to the Whole. You are part of it. Nothing can hurt you nor destroy you. And you are growing to a consciousness of your union with God—not a mere intellectual understanding, but a real, actual, living knowledge. Peace be with thee!

LESSON VII. BHAKTI YOGA.

As we have stated in previous lessons, the Yogi Philosophy is divided into several branches or forms, each specially adapted to the requirements of certain classes of students. And yet, each path leads to the same end—unfoldment, development, and growth. The man who wishes to grow by force of will, or by the steady pressure of the mind upon the sheaths enfolding the Higher Self, will be attracted to Raja Yoga. Another who wishes to grow by knowing—by studying the Riddle of the Universe, and by an intellectual comprehension of the principles underlying Life, naturally is attracted toward Gnani Yoga. A third whose "religious nature" is largely developed, prefers to grow into an understanding and union with the Absolute, by the power of Love—by the inspiration that comes from the love of some conception of God, and some form of worship that may accompany that conception of Deity. Such an one is a follower of Bhakti Yoga.

Of course one may be an ardent Raja Yogi, or a learned Gnani Yogi, and at the same time be filled with such a reverence and love of the Absolute that he is an advanced Bhakti Yogi. In fact, we fail to see how one may avoid being a Bhakti Yogi, if he studies any branch of Yoga. To know God is to love Him, and the more we know of Him, the more we must love Him. And, likewise, to know ourselves is to love God, for we perceive our relationship with Him. And the more we develop ourselves, the more we find ourselves filled with a love of the Absolute.

Bhakti Yoga supplies the craving of the human heart for the love for, and of, the Absolute, which craving manifests itself in what we call the "religious instinct"—the instinct of worship. All men have this instinct, manifested in various forms. Even those who style themselves "free-thinkers," "agnostics," as well as those who deny the existence of God at all, and who accept the intellectual conceptions of the materialists, feel this instinctive urge, and manifest it in the love of "Nature," or Art, or Music, little dreaming that in so doing they are still loving and practically worshiping some of the manifestations of the God they deny.

But when we say that Bhakti Yoga is the science of the Love of God, we do not mean that it is a science which separates those who love and worship some certain conceptions of Deity, from others who may love and worship certain other conceptions of Deity. On the contrary, the true Bhakti Yogi recognizes that the love and worship of any conception of Deity is a form of Bhakti Yoga. To the Bhakti Yogi all men are worshipers of the Absolute—the Center of Life—Spirit—God. Notwithstanding the crude and barbarous conception of Deity the ignorant savage may have, the Bhakti Yogi sees that that man is worshiping and loving the highest conception of Deity possible to him in his undeveloped state, and that he is doing the best he can. And consequently he sees in the savage a brother Bhakti Yogi, in the elementary stages of knowledge. And he feels a sympathy with and an understanding of that savage mind, and his love goes out toward that humble brother (doing the best he knows how) and instead of denouncing him as a heathen and an unbeliever, he calls him "brother," and understands him. You may see, readily, that there are no closely drawn lines among the Bhakti Yogis—no feeling of sectarianism—for they feel that the whole race may be included in their body, and they are ready to extend the right hand of fellowship to all.

The Absolute is unchangeable—the same yesterday, to-day, and to-morrow—but Man's conception of the Absolute is constantly changing as the race makes evolutionary progress. A man's God is always just a little in advance of the man—some have said that a man's God is the man at his best, and in so saying they have expressed the idea cleverly. The God of the Old Testament is a different being from the God of the New Testament. And the God of the Christian Church of to-day, is far different from the God of the Church of fifty years ago. And yet, God is the same—no change—the difference comes from the growth and development of the minds of the men and women composing the Church. As Man advances he sees higher attributes in God, and as he always loves and worships the highest and best in his conception of Deity, he transfers his idea from the lower idea of yesterday to the higher idea of to-day. And, to-morrow, still higher ideas will be grasped, and the God of to-morrow will be a still higher conception of Deity than the God of to-day. And yet, God has not changed, and will not change the slightest, but Man has and will change his conception of Him.

The ignorant savage believes in a God that seems to us like a Devil—but it is a God something like himself—only a little bit better. And he carves some hideous image to represent that God, and he falls down and worships it—perhaps offers sacrifices to it—perhaps sprinkles human blood upon its altar, imagining that, like himself, God loves to see the blood of his enemies.

The savage's enemies are always his God's enemies—and this idea follows man for a long time, as we may see by looking around us a little in our own countries to-day. After a while the savage, or rather his descendants, increase in knowledge and understanding, and they cast down the God of their fathers, and erect one more in keeping with the higher conception of Deity that has come with knowledge and unfoldment. The improvement may be but slight, but still it is a move in the right direction and the new God is just a little bit better—just a little bit kinder—just a little bit more loving—than the one that went before. And, so on, step by step the race rises to higher and greater conceptions of God—each step marking a throwing down of old ideals and a building up of new and better ones. And yet God remains the same—although higher conceptions of Him come into the minds of Man.

The less developed races cannot form the concept of One God—they can see Him only as many Gods, each portraying and exhibiting some particular attribute of the One—some phase of Life—some form of human feeling, passion, or thought. They have their gods of war—of peace—of love—of agriculture—of trade—and what not. And they worship and try to propitiate these various gods, not realizing that underneath it all they are obeying the religious instinct that will in time lead the race to a worship of the One—the Absolute. They clothe their gods with human attributes (even after they have evolved from the worship of many gods into the worship of some one particular conception). They imagine that God divides men into two classes, friends and enemies, and rewards His friends and punishes His enemies. They make their God do just what they would do if they had the power to reward and punish. They imagine that they are the chosen people and special favorites of God, and that He goes with them to battle and will help them to triumph over their enemies. They imagine that God delights in human blood, and that he commands them to put their enemies to the sword, even to the extent of killing the women and little children, yea, even to the ripping open of pregnant women, and the putting their unborn babes to the sword. Their God is a bloody and savage God—because they are bloody and savage themselves. And yet the Absolute— God—moves on unchanged, and these people are worshiping and loving him the best they know how, calling him this name and that name, according to race and time. And the enemies of these people are likewise worshiping their own conception of God, calling Him by some name of their own, and imagining that He is helping them to fight their enemies and their false God. And yet these two Gods are both products of the minds of the two warring tribes, both being created in obedience to the unfolding "religious instinct."

We may shudder at these tales and thoughts, but are we so very much in advance of this idea of the savage? In modern wars we find the two peoples praying to their God for success over their enemies, each imagining that God is on their side. In the great war now being waged between Japan and Russia each nation is praying to its particular conception of God, beseeching that He march with them to battle against His enemies. They do not realize that they are both worshiping the same God, under different names, and that this real God loves them both equally well. In the late Civil War in the United States, each side prayed for victory, and believed that God must be with them. Churches were rent in twain by the war, and there was thought to be a God of the North and a God of the South—the one hating slavery and wishing to kill those who favored it—the other believing slavery to be a Divine Right and privilege, and wishing to defeat those who would abolish it. And yet, each side was merely seeing God through their own spectacles, and seeing him as themselves, somewhat magnified. And now both sides again agree upon certain conceptions of God, and see slavery as something that had its rise, progress, and fall, in the evolutionary progress of Man. And yet, God has not changed—but Man's conception of Him has.

Men have persecuted others because they had a different conception of God from the persecutors. And the persecuted, in turn, when they gained power, persecuted weaker men who held to a third conception of the same God. And each thought he was doing his God's will in persecuting, and the persecuted thought that they were being persecuted in their God's cause. The Puritans were driven out of their native land because of their peculiar conceptions of Deity, and when they had established themselves in a new land, they proceeded to punish the peaceful Quaker Friend whose conception of Deity offended them. And each thought he was pleasing God by punishing those who did not agree with him in his conception of Him. How childish it all seems to those who have attained the broader view, and are able to see all men as children of God, each doing the best he can, and worshiping the highest conception of Deity possible to them. And yet none are to be blamed for this narrowness and blindness—they, too, are doing the best they can. And all are worshiping God—the one God— the true God—the only God possible—the Absolute. And all are doing this because of the urge of the religious instinct pressing forward for unfoldment and growth. All these people are followers of Bhakti Yogi (in its elementary forms) although they know it not. They think they are worshiping different conceptions of Deity—different Gods—but they are not—they are all loving and worshiping the One—the Absolute—the Reality. Seen through the different spectacles of the mind, the Absolute presents different and often grotesque forms to the viewers, but all the while the Reality remains unchanged—The One—The Eternal One—The Absolute.

And however crude and barbaric be the form of worship, it all ascends to the One. Whether the visible object be stick, stone, image, tree, snake, or some other form of man's desire for an outward form for his inward belief, the real thing worshiped is the One—unchangeable—eternal—omnipotent— omniscient—omnipresent. And the man who worships his highest conception of Deity does well. He does the best he knows how, and is as worthy of respect as his more enlightened brother who also worships his highest conception of Deity. And the conceptions of both the savage and the advanced man, will grow higher and better, year by year, and the mind of each unfolds so as to allow the spiritual knowledge to flow into it. Let us lead our humbler brethren to better things, if we may and if they are capable of receiving such instruction. But let us condemn them not, for they are our brothers—children of God—all on the Path, and also are we. We are but children in various stages of growth—each doing that which his age impels him to do—each having the understanding that belongs to his age—each doing the best he knows how. Let us not sneer, nor condemn, nor hate—but let our love flow out toward all our brothers, though they may be but infants unborn in spiritual knowledge. This is Bhakti Yoga in one of its phases.

Bhakti Yoga is divided into two great branches or stages. The first is known as Gauni Bhakti, and the second, and higher, is called Para Bhakti. The first, Gauni Bhakti, is the preliminary stage, and consists of the science of the love and worship of God by means of the mental conception of God as a personal being—a "personal God." The second, or higher stage, Para Bhakti, consists of the worship and love of an impersonal God— the Absolute. Of course the same God is loved and worshiped in both cases, but the mental development of the follower of Gauni Bhakti does not admit of his forming a mental concept of an impersonal God, and he, doing the best he can, forms a mental image of a personal God. There are many sub-stages to both of these main stages, the conception of God depending upon the mental and spiritual development of the man. We will go over the question briefly in order that the student may distinguish the great difference between the two great stages of Bhakti Yoga, and at the same time may recognize that both ideas are of the same stock, the difference being a matter of mental and spiritual growth.

Primitive man feeling the urge of the religious instinct, but being unable to think clearly on the subject, vents his instinctive worship upon crude symbols. He worships sticks and stones—thunder and lightning—the sun, moon and stars—the winds—and other natural objects. A little later on the race begins to feel that God is some sort of person—some great big man, living somewhere in space—unseen but seeing.

The mind of the savage conceives the idea of a God possessing the same characteristics as himself—only much bigger and stronger. The savage being cruel and bloodthirsty can imagine only a cruel and bloodthirsty God. If he is a black man his God likewise is black. If he is a Mongolian, his God has slanting eyes, and perhaps wears a queue. If he is an Indian, his God is red, with painted face and feathers, and carries a bow and arrows. If he is an uneducated Hindu, his God may ride a bull or an elephant, and be nearly naked. And so on, the God of every people bearing the characteristics of that people. Each nation, feeling the religious instinct, creates a conception of a personal God—and each conception of a personal God resembles those who create him, Each of these created Gods loves and hates the persons and things loved or hated by his creators. Each of these Gods is an ardent patriot of the country to which he belongs, and hates and despises all other countries and peoples.

These created Gods often are given grotesque forms and shapes. Some have a dozen arms—some have several heads. They are armed with the weapons of the times to which they belong. Some hunt and chase—others indulge in warfare. They are supposed to grow angry, jealous, and to manifest hate, envy, and often change their minds. They are revengeful and, in short, are given all the attributes of a man of low development. And why not? The people who form these mental concepts cannot imagine a God very much in advance of them. These Gods generally demand flattery and sacrifices, and have a large following of priests and attendants to sing their praises, and to render homage. The priests are supported by the people, under supposed Divine orders, and claim to have the ear of the Deity, and to dispense favors. They all seem to think it a part of their duty, to chant the praises of their Deity and to boast about his power, and claim that he can overcome the Gods of other peoples. These Gods seem to like to have men grovel in the dust before them, and loudly proclaim their slavery—following the desires and examples of the kings and chiefs of the time.

They can be flattered and bribed into giving favors, and if the sacrifices and offerings are not sufficient, they visit some terrible affliction upon the people, in order to make them pay their tithes or to furnish a sufficient number of objects for sacrifice. These Gods delight in the smell of burning flesh, and the aroma of the burnt ox or sheep is a delight to them. They also favor incense and perfumes. Once in a while they demand that blood—human blood, often—be sprinkled upon their altars. They give revelations through their high priests, and woe unto him who doubts them. Many of the priests are sincere and honest, but many more are not, and use the superstitious people as a milch cow, to support them in comfort. Heavens and hells have been invented—the first to bribe the people to follow the laws of the church of priests, and the second to frighten them if the bribe failed. Temples are erected, and certain places are supposed to be "holier" than others and especially favored by God. Non-attendance at the temple is a serious offense, and God is particular to punish the stay-at-homes. Devils have been invented as a means of frightening people, and to account for "evil," although, in some of the creeds, the devils are not much worse than is the conception of Deity.

Nearly all people have made images of their Gods, and the less learned of the people, could see but little difference between the image and the personal God somewhere afar off. The image was right before them, and partook of reality, while the Deity itself was a poorly understood being.

We are not mentioning these things in the spirit of unkindly criticism, or of ridicule. Not a particle of such feelings animate us in this writing. We merely mention the facts in order to show the student the rough places traveled over by Man in his search for God. No matter how crude the conception of Deity—no matter how cruel and barbarous the form of worship—no matter how buried in superstition are these forms of religion—each is a step in the progress of man to Union with God, and must be recognized as such. Man has discarded sheath after sheath of religious ignorance, each sheath revealing a better form than itself. And this process is still going on, and will go on. We are growing out of old forms into better ones. This is a part of the evolutionary process.

The materialist points out these same facts, and argues that all religions are false because the history of the past shows the falsity of the old conceptions of age after age. But he does not see that his own conceptions of matter and Nature are likewise steps in the evolutionary process, and that his present position is merely a step on the ladder, just as were the forms and conceptions at which he sneers. He like the savage and his successors, is seeking God, but he does not realize it.

The student of religions will notice that Man's conception of God is growing greater, broader, grander and kinder each year. Even in our own times is this so. The last twenty years has wrought a mighty change in this respect. We no longer hear of God burning infants a span long in eternal flames. We hear very little of hell, in these days. We hear more and more of the Loving God, and less and less of the God of Hate and Anger. The people are being taught to love God instead of to fear Him. The change is going on rapidly. And better things are ahead of us. But we must not forget that each form of religious teaching— each creed—each church—no matter how crude may seem their teachings and forms—fills a needed place in the religious evolution of the race. Each suits the requirements of those following them, and each should be respected, accordingly. When the pews outgrow certain forms and conceptions, the pulpits drop the objectionable teachings and modify and alter matters so as to fall into line. The preachers, as a rule, see quite a way ahead of their flocks, but know that the time is not yet ripe for the change. The change comes gradually. The teachings of the churches to-day—even the most orthodox—would seem like heresy and even blasphemy to our forefathers. Outgrown creeds fall aside, and new ones take their place, and yet the church organizations remain under the same old names. It is like the story of the boy who had a knife which had been repeatedly repaired. It had had four new handles and six new blades, and yet it was still the same old knife. Many of us, when we outgrow certain old conceptions, display an impatience and even contempt for those remaining in the fold from which we have strayed. This is all wrong. Those who remain are just where they belong—it is the best place for them for the time being. When they outgrow their creed, they will drop it from them like a worn-out garment. Intolerance on our part would be just as absurd as the intolerance shown by these people. The true student of Bhakti Yoga will feel the keenest sympathy and the greatest tolerance for all who are seeking God, no matter by what road they are journeying, or what may be the methods of their search. The undeveloped men try to prove their love of God, by starting in to hate all men who differ from them in their conception of Deity. They seem to feel that such non-belief, or difference of belief is a direct affront to God, and that they as loyal servants of God must resent same. They seem to think that God needs their help against His "enemies." This is a most childlike attitude, and is entirely unworthy of those who are reaching the age of spiritual maturity. The developed man, on the contrary, recognizes the relationship of all lovers of God—regardless of their conceptions—and sees them as fellow travelers on the same road. The way to love God is to Love Him instead of hating some fellow man.

The worship of a personal God, whether such worship be of a God of the savage, or the personal God of the educated man, is all a form of Gauni Bhakti. It is only when man drops off the "personal" idea of God that he passes into the stage of Para Bhakti, and has an understanding of God in His higher sense. Not that God is devoid of personality—He goes beyond personality, not contrary to it. The Absolute may be loved as one loves a father or mother—as one loves a child—as one loves a friend—as one loves a lover. He includes in His being all the attributes calling for such forms of love, and responds to each demand. In fact no demand for a return of love is necessary between Man and God. Just as man steps out into the sunshine and opens himself to its rays, so does the man who loves God step out in the rays of the Divine Love and receive its benefit.

The very act of loving God opens up one to the Divine Love. If one feels the need of the protecting love of the Father, all he need do is to open himself to such love. If one needs the tender and sympathetic love of a mother, such love comes to him if he but opens himself to its inflow. If one would love God as one does a child, such love is open to him in the same way, and many who have felt the need of such a bestowal of love, but who have feared the apparent sacrilege of thinking of God as one does of a loved child, may find that such a giving of love will ease many a heartache and pain, and will bring to them the comforting response that comes from the answering pressure of the loved child. The Western religions take no account of this last form of love, but the religious Oriental knows it, and it is no uncommon thing to hear a Hindu woman (using the poetical language of her race) speaking of herself as a "Mother of God." Startling as this may seem to the Western mind, it is but a recognition on the part of these women of the fact that God supplies every need of the human heart in its desire for Love. And one may love God as a friend and brother and companion. And one may feel toward God the burning love of a lover. All these forms of love of God are known to the Bhakti Yogi. Our Western conceptions of God have allowed us only to feel for Him the love of a child for a Father—while every human heart, at times, feels the need of a Mother-love from God. God is not a male being—nor is he a female. Both of these forms are but partial manifestations of Him, and he includes all forms within Himself—and many unknown to us to-day. The Bhakti Yogi knows that by this constant love of God he will grow nearer to Him, and will in the end come to a consciousness and "knowing" of the true relationship between them. The lover of God who has not advanced beyond the Gauni Bhakti stage, knows nothing of the wealth of love and nearness experienced by the one in the Para Bhakti stage. The one may be compared to the little child who is fond of its playmate, and thinks he knows what love is—the other is like the same child, grown to maturity, who feels the sweep of deep, pure and noble love for his true mate. The one touches God at but one point, at the best, while the other finds that God responds to every human need, and may be touched at a thousand points—He is always there, just as is the sun, and all that one needs is to step out into the sunshine. Nothing is asked by the sun, but the stepping out, and nothing is asked by God but the same thing—the need of Him.

The Western student must not suppose that this Bhakti Yoga love of God is akin to the hysterical, emotional thing he sees in his own countries among the followers of certain sects of church-people. On the contrary the followers of this form of Yoga are generally men of dignified bearing, and deep knowledge. They do not roll around shouting "Glory, glory," and working themselves up into a frenzy of emotional excitement. Instead, they go through life—doing their work, and living their lives—but filled with a deep and abiding sense of the love of God, coming from their consciousness of their relationship to, and nearness to Him, and from the consciousness of His accessibility. They realize that in Him, indeed, do they live and move and have their being, and that He is not a being afar off, but is right here, all the time, nearer than one's very body. They are not "goody-goody" people, but men and women who see God everywhere, in everything, and who feel that they are worshiping Him in every act. They seek diligently the Kingdom of Heaven, but they realize that the Kingdom of Heaven is within themselves, and also all around them. They feel in Heaven every moment of their lives. They worship God, all the time, everywhere; in every act—they know that every act is a service to Him, and that every place is His Temple. They feel constantly filled with the Power of God—constantly within his sight and knowledge—constantly in His Presence. And they fear not—Love fills them so completely that there is no room for anything else. Love casts out all Fear, for them. Every day is Sunday to such people—every hill, plain, field, and house is the Temple. To them every man is His priest—every woman His priestess—every child an attendant at His altar. They are able to pierce the disguise of man, woman and child, and to see the soul underneath the often hideous fleshly covering.

The Bhakti Yogi does not feel that God demands Man's love, or that He holds favors and benefits as a reward for those who love Him, or reserves punishments and penalties for those who do not manifest such love. On the contrary, his idea of God would cause him to regard such an idea as unworthy of a true lover of God. He knows that God is above such primitive feelings and characteristics. He knows that the love of God extends to all of his children, without regard to whether or not they love Him or worship Him. They know that God does not demand services or duty; worship, or even reverence. They compare God to the sun which is no respecter of persons or motives, and which shines on the just and unjust alike—his rays being open even to those who deny his existence. But the Bhakti Yogi also knows that there is a reward and benefit awaiting those who open themselves to God's love—not as an act depending upon God's favor, but as an effect resulting from the act of Man. Just as the man who steps out into the warm rays of the sun is relieved of cold, and is thus rewarded for his act, so is the man rewarded who steps out in the sunshine of God's love which is there awaiting his coming, and is thus relieved of the cold resulting from a failure to take advantage of the warmth of such love. It is not to be wondered that throughout many Oriental writings the Sun is used as a symbol of the Absolute. We find this symbol used in nearly all sacred writings, even in the Bible, which, of course, is of Oriental origin.

Some of these ideas about God may seem strange to the Western student, but if he will take the trouble to look into the matter he will find that this idea runs along through the Christian teachings like a golden thread upon which the beads of the teaching is strung. Christ's teachings are full of this truth, which, however, has been lost sight of during the centuries. The early Christians saw these truths plainly, as may be seen by a reading of the works of some of the early fathers of the church, but the theologians have built much rubbish around the early teachings so that unless one looks under the surface the central truths are not seen.

The Bhakti Yogi prays to God. In the elementary stages of Gauni Bhakti he may word his prayers so that they seem to be asking God for favors—this, later, is discarded. The man of crude spiritual discernment may come to God as a beggar, asking for this thing and that (usually material benefit). A little later on, Man sees that this is not the way to approach God, and he asks to be given strength and courage and to be helped in spiritual unfoldment. In this stage the man thinks that God rewards the prayer by bestowing strength and courage and the rest, just as a king may bestow gifts to those asking for them. But the Yogi who follows the road of Para-Bhakti does not expect rewards of this kind, and yet he obtains the richest rewards. He knows that prayer does not help God, nor does God delight in being besought and praised in prayer. And yet prayer is of the greatest benefit to Man, for, by means of it, he brings himself in tune with the Infinite, and opens himself to the strength, courage, and wisdom that comes from the nearness to God—the nearness to the Centre of Power and Wisdom. This is the secret of prayer.

The man who prays earnestly—from the heart—brings himself into a closer touch with the Absolute. No word may be uttered, but the mental condition of prayer brings man into a form of union with God, and allows the strength and wisdom of the Infinite to flow freely to him. And yet the most of us prefer to use words, and find them a great help in producing the proper condition of mind. But the words are merely helps to that end. God does not need to be spoken to in words—when the finite mind calls to the Infinite Mind its message is heard and understood.

Prayer to be efficacious must not be mere lip-service—mere parrot-like repetition of words, for such performances do not tend to open up the mind to the inflow of the Divine Strength and Wisdom. One must have a heart-to-heart talk with God. Not that God needs to be told what we want—He knows far better than we do—but by a heartfelt confession and talk we open up our mind properly—we uncover the empty vessels needing filling, and the Divine pours into the void. The Divine Power and Wisdom is ours, if we but open ourselves to it.

That is all there is to it. It is as free as the air and sunshine, but we must remove the barriers that we have erected. We have imagined God to be afar off from us, and we must cultivate the consciousness that he is right Here—Now. Talk to God as you would to your Father, or Mother, or loved Child, or Friend, or Husband or Wife, or Lover. He is all this and more, and whatever form represents to you the closest relationship, that is the form to use. Realize the sense of the nearness of God, and He will be near. Fine words are not necessary—use the same words that you would in addressing the person dearest to you and who loves you the best. God does not sit as a king on his throne, expecting you to prostrate yourself at his feet and stammer out your message. He bids you seat yourself beside Him, and He places His arm around you—makes you feel at home—and you forget your fear and bashfulness and tell him your story in your own words.

Do not imagine that God needs your advice or suggestions. You must have the utmost confidence in Him, and know that He will abide with you, and guide your steps. Your mind will be filled with the knowledge that will enable you to know how to act—you will then be given the strength to act. If the mind does not seem able to grasp the situation—if no way opens out before you—open yourself to the inflow of the Divine, and you will be led by the Spirit to see the first step to be taken—then take that first step in confidence. This is not mere "churchy" talk, such as has been poured into your ears from every pulpit as a matter of form. It is a great reality, and thousands live in this way. You gradually will gain courage and confidence in leading this life, and will begin to realize what a great field has been opened to your view.

The main idea in considering one's relation to God, is the fact that God is the great Centre of Life. He is the centre, and we are like atoms in the rays emanating from that centre. We are not apart from Him, although we are not the centre itself. We are connected with Him, as the rays are connected with the sun. The power and wisdom flowing out along the rays are ours, if we but elect to use them, and allow them to use us. The little wheel in the centre of the symbol used by the publishers of these lessons (found on the front of the cover of all their books)—the little wheel within the triangle—represents this truth. The symbol is imperfect, for it shows that the rays terminate, while the rays of the Absolute never terminate— they are infinite. But infinity cannot be represented by finite symbols, and so a circle must be drawn around the rays, which circle represents the finite understanding of Man. If you will but fix this idea of God and His emanations in your mind, you will find yourself gradually growing into a better realization of the matter. The Centre is pure Spirit—God—and as we unfold spiritually we draw nearer and nearer to that centre. Those in whom the Spirit has not manifested so freely as in us are farther removed from the centre than are we. And those who are further advanced spiritually are still nearer it than are we. The further from the centre, the more material is the atom. The nearer the centre, the more spiritual does it become. There are far off from this planet, atoms of a still greater degree of materiality than we can dream of. And closer in to the centre are beings so far advanced beyond Man in the spiritual scale as to be impossible of comprehension to his intellect. Man, as we know him, is only midway between the two extremes of conscious life. There are intelligent beings as far above us in the scale as we are above the jelly-fish. And yet even the jelly-fish, and still lower forms, are within the circle of the Divine Love. Then why should we fear—why should we lose courage? We cannot die—we cannot be wiped out of existence—we are parts of a mighty Whole, ever advancing toward the centre—ever unfolding and growing. The why and wherefore of it all is wrapped within the Central Intelligence, although as Man advances spiritually he begins to grasp fragments of the truth. As he advances toward the Centre he grows in Power and Wisdom—both Divine attributes. All Power and Wisdom emanate from the Centre, and the nearer we approach the Centre the more powerful are the rays that beat upon us. The Divine Attributes—Omnipotence, Omniscience, Omnipresence—are partaken of by us in an increasing ratio as we approach the Centre. This is a hint of a mighty truth—are you prepared to receive it?

Do not for a moment imagine that the lover of God need assume an unnatural mode of life in order to please Deity. Let him lead a perfectly natural life, entering into all the occupations, recreations and pleasures that he may see fit. Be free to choose, and neither force yourself into things, nor away from them. Do not imagine that a stern, serious expression is more pleasing to God than a smiling, cheerful face. Just be natural—that's all. The man or woman who feels the love of God flowing through him, is apt to be of a happy, cheerful disposition—radiating sunshine everywhere. He need not be afraid to laugh, and sing, and dance, if he feels like it, for these things are all good if we use them and do not let them use us. Let us enjoy the sun, the rain, the heat, the cold. Let us delight in the plain, the mountain, the sunrise, the sunset. Let us enjoy to the full the things of Nature. The closer we get to God, the closer do we enjoy the things of Nature. Let us lead the natural, simple life. Let us make the best of everything, and turn everything to good account. Let us be sunny—let us be sweet. Let the keynote of our life be

"Joy, joy, joy!"

Edward Carpenter, in one of his poems, voices this sense of joy that comes to him who feels the great love of God surging through him, and who recognizes the nature of this God, and who feels his relationship to Him. He says:

"I arise out of the dewy night and shake my wings. Tears and lamentations are no more. Life and death lie stretched before me. I breathe the sweet aether blowing of the breath of God.

"Deep as the universe is my life—and I know it; nothing can dislodge the knowledge of it; nothing can destroy, nothing can harm me.

"Joy, joy arises—I arise. The sun darts overpowering piercing rays of joy through me, the night radiates it from me. I take wings through the night and pass through all the wildernesses of the worlds, and the old dark holds of tears and death—and return with laughter, laughter, laughter. Sailing through the starlit spaces on outspread wings, we two—O laughter! laughter! laughter!"

The true lover of God is an optimist. He looks for—and finds—the bright side of things. He is able to extract sunshine from the darkest corner. He walks through life with a smile, a cheerful song, an abiding faith in the Absolute. He loves all of Life, and carries a message of hope, and courage, and a helpful suggestion to all. He is broad and tolerant—merciful and forgiving—devoid of hate, envy, and malice—free from fear and worry. He minds his own business, and grants all the same privilege. He is full of Love, and radiates it to all the world. He goes through life in his own sunny way, joyfully meeting things that drive others to despair and misery—he passes over the stony road unharmed. His peace comes from within—and all who meet him feel his presence. He does not seek after friends or love—these things come to him as his right, for he attracts them. He is as much at home in the tenement of the laborer as in the palace of the wealthy—both places seem as home to him, and their occupants on a level. Brother to both saint and sinner is he, and he loves them both—for he feels that each is doing his best. He looks for good in the sinner, rather than for sin in the saint. He knows that he himself is not without sin, so he casts not the stone. The outcast recognizes in him a brother— the woman who has passed through the fiery furnace trusts him and is not afraid, for she knows that he understands. He, being near the sun, knows that it shines on saint and sinner— he feels that when God withholds his sunbeams from his most disobedient child, then may man withhold his love from his most degraded sister or brother. He does not condemn— he does not attempt to usurp God's prerogative. He works and works well. He finds joy in his work. He likes to create things—and he is proud of that desire for he feels that it is an inheritance from his father. He does not hurry, nor is he rushed. He has plenty of time—all the time there is—for eternity lasts a long time, and he is in it now. He has an abiding faith in the Absolute. He believes in Infinite Justice and Ultimate Good. He knows that the Father is near him, for he has felt the pressure of the Unseen Hand. In the darkness of the night he has felt his Father's presence—by the glare of the flash of illumination he has seen His form for a moment, and that memory is burned into his mind. He is simple, loving, kind. He is a prophecy of the future. If you would be like him—if you feel the call—do not resist, but answer cheerfully, "I hear; I obey; I come." When you feel the impulse, do not resist—open yourself to the Sun— receive its rays—and all will be well. Be not afraid—have within you the love that casteth out fear—place your hand in that of the Absolute, and say: "Lead Thou me on." After long ages of wandering, you are coming home.

Perhaps you think that you do love God—do know how to love Him. Listen to this Hindu fable, and then see if you do. The fable runs thusly:

Once upon a time a chela (student) came to a Yogi guru (teacher) and asked to be taught the higher stages of Para-Bhakti. He said that he did not need the preliminary stages, as he already knew how to love God. The Yogi merely smiled at the youth. He came again and again, making the same demand, and receiving the same answer. At last he became very impatient, and insisted upon an explanation of the Yogi's conduct.

Then the Yogi took the youth to a great river, and leading him out into it, he plunged him beneath the water, and firmly held him there. The young man fought and struggled, but could not raise his head above the surface. At last the Yogi raised him out of the water, and asked him: "Son, what didst thou desire most when under the water?"

"A breath of air," replied the youth, gaspingly. "Yea, verily," said the Yogi, "when thou desirest God as much as thou didst desire the breath of air, then wilt thou be ready for the higher stage of Bhakti—then indeed wilt thou love God."

Peace be to thee!

LESSON VIII. DHARMA.

"Dharma" is a Sanscrit word which is translated into English as "Virtue"; "Duty"; "Law"; "Righteousness"; etc. None of these English words convey just the exact meaning of Dharma. We cannot improve on these definitions, but we may adopt one which fits closer into our particular conception of the truth of Dharma, so we will consider that, for the purposes of this lesson, "Dharma" means "Right-Action." To be more definite, we might say that Dharma is the rule of action and life best adapted to the requirements of the individual soul, and best calculated to aid that particular soul in the next highest step in its development. When we speak of a man's Dharma we mean the highest course of action for him, considering his development and the immediate needs of his soul. We think that this lesson will be timely and will answer the demands of many of our students. We hear, on all sides, the old question, "What is right?" People are not satisfied with the old answers, which seem to belong to the past, and which make certain forms, ceremonies and observances equally as important, if not more so, than right-action and right-thinking. The advanced student sees the absurdity of the old divisions of "right and wrong," and knows that many things which have been condemned as "wrong" are "wrong" only because certain men arbitrarily have called them so—and that many things that have been called "right" are "right" only from the same reason. He looks around him and sees that right and wrong seem to differ with latitude and longitude, and that the conceptions of right and wrong vary with the ages and constantly are changing; being modified, improved upon, or rejected. This being the case, the student is apt to be puzzled regarding a code of ethics—he has lost his old landmarks and standards, and finds himself puzzled to determine with what to measure right and wrong. On one side he hears the old doctrines of this or that mere matter of form of observance, dogmatic and unreasonable, which his soul rejects as outgrown and inadequate for its present needs. On the other hand, he hears the new doctrine of "All is Good" being preached vigorously, often by those who have not the slightest conception of the real meaning of the words—and this new doctrine is not satisfactory to the average student, for his conscience tells him that certain courses of conduct are "right" and others "wrong" (although often he is not able to tell just why he so considers them). And so the student is apt to become quite puzzled.

To add to his confusion, he recognizes the fact that what may seem "right" to him, is utterly incomprehensible to some men of his acquaintance who are not so far advanced spiritually— they are not able to grasp his high standard and ideals. He also notices that some of the things that, even to him, seem the natural and right things for these undeveloped men to do (that is, seem better than other things they have been doing) would be "wrong" for him, the advanced man, to do, because they would mean going backward. Among other things, he sees these undeveloped men being influenced to "right" doing, and deterred from "wrong" doing, by promises of reward and threats of punishment, which appear most unworthy and selfish to those who believe in doing right for right's sake. And yet, he is forced to see that these people apparently need some such artificial stimulus and deterrent, for they are incapable of grasping the higher ideals of ethics.

These, and countless other questions, arise to perplex the student, and to make him feel that the old foundations have slipped from under his feet, and no other safe foothold has presented itself to view. We think that this little lesson on that phase of the Yogi Philosophy which is called "Dharma," will help him to find his way—will aid in pointing out the path that he has lost sight of, momentarily, by reason of the thick growth of underbrush which covers the particular spot now being traveled by him. The subject is too large to cover in the space before us, but we hope to be able to point out a few general principles, which may be taken up by the student, and followed out to their logical conclusion.

Let us take a brief view of the general question of Ethics, and some of the theories regarding the same. Ethics is defined as "The Science of Conduct," and it treats of the desire to render harmonious the relationship of a man and his fellows. There are three theories of Ethics among Western people, known as follows: (1) The theory of Revelation; (2) The theory of Intuition; and, (3) The theory of Utility. As a rule, the advocate of any one of these three systems claims his particular system to be the only true one, and the other two to be errors. The Yogi Philosophy recognizes truth in each and all of the three systems, and gives each its place in what it calls "Dharma." In order to get a clearer idea of Dharma, we must take a brief look at each of these three systems, taken separately.

The system of Ethics based upon the Theory of Revelation, holds that the only basis for morality and right-conduct is Divine Revelation, coming through prophets, priests and teachers, called by many names. The laws given out by these men, as having been received by them from God, have been accepted, more or less submissively, by all races in certain stages of their development, although their conception of the God, who had given out these laws, differed very materially. These laws, so far as their great underlying principles were concerned, resembled each other very much, although they differed widely in detail, and minor laws and precepts. The great religious books of all races contain a more or less complete code of ethics, which the people are enjoined to obey implicitly without regard to reason or their own opinions, these codes, however, being subject to the interpretation of the highest religious authorities of the race. Each race regards the precepts of its religious books, as interpreted by its priests, as supreme authority, and, of course, view the similar claims of other races as spurious. The majority of these religions have split up into sects and denominations, each having its favored interpretation of the sacred teachings, but all rely on the original revelation as the only truth concerning ethics. And then, again, each race has modified its original conception of the revealed teachings, fitting their ideas to the constantly changing requirements of the age. As a race evolves its wants and needs change, and its sacred teachings are twisted and bent to fit the changed conditions. The priests, in such cases, say that God undoubtedly meant "this and that," instead of "thus and so" as their fathers had supposed. So that after a time the authority of the code of ethics rests largely upon the interpretation of priests and teachers, rather than upon the words of the supposed Divine revelation itself. The followers of the other two schools of ethics object that if Deity had intended to promulgate a code of ethics—a rule of conduct—applicable to all men in all time, He would have worded it so clearly that it could not be misunderstood even by the most ignorant, and His wisdom would have enabled Him to have foreseen the growing needs of the people, and, consequently, He would have provided for such needs, either in the original revelation itself, or in "supplements" thereto. We will consider the advantages and disadvantages of this theory later on in this lesson.

The second system of ethics advances the theory that Man knows right and wrong intuitively—that Deity imparts to each man, through his conscience, an instinctive knowledge of good and evil, that he may govern himself accordingly. This school urges that men must refer the details of his conduct to his own conscience. It overlooks the fact that the consciences of no two people are exactly alike, and that such a theory implies that there may be as many different standards of morality and conduct as there are people, and that the statement "My conscience approves of it" would preclude any argument as to ethics. As to what conscience is, the writers differ. Some say that it is the higher portion of the mind speaking to man. Some say that it is merely the sub-conscious mind repeating what has been suggested into it, and that consciences grow with experience and change with environment. Some claim that it is the voice of God speaking to the soul. Others have still other explanations and theories. We shall consider this theory at greater length a little further on in this lesson.

The third system of ethics rests upon the theory of utility, or what is known as utilitarianism, which latter word is defined as "the doctrine that virtue is founded on utility," or "the doctrine that the greatest happiness of the greatest number should be the aim of all social and political institutions."—(Webster.) This is the theory upon which human law is supposed to be based. Blackstone, the great expounder of the English Law, states that human laws are based upon "the law of nature," which law of nature he tells us are based upon the laws of God—eternal immutable laws of good and evil—which the Creator causes to become evident to Man by means of human reason. Blackstone goes on to say that "This law of nature, being coeval with mankind, and dictated by God himself, is of course superior in obligation to any other; no human laws are of any validity if contrary to this; and such of them as are valid derive all their force, and all their authority, mediately or immediately, from this original." All this sounds beautifully simple, and one is led to wonder how it is that civilized life is not heaven on earth, until he remembers the state of modern law-making and law-administering, which, however, is an improvement on that of former days. It seems so easy to speak of the "law of nature," but so difficult to apply that law to details of life, and to administer it. Blackstone, himself, recognizes this fact, and says; "If our reason were always clear and perfect, the task would be pleasant and easy; we should need no other guide but this: But every man now finds the contrary in his own experience; that his reason is corrupt, and his understanding full of ignorance and error." The man who has had much experience in courts and the processes of "justice" will be apt to agree with the great English lawyer, in his last quoted remarks. While it is true that the laws of a nation represent the average of its best conceptions of ethics, still the conceptions change more rapidly than the law, and the latter is always a little "behind the times" as compared with public opinion and conception of right and wrong. And many are the loop-holes of man-made law, and the shrewd lawbreaker may safely commit almost any of the great offenses against the current conceptions of morality, providing he does it cleverly enough. Some men have a code of ethics of their own, which holds that no "wrong" is committed providing no law is technically broken, and so they scheme and plan, aided by "able counsel," to attain their ends without violating the letter of the law. This danger being avoided, their consciences are easy. This is a very easy and simple theory of conduct, for those who can live under it. Justinian, the great Roman law-giver, reduced the whole doctrine of human law to three general precepts, as follows: "Live honestly; Hurt nobody; and Render to every one his due." This is a simple and beautiful code, and its honest adoption by mankind would make the world over in a day, but nearly every man is inclined to place his own interpretation upon each of the three precepts, and, consciously or unconsciously, stretches them in his own favor and against his fellows. It is very difficult for one, in the present state of the world to tell just what it is to "be honest"; to live so that he will "hurt nobody"; or to "render unto everyone his due"—or even to tell just what everyone's due really is. However, as an example of the reason's conception of proper conduct, Justinian's precept is well worth remembering, with the purpose of following it as closely as may be. It will appeal to those who instinctively wish to give all "a square deal," so far as may be, but who are unable to grasp the still higher teachings. But even those who can manage to live up to Justinian's precepts, will fall far short of satisfying their neighbors, who will insist upon the observance of certain other things—many of them most ridiculous things—that have grown to be the custom, or which are insisted upon by certain so-called religious "authorities," not to speak of the civil ones.

The followers of the Utilitarian school of ethics differ one from the other in their explanations of the cause and history of ethics and rules of human conduct, some thinking that it arose from God speaking through man's reason, and others taking the more material view that ethics, laws, morals, and rules of conduct are the product of the evolution of the race— the result of accumulated experiences, the trying of this and of that until a fair average has been obtained. Of course to the latter class, morals and rules of conduct are purely matters of the reason of Man, having nothing to do with Divine Law, or Spiritual Knowledge. Herbert Spencer, the great English scientist, is perhaps the best exponent of this last named school, his work, "The Data of Ethics," being a masterpiece of reasoning along these lines.

Dharma takes cognizance of each and all of these three schools of ethics, seeing that each has a bit of truth in it, and that all, combined, and welded with the cement of the occult teachings, make a mighty whole. We will show how these apparently conflicting systems may be reconciled. But before doing so it may be better to take another look at the three systems above mentioned, making an analysis of the objections to each as a complete theory, so that we may see the weakness of any one theory taken by itself as well as the strength of the three when combined and joined together with the teachings of Dharma. Let us take them up in the order given above.

(1.) The Theory of Revelation. The principal objection urged against this theory, by the advocates of the other theories, is that there is not sufficient proof of the truth of the revelation. Priests always have claimed to be the mouthpieces of the Almighty, and the revelations have come through these priests in all ages. The advocates of the utilitarian theory of ethics claim that these so-called revelations (when the rule of conduct given out was really for the good of the people, rather than for the benefit of the priests) were really the result of the superior reasoning of the prophet, who, being head and shoulders above his people, could see what was best for their needs, and accordingly compiled such rules of conduct into more or less complete codes, stating that they had been given direct by God through the prophet, the priest placing the authorship upon God rather than upon himself, knowing that the people would be more apt to respect and obey a Divine command than one emanating from a mere man. The advocates of the intuitional theory hold that the so-called "revelations" really arose from the conscience and intuition of the prophet, who being a more advanced man than his people would be apt to sense more clearly the voice of the spirit, but who would attribute the voice of conscience to God, and who, accordingly would so give out the message. The intuition of the people would enable them to see the "rightness" of the so-called Divine message, and they would accept same with the approval of their consciences. Another objection raised against the

Theory of Revelation is that there are many so-called revelations, differing materially in detail—each religion having its own set of revelations, through its own prophets and teachers. It is held that if God wished to reveal a code of morals to His people, his revelations would agree, and would be given in such a way that there could be no mistaking them. It is also held that it is impossible to regard any one of these numerous revelations as authoritative, owing to the impossibility of selecting any one from the great number, as each prophet made equally strong claims that he received the revelation direct from God, and there is no Supreme Court to pass finally upon the matter. It is also objected to that many of the things claimed to have been directed by God have no real connection with morality, but deal with the details of the life of the people, such as the mode of slaughtering animals; the selection of kinds of food; various religious ceremonials, etc., which are as strictly enjoined as are the rules of conduct, and are equally entitled to be regarded as examples of "right and wrong." Then, again, there are many things sanctioned in these so-called revelations that are contrary to our modern conceptions of morality. Divine commands were given to kill enemies in a most barbarous fashion, which the law of nations now prohibits, and only savage nations now follow. In such a case it would seem that the intuition or reason of man has raised a higher ideal than did God. The same is true of polygamy and slavery, which are not prohibited by the so-called Divine revelations, but which are sanctioned and allowed. A number of similar objections are urged against the theory of the divine revelation of ethics, but the main objection seems to be that there is not sufficient proof of the truth of the revelation, and that reason teaches that the so-called revelations were simply the result of the human reason of the prophets, and were promulgated either with the idea of keeping the people orderly and prosperous, or else, to keep the priesthood in power and authority, or both reasons. The Yogi Philosophy of Dharma recognizes these objections, but answers them in its system, as we shall see later on.

(2) The Theory of Intuition. The objection to this theory, most frequently advanced, is that the conscience is merely the result of one's teachings; environment; race; temperament; age; etc,—that the conscience of one man may make it seem wrong to kill a fly, while that of another may make it seem right to kill an enemy—that the conscience of one may make it seem wrong not to share one's all with a stray comer, or to hold any property as one's own, while the conscience of another (a Whitechapel pickpocket, for instance), may cause him to perfectly justify himself in stealing whatever he may lay his hands upon, and even reprove him for not taking advantage of an opportunity to do so. The conscience of certain of the criminal classes is akin to that of the cat which sees no harm in stealing the cream or bit of meat, and is only deterred by fear of punishment. The student of human nature, people and history, knows that conscience is largely a matter of race,

time, environment and temperament, and he would hesitate at accepting the voice of the conscience of any particular man as a fit source or authority for a code of morals for all people, at all times. He sees that the rules of conduct emanating from the conscience of an undeveloped man would be far below the standard of the average man of our own times, while that given forth by the conscience of a highly developed man would be impossible of compliance with on the part of the average of our race today, by reason of its high precepts and fine distinctions of thought and conduct. And then "conscience" has made people do some things which our own "conscience" of today tells us is "wrong." People have been burned at the stake—have had holes bored in their tongues—have been tortured physically and mentally at the dictates of the consciences of the persecutors, who were just as sincere as those whom they persecuted.

If the principle of "conscience" were implicitly followed, the "conscience" of the majority might make things very unpleasant for the minority, as it has happened many times in the past.

So, you see, the theory that "conscience" as an infallible guide may be attacked severely by its opponents. And yet, the Yogi Philosophy of Dharma, while recognizing these objections, also sees much truth in the theory of intuition or "conscience," and welds it into place in its system, as we shall see later on in this lesson.

(3) The Theory of Utility. This theory often is attacked severely on the ground that it is a purely selfish idea—that the basis of morality offered is "happiness"—the happiness of the individual modified by the happiness of those around him— "the greatest happiness to the greatest number," in short—and that such a basis fails to recognize the higher destiny of man, being based entirely upon his earthly and material existence. To this the utilitarian very naturally answers that any code of conduct has a more or less selfish basis, inasmuch as a man doing certain things, and refraining from doing certain other things, by reason of hope of Divine approval and reward, or fear of Divine displeasure and punishment, is as selfish as one who is actuated by the idea of material happiness or unhappiness. Another objection urged is that acting under it the average man would be impelled to get as much happiness for himself as possible, and to bestow as little happiness upon others as he could help, as there would be no reason why he should act otherwise—in fact, that he would obey the letter of the human law, and not go one inch further. Theoretically this objection might be correct, but, in spite of cold theory, man is open to higher impulses and motives coming from regions of his soul that the utilitarian philosophy, as well as its opponents, fail to recognize. A form of this same objection is found in the idea that the utilitarian philosophy appeals only to the developed intelligence (that is, according to the view of the Yogi Philosophy, to the highly evolved soul) and that the ordinary man would not be influenced by it to high action,

but, if he grasped it at all, would use it as an excuse for his own selfishness, caring nothing for the welfare of his fellow men, or for the benefit of the generations to come. The objectors hold that according to this theory a man working for the good of his kind is the greatest kind of a fool, for he is throwing away his happiness and material gain for a sentiment. (This objection loses sight of the fact that the advanced man finds much of his greatest happiness in making others happy.) A further objection is urged against this theory of ethics to the effect that the happiness of the majority is an unworthy limitation, inasmuch that even though the majority be happy the minority may not be so, and, in fact, a certain number of them must be very unhappy and miserable. This objection finds a response from those of spiritual advancement, for such people know that no one can be thoroughly happy unless all are happy, and that there can be no ideal happiness if even one of the race is crowded out of it by any set code or rule. The followers of the theory that all morality is derived from Divine revelation, and there is no morality to be found outside of it, object to the utilitarian view because they say "it leaves out God and His wishes." Those favoring the Intuitional Theory object to the Utilitarian Theory because it refuses to recognize the existence of the "conscience" or higher reason in man, and instead, places the basis and foundation of all morality and rules of conduct upon the cold human reason, and that, consequently, there can be no "good" or "bad" except as measured by the intellectual standard, which standard could be altered, changed, improved upon, or abolished by Man's reason. These objections are recognized, and answered in the Hindu Philosophy of Dharma, which, while recognizing the weakness of the theory when considered as the "whole truth," still finds much truth in it and places it as one of the pillars of Dharma, the other two theories forming the other two supports of the structure.

Dharma claims to set in order this apparent confusion. It recognizes each view as a partially correct one—parts of the whole truth—but too weak and incomplete when standing alone. It reconciles the conflicting schools by taking the materials that are found in each, and using them to build a complete system. Or, rather, it finds a complete structure erected, in the order of the Universe, and sees that each school of thinkers is looking at but one of its pillars, mistaking its favored pillar for the sole support of the structure, the other two being hidden from sight by reason of the particular point of view of the observer. And this teaching of Dharma is much needed at this time by the Western people who are in a state of great mental and spiritual confusion on the subject of morality and conduct. They are divided between (1) those who rely on revelation, and who disregard it in practice because it is not "practical"—these people really advocate revelation as modified by experience and custom; (2), Those who claim to rely on intuition and conscience, but who feel that they are resting on an insecure foundation, and who really live on custom and "the law of the land," modified by their "feelings"; and, (3) those who rely on pure reason, modified by the existing laws, and influenced greatly by the impulses which come to them from the higher regions of the mind, notwithstanding that they deny these same higher states of mentality. Let us hope that a study of Dharma will help to straighten out matters for some of us. Of course, this little lesson is merely a hint of the truths of Dharma, but we trust that it may help some to adjust the matter in their minds, and make it easier for them to get their moral bearings, and to take advantage of the truths that are pouring in on them from the three sides of life. Let us now see what Dharma has to offer.

In our brief consideration of the subject, we must ask the student to give us the "Open Mind." That is, be willing to lay aside, for the moment, his preconceived ideas and theories, and to listen to our teachings without prejudice, as far as possible, without being unduly influenced by his previously entertained theories. We do not ask him to accept our teachings unless they appeal to his reason and intuition, but we do ask him to give us a fair hearing—that is, the hearing of an unprejudiced judge instead of that of a paid advocate ready to pick flaws and make objections before we state our case. That is all we ask, and it is no more than any fair-minded student should be willing to grant. We are not attempting to tell you how to act, but wish merely to present the general principles of Dharma for your consideration.

Perhaps the better way to begin our consideration of the philosophy of Dharma would be to give you an idea of how that philosophy views the three above mentioned theories of the basis of morality and rule of conduct. We shall take up each theory in turn. But before doing so we must ask you to bear in mind the fundamental theory of the Yogi Philosophy that all souls are growing souls—souls in different stages of growth and advancement along The Path. Spiritual evolution is in full force, and each soul builds upon its yesterdays, and, at the same time, is laying a foundation for its tomorrows. Its yesterdays extend back over its present earthly life away back into its past existences. And its tomorrows reach far ahead of the remaining days of its present earthly life into its future embodiments or incarnations. Life is not a mere matter of a few years in the flesh—the soul has countless yesterdays of existence, and has the whole of eternity before it, in a constantly progressing scale, plane after plane of existence being before it, in an ever ascending spiral. We do not purpose dwelling upon this fact, but mention it that you may be reminded that the embodied souls we see around us in the shape of men and women represent different scales of ascent, development, and unfoldment, and that of necessity there must be widely differing needs and requirements of the soul. The advancing ideals of morals, conduct and ethics are seen by the Yogis as indications that the idea and delusion of separateness is falling away from the race, and that the consciousness of Oneness is dawning in the minds of men. This dawning consciousness is causing the race to see "wrong" in many things that were formerly considered "right"— it is causing men to feel the pains and sorrows of others, and to enjoy the happiness and pleasure of those around them—it is making us kinder and more considerate of others, because it makes us more and more conscious of our relationship with each other. This is the cause of the increasing feeling of brotherhood that is possessing the race, although those who feel it may not realize the real cause.

The evolution and unfoldment of the soul results in higher ideals of thought and conduct for the race, and accounts for the changing conceptions of morality which is apparent to anyone who studies history, and who notices the signs of the times. An understanding of this theory of Dharma, enables us to understand comparative morality, and prevents us from condemning our less developed brethren who have cruder ideals of conduct than ourselves. The higher the degree of unfoldment, the higher the ideal of conduct and morality, although the unfoldment causes the soul to cast off many old forms and ideals which seemed the best for it in the past. Bearing these facts in mind, let us consider the three sources of authority.

The Yogi Philosophy recognizes the theory of Revelation as one of the pillars supporting the edifice of Dharma. It holds that at different times in the history of the race the Absolute has inspired certain advanced souls to give forth the teachings needed by the race at that particular time in its history. These inspired men were souls that had voluntarily returned from higher stages of development in order to render service to their less developed brethren. They lived the life of the people around them, and took the part of prophets, priests, seers, etc. Accounts of these people come down to us from the ages, distorted, magnified and elaborated by legends, superstition, and myths of the people among whom they lived. They seldom wrote, but their teachings often written down by others, (often after long years had past), and, although colored by the views of the compilers, these writings still give a fair idea of the teachings of the particular prophet or teacher. These prophets were of varying degrees of advancement, some coming from great heights of attainment, and others from comparatively lower planes, but each carried a message to his people, suited to their needs at that particular time. These messages were accepted, more or less, by the people, and the teachings worked a change in them, and helped to lay a foundation for future generations to build upon. It is no discredit to these prophets, or to the source from which they received their information, to say that we have advanced far beyond many of their teachings, and today are enabled to discard nearly all of their precepts, with the exception of a few fundamental ones which were intended to last. The religious sects are apt to insist upon the infallibility of these teachings, and to hold that they were intended as rules of conduct and standards of morality for all people, at all times. A moment's thought will show the folly of this idea. Take Moses for example, and see how the details of his teachings were intended for the people of his time, and how well they fitted into their requirements, and yet how absurd many of them would be if applied to our life today. Of course, the fundamental principles laid down by Moses still obtain in full force, but the minor rules of conduct laid down for the Jewish people have been outgrown and no one pretends to observe them. Many critics of the theory of revelation find fault with many of the rules laid down by Moses, and point to their savage and barbarous nature, many of which are revolting to the ideals of today. And yet, these teachings each had a definite purpose, and were intended for the aid of the slowly evolving souls in the flesh at that time. The object of all of these teachings was to help man along in his evolution—to give him something just a little higher than his then mode of living to serve as an ideal of conduct. Some of these teachings which seem so barbarous to us today, if examined closely in the light of the condition of the race at that time, will be seen to be just a few steps in advance of the customs of the race at the time the teachings were given. To us on the higher rounds of the ladder, these teachings are seen to be on a lower plane than ourselves, but if we were to stand on the round occupied by the race at that time, we would see that the teachings were a round or two higher still. It is unreasonable to insist that the highest conceivable ideals should have been given the race in its infancy—just imagine the highest ideals of Christ submitted to the semi-barbarous tribes of Israel. But here let us call your attention to a remarkable fact, namely, that in the majority of these crude ancient teachings may be found an esoteric or secret teachings intended for the few advanced souls of that generation, and those to follow—just enough to show that the teachers understood the higher teachings. These esoteric teachings are found embedded in the exoteric teachings intended for the multitude. It has ever been so. The teachings of Christ are not understood by the masses of today, not to speak of yesterday. Look at the history of Christianity and see how the so-called followers of the Christ misunderstood his teachings—see how barbarous and savage have been their conceptions, and are even to this day. And yet, the advanced soul in every generation for the last nineteen hundred years has been able to read the esoteric teachings between the lines of the imperfectly reported, and often distorted accounts of the sayings of Jesus. And yet, Christ's teachings have done wonderful work, in spite of the lack of understanding. The ethics of the Sermon on the Mount are not in force today—the race has not grown up to them—but future generations will live by their light and guidance.

At this point, let us call your attention to a fact. The teachings of all the prophets were intended to help man in casting off the old sheaths of the lower planes of the mind, and to help him to work his way to a higher stage of growth. The evolution of the soul was the end aimed at, and all observances were intended for that purpose. One step at a time was, and is, the rule. The word spoken was not the final word, but was intended to fit in a certain place. This is the key to much that has perplexed you in the past. Another important point to remember, is that all the teachings were intended to raise man up and all were for his own benefit. They were not intended to make man perform certain duties toward God, as we have been taught to believe. God was not worrying about man's lack of consideration toward him. He was not vain-glorious, and demanding worship and burnt-offerings to tickle his nostrils. Such ideas belong to the infancy of the race. God gets along very well without man's worship and praise. Man alone is the gainer by the love of God— the Absolute is not injured or benefited by man's actions. If the teachers and the prophets commanded that man worship God, it was solely for the purpose of bringing man's attention to the fact that there was a Power above, the fact of the attention being so directed causing man to obtain the advantage of the upward attraction of the Absolute in his unfoldment. Get out of your mind the idea that God needs your praise and worship in order to satisfy His love of approval and your statements of His exalted position. All the benefit of prayer, worship and love of God is on the side of Man—it is all one-sided.

To understand the teachings of the prophets of all religions, we must put ourselves in the place of the prophet and see the kind of people he had to deal with. Then will we understand that the crude commands were calculated to bring them up just one step in the scale—and they did. But because the teachings were so intended, and accomplished their purpose, we must not allow ourselves to be bound by the letter of them at this time. If we grow to an understanding of the matter, along the lines pointed out, we will be able to discard the chaff of the teachings (which was the wheat in the past) and to seize upon the scattered grains of wheat still to be found in the measure. Let us make use of all the good in the old teachings for there is still much good to be found in them—they have not as yet outlived their usefulness. But let us not bind ourselves with the worn-out teachings of the past—let us not forget the spirit of all teachings and tie ourselves to the dead letter of the old law. Let us not commit the folly of claiming that because a teaching was inspired, that it is an infallible rule of conduct for all time, and all people—let us remember the other two pillars of Dharma, intuition and reason. But, at the same time, let us not sneer at the old teachings, and deny their inspiration, simply because they belong to a long past age and time. Let us recognize the thing for what it is, and govern ourselves accordingly. And let us not suppose that the day of revelation and inspiration has passed. There is as much inspiration in Emerson as there was in the Hebrew prophets—each was ahead of the times, and the message of each is but imperfectly understood by the multitude—each struck a higher note in the scale. We select Emerson merely as an instance—there are many others in our own times. But there is this difference between the prophet of old and the modern seer and teacher. The ancient prophet had a following that were compelled to accept the teaching in blind faith, illuminated with but a faint degree of spiritual insight, while the people of today are able to measure the value of the teachings by the light of their souls, and the aid of the reason— that is, some of the modern people may do this, the others must be content with the old teachings, for they belong to a past age of development, and not having kept pace with their brothers must remain content with the tales of the spiritual childhood. And even this is good.

The Yogi Philosophy recognizes the Theory of Intuition or Conscience as the second pillar supporting the edifice of Dharma. As we have already said in the consideration of this particular theory, many persons who have devoted thought to the question of ethics are repelled by the difficulties surrounding the theory of Revelation (considered by itself) and not being willing to accept as authoritative, infallible, and final, the so-called revelations given to primitive peoples in the past ages, they deny the inspiration of these revelations and look around them for some other theory and rule of conduct. Many of such people accept the Utilitarian Theory, as appealing to their reason, although it does not seem to fill the needs of their souls so full as might be desired. Others being repelled by the coldness and selfishness of the last mentioned theory, and yet not being willing to go back to the old Theory of Revelation, adopt the Theory of Intuition or Conscience, and accept the idea that "conscience" or "intuition" is the direct and sole arbiter of morality and conduct, and believe that the human laws are really based upon the same. Some take the radical position that the voice of "conscience" or "intuition" is really the voice of God speaking to Man, and should be obeyed implicitly—that God makes his revelations to each man. As we have stated before, this position has been severely attacked upon the ground that the conscience of no two people agree, and that it is dependent upon environment, age, race, public opinion, education, etc., and that therefore it cannot be an infallible guide nor one safe to follow, as every man would have his own laws which no other man would be bound to take into consideration, etc., etc. Dharma reconciles these two apparently conflicting opinions. Let us see what it has to say about Intuition or Conscience.

We had hoped to take up the question of the Theory of Conscience or Intuition, and also the Theory of Utility, in this lesson, reserving the next lesson for an elaboration of Dharma, but we find that we have exceeded our space. Therefore, we will be compelled to postpone the consideration of Conscience and Utility until our next lesson, in which these features will be combined with the remarks upon the practical phases of Dharma. We trust that our students will not pass over these two lessons as too "dry" for careful study. They are most important, and are needed by every student who is endeavoring to "get his bearings"—who wishes to lead the life that brings happiness— who desires to proceed along the Path of Attainment. The subject of Conscience or Intuition is particularly interesting, and we expect to bring out some important points on this subject in our next lesson.

We beg that you give us attention and patience—you will be rewarded for so doing. Peace be with you.

LESSON IX. MORE ABOUT DHARMA.

Our last lesson closed just as we were about to consider and examine into the Theory of Intuition or Conscience—the second pillar supporting the edifice of Dharma. We will now take up the subject at that point. Every man is more or less conscious of an inner voice—a "knowing" apparently independent of his Intellect. This voice speaks to him either in an authoritative or a coaxing tone— either commands him to do so and so, or to refrain from doing something. Sometimes it impels him to higher action, and sometimes it seems to tempt him to perform an unworthy act. In its higher phases, we call this voice "conscience." In its lower phases, we are apt to regard it as "temptation." The old tales held that each man had a good angel on one side of him, and a bad one on the other, one whispering into his ear telling him to do the "right" thing, and the other urging him to do the "wrong" one. The old tales symbolize the truth, as we shall see as we proceed with our consideration of the matter. In addition to the "voice of conscience," or the "urging of the tempter," we find that there is a "leading" in matters of ordinary action and conduct in which the question of "good" and "bad" does not arise—the decision upon some of the affairs of ordinary life, work, business, etc. This third manifestation we are apt to call "intuition." Many people use the three terms and have a clear understanding of the difference between each form of manifestation, but are unable to explain just what these promptings are, or from whence they come. The Yogi Philosophy offers an explanation, and Dharma depends to some extent upon that explanation, as it rests partially upon the pillar of Conscience or Intuition—the second pillar—the first pillar being Revelation; the third being Utility. These three pillars represent, respectively, the voice of The Lord; the voice of man's intuitive faculties; and the voice of man's reason. Let us now see what the Yogi Philosophy has to say regarding this question of Intuition, and the nature of the message coming from that part of the soul.

In order to understand the nature of Conscience, Intuition, Temptation and other feelings coming into the field of consciousness from the sub-conscious regions of the mind, we must turn back a few pages in our lessons. In the first series of The Yogi Lessons (generally known as "The Fourteen Lessons"), in The Second and Third Lessons, we told you something about the different "minds" in man—the different planes along which the mind of man functions. You will remember what we said about the Instinctive Mind, the Intellect, and the Spiritual Mind. We have spoken of them repeatedly in the several lessons comprising the first course, and the present course, of lessons, and we trust that you have a fair understanding of the nature of each.

"Temptations," or the impulse to do "evil" or "wrong" things, come from the lower regions of the mind—that part of the Instinctive Mind that has to do with the animal passions, tendencies, emotions, etc. These passions, emotions, tendencies, etc., are our inheritance from the past. They are not "bad" in themselves, except that they belong to a part of our soul history which we have left behind us, or out of which we are now emerging. These things may have been the highest "good" possible to our mental conception at some time in the history of our evolution—may have been necessary for our well-being at that time—may have been much better than other states of feeling and acting which we passed, and accordingly may have seemed to our minds at that time as the voice of the higher self beating down upon the lower consciousness. These things are comparative, you must remember. But, now that we have passed beyond the stage in which these things were the highest good, and have unfolded sufficiently to take advantage of higher conceptions of truth, these old things seem quite "bad" and "wrong" to us, and when they come into the field of consciousness from these lower regions of the mind, we shudder at the thought that we have so much of the brute still in us. But there is no need to feel that we are "wicked" because these thoughts and impulses arise within us. They are our inheritance from the past, and are reminiscences of the "brute" stage of our unfoldment. They are voices from the past. If you feel the struggles of the brute within you to be unleashed, do not be disturbed. The fact that you can see him now as something different from your normal self, is encouraging. Formerly you were the brute—now you see him as only a part of you—a little later on, you will cast him off altogether. Read what we have said on the subject on page 29 (Lesson i) of the present series of lessons. In other pages of the present lesson we will take up the subject of the comparative nature of "right" and "wrong," so that you may see how it is that a thing that was once "right" may now be "wrong"—how what seems to be very "good" and "right" just now will appear "bad" and "wrong" later on in our unfoldment (that is speaking relatively, for when we unfold we begin to see that "right" and "wrong" and "good" and "bad" are relative terms, and that there is no such thing as "bad" viewed from the Absolute. And yet, as we progress, the things we outgrow are "bad," and those into which we are growing seem "good" until they too are discarded). All that we wish to do now is to point out to you that "temptation" is merely the urge of some past experience for repetition, because the tendency is not entirely dead. It raises its head because of the flickering of expiring life, or because the dying thing has been aroused by some outside suggestion or circumstance. Let the beasts die, and do not become alarmed at their struggles.

Intuition may come either from the impulses of Spiritual Mind projecting itself into the field of consciousness, or from the sub-conscious region of the Intellect. In the latter case, the Intellect has been working out some problems without bothering the consciousness, and having worked the matter into shape, presents it to the consciousness at the needed time, carrying with it an air of authority that causes it to be accepted. But many intuitions come to us from the Spiritual Mind, which does not "think" but "knows." The Spiritual

Mind gives us, always, the best that we are able to accept from it, according to our stage of unfoldment. It is anxious for our real welfare, and is ready and willing to aid and guide us, if we will allow it. We cannot go into the subject now, and merely mention it to show the shades of difference between Intuition and Conscience. Conscience deals with questions of "right" and "wrong" in our minds, but Intuition deals with questions of proper action in our lives, without regard to ethics or morals, although not contrary to the best we know of those things. Conscience informs us as to whether or not a thing conforms to the highest ethical standards possible to us in our present unfoldment—Intuition tells us whether a certain step or course is wise for our best good. Do you see the difference?

Conscience is the light of the Spiritual Mind, passing through the screen of the enfolding sheaths of our soul. This is a clumsy definition, which we must endeavor to make clearer. The light of the Spiritual Mind is constantly endeavoring to work its way to the lower mental planes, and some of its light reaches even the lowest regions, but the light is seen but dimly at such times, owing to the confining sheaths of the lower nature which prevent the light from working through. As sheath after sheath is cast off, the light is seen more clearly, not that it moves toward the soul, but because the centre of consciousness is moving toward the Spirit. It is like a flower that is casting off its outer petals, and dropping them to the ground as they unfold. In the center of the flower let us suppose there is something possessing light, which light is endeavoring to force its way through to the extreme rim or row of petals, and beyond. As the successive layers, or petals, fall off, the light is enabled to reach the remaining ones—and at the end all is light. This is a forced figure of speech but we are compelled to use such. Let us take another, equally clumsy, but which may be plainer to you. Imagine a tiny, but strong, electric light bulb confined in many wrappings of cloth. The light is the Spirit—the glass bulb the Spiritual Mind, through which the Spirit shines with a minimum of resistance and obstruction. The outer layers of cloth are very thick, but each layer is thinner than the one next further away from the light—the layers nearest the light are quite thin, until they grow almost transparent. Try to fix this figure in your mind. Now, very little light reaches the outside layer of cloth, but still that which does reach it is the best light it is capable of receiving or conceiving. We remove the first layer of cloth. The second layer is found to receive and show forth more light than the one just cast aside. We remove the second one, and we find the third one still brighter, and able to radiate considerably more light. And so on, and on, each layer when removed bringing to view more light and brighter light, until at last all the layers are removed and the light of the Spirit is seen shining brightly through the glass bulb of the Spiritual Mind. If the layers of cloth had been able to think, they would have thought of the whole bundle of cloth (with the lamp in the center) as "I." And each layer would have seen that "closer in" was something a little lighter than is ordinary self, which light would stand for the highest conception of light possible to the outer cloth—its "conscience," in fact. Each layer of cloth would be conscious of the next inner layer being brighter than itself. The second layer would appear very "good" to the first one, but to the fourth or fifth the second would be darkness itself (by comparison), quite "bad" in fact. And yet each would have been "good" because it carried light to the layer still more in the dark. Conscience is the light of the Spirit, but we see it more or less dimly because of the layers surrounding it—we see only as much as filters through the cloth. And so we call the next inner layer "conscience"—and so it is, relatively. Do you understand the matter any clearer, now? Can you see why the "consciences" of different people differ? Does the fact that the different layers of cloth manifest varying degrees of light, make you doubt the brightness and reliability of the light itself? Think over this clumsy illustration for a while, and see whether your mind does not open to a clearer idea of the value of Conscience. Do not despise Conscience or its voice, just because you see that the Conscience of the lowly and undeveloped man allows him to do certain things that you consider "bad." That "bad" is "good" when compared to the next lowest stage of unfoldment. And do not feel self-righteous because your Conscience holds you to a very high code of ethics—there are beings today, in the flesh, that view your code of ethics as you do those of the Bushman. You doubt this! Let us give you an illustration. You call yourself "honest" and "truthful." Can you truthfully say that you have ever lived a month without telling an untruth? Come now, honor bright—"white lies" and an evasion of "the whole truth" count as well as the big lies—have you ever been absolutely truthful and honest for a whole month? Trade lies— professional "necessities"—"business talk"—"politeness"—and all the rest count against you in this test. Oh, no, we do not condemn you—in fact, we cannot see how you could be much better in the present stage of the unfoldment of the race—you are doing the best you know how—to be able to see that you are not strictly honest and truthful is a mighty advance. And this test is only a trifling one—the race is committing much greater crimes, when viewed from a few steps up the mountain side. Are any people suffering from want in the world? Are any of your brothers not receiving their share of the benefits that have come to the race? Are things fully as "good" as they should be? Can you not suggest a single improvement in the state of affairs? Oh, yes, we know that you alone are not able to remedy things—but you are a part of the race and are enjoying the privileges that come to the race—you are one of the crowd in the car that is rolling over the victims of the present state of affairs. But, as you say, you cannot help it—the race must grow into better things—must work itself out of the slough. And the pain of it all will cause it to work out—it is beginning to feel that pain now, and is getting very uneasy about it. All that you can do is to see the thing, and be willing for the change to come when it does. God has the loose end of the ball, and is unwinding and unwinding. You must have faith, and be willing for the unwinding, bring it to you what it will, for the seeing and the willingness will save you from much of the pain that must come to those who will not see and who are not willing— but even this pain will be good, for it is part of the unfoldment. Well, to get back to our subject, do you feel so very superior and "good" now? Well, the lesson is: "Condemn not"—"Let him that is without sin cast the first stone." None of us is so very "good." And yet, all are on the upward path. Let us live friends, one day at a time; doing the best we know how; sowing a word here and a deed there; let us not be self-righteous; let us not condemn; let us do our best, but give to every other man the same privilege; let us "mind our own business;" let us cease to persecute; let us be filled with love, tolerance and compassion; let us see all as part of the All; let us see that each is doing the best he knows how, considering the stage of his unfoldment; let us see the Divine in the humblest, vilest, and most ignorant person—it is there, it is there, hidden but pressing forward toward unfoldment; and, finally, "let us be kind—let us be kind." This is the lesson of the electric light within the bulb, covered with layer after layer of the cloth. Take it with you—make it a part of yourself. And Peace will be yours!

A consideration of the above illustration will show you that Conscience is the voice of the Spirit as heard through the confining walls of the lower principles of Man's nature. Or, to state in another way: Conscience is the result of man's past experience, growth and unfoldment, plus such light of the Spirit as is possible for him to perceive. Man in his unfoldment has profited by past experiences—has formed new ideals—has recognized certain needs of the growing soul—has felt new impulses arising within him, leading him to higher things— has recognized his relationship with other men and to the Whole. These things have accompanied the growth of the soul. And each stage of the soul's growth has given Man a higher conception of what is "right"—has exacted a higher ideal on his part. And this highest ideal is what he feels to be "right," even though he does not always live up to it. The light of the Spirit illuminates this highest peak of ideality possible to him, and makes it stand out clearly to the soul as a point to be aimed at—to be climbed toward. This highest peak, thus illumined, is as a goal for him to march toward. It is the highest thing that he is able to perceive. It is true that as he advances, the light mounts higher and shows him still higher peaks, the existence of which has not been suspected by him. When he attains to what now seems to be the highest possible point, he will see that he has merely gained the top of a foot-hill, while far above him, towering higher and higher, rise the peaks of the real mountains, the topmost point being brightly illumined by the light of the sun of the Spirit. There are other intelligences whose task it is to surmount heights unseen by us—the goal of those far behind us (that is the highest peak seen by them) seems far beneath us, for we have left it behind long since. So we must understand these things—this state of affairs, if we would form a clear idea of the acts, ideals, and "conscience" of others. We must cease to condemn—our duty toward others is not to blame them for not having reached the heights that we have attained, but to send them a cheering message of hope and joy, and to help to point out the way. That is what the Elder Brothers are doing for us—let us do the same for those behind us on The Path.

In conclusion, we call your attention to the fact that Conscience is but one of the pillars supporting the edifice of Dharma. It is an important pillar, but not the only one. It is to be taken into most serious consideration, but it is not an infallible guide. It points out the highest we have grown to see, but the point seen by us is not necessarily the highest, nor must we rest content with what we see. That which is behind Conscience is Infallible and Absolute, but Conscience itself is Relative and Fallible, because of our lack of growth—because of the confining sheaths which prevent the light of the Spirit from shining upon our souls. But, nevertheless, let us look toward that light, and follow it. Let us say in the words of the old familiar hymn of our childhood:

"Lead, kindly Light, amid the encircling gloom
Lead thou me on.
The night is dark, and I am far from home;
Lead thou me on.
Keep thou my feet; I do not ask to see
The distant scene; one step enough for me.
Lead thou me on."

The third pillar of Dharma is the theory of Utility, of which we have told you in our last lesson. Dharma acknowledges the value of Utility as a pillar, while seeing its weakness as a sole support for ethics. Human law, as set forth in statutes, laws, etc., rests almost entirely upon the basis of Utility, although some of the writers try to make it appear that it rests upon Divine command. The law is the result of man's endeavors to frame a code of conduct to fit the requirements of the race. Human law is a matter of evolution—it has grown, changed and unfolded from the beginning, and always will do so, for it is fallible and not absolute. Just as Conscience is always a little ahead of man's growth, so is human law always a little behind. Conscience points out a step higher, while laws are framed to fit some need that has arisen, and are never enacted until the need of them is clearly seen. And laws generally are allowed to remain in force for some time (often a long time) after their need has disappeared. Human laws are the result of the average intelligence of a people, influenced by the average "conscience" of that people. The intelligence sees that certain wants have arisen and it attempts to frame laws to cure the "wrong," or possible "wrong." The conscience of the race may cause it to see that certain laws that have been in force are unjust, unreasonable, and burdensome, and when this is clearly seen an attempt is made to have such laws repealed, altered, improved upon, or superseded by others better adapted to the new wants of the race. Corrupt laws are sometimes introduced by designing and unscrupulous persons, aided by immoral legislators—corrupt and ignorant judges often misinterpret the laws—mistakes are often made in making, interpreting and enforcing the laws. This because men and the human law is fallible, and not absolute. But take the general average, the laws of a people, both in their making, interpretation, and administration, represent the highest average of which that people is capable. When the people, or the average of them, outgrow a law, they do away with it—when the average of the race demand a new law, they get it, sooner or later. Reforms in law move slowly, but they come at last, and they are not so very much behind the average intelligences of the people. Of course, such part of the people as have risen above the average, see the human law as very faulty, and often very unjust, from their point of view, just as do those below the average, from an entirely different reason—to the first the law at any stage of the race is imperfect because it is behind the requirements of justice and the needs of the race, while to the second class it is imperfect because it is in advance of their ethical conception. But, on the whole, the laws of a people fairly represent the needs, ideas, and intelligence of the average man composing that race. When that average man grows, the laws are changed to fit him—that is, he causes the laws to be changed, for he recognizes their imperfection. Some thinkers have thought that the ideal condition of affairs would be "an absolute monarchy, with an angel upon the throne;" while another set of thinkers picture a community so highly advanced in intelligence and spirituality that human laws would be thrown aside as an impertinence, because such a people would need no laws, for every man would be a law unto himself, and being ideal individuals, ideal justice would reign. Both conditions above mentioned presuppose "perfection," either upon the part of the ruler or the people. The laws of a country are really desired or permitted by the average opinion of the people of that country—this is true of autocratic Russia as well as of so-called democratic countries, for the real will of the people makes itself heard, sooner or later. No people have a yoke imposed upon them, unless their necks are bent to receive the yoke—when they outgrow the yoke, it is thrown off. We are speaking of the average of the people, remember, not of individuals. So you see, the laws of a country generally represent the needs of the average citizen of that country, and are the best of which he is capable, and consequently, those which he needs at the present moment—tomorrow he may be worthy of and need better forms. The law is fallible and imperfect, but is necessary as a supporting pillar to the temple of ethics. It is the average conception of ethics, crystallized into a temporary shape, for the guidance of the people making the shape. Every law is a compromise and bears more or less upon some one.

The theory is "the greatest good to the greatest number." The advocates of the Utilitarian school of ethics point out that man calls a thing "wrong" because it gives him pain or discomfort to have that thing done to him. For instance, a man doesn't like to be murdered or robbed, and consequently gains the idea that it is a crime for any one to kill or rob, and gradually enacts laws to prevent and punish the same, he agreeing to refrain from robbing and killing in return for the immunity from such things granted him by the general acceptance of the conception of the thing as "wrong," and the enacting of laws prohibiting the same. In the same way he sees that the community is harmed by the neglect of a man to support his children, and so he grows to call that thing "wrong," and moral sentiment causes laws to be passed to punish and prevent this offense. And so on—this is the reasoning of the Utilitarian, and his reasoning is all right so far as it goes, for indeed this is the history of laws and lawmaking, as well as one side of the growing conceptions of right and wrong. But there is something more to it than this selfish idea (which though selfish is right in its time and place, as, indeed all selfish things are or have been). The Utilitarian overlooks the fact that the unfoldment of the race soul causes it to feel the pain of others, more and more, and when that pain of others grows intolerable, then new ideas of right and wrong present themselves—new laws are passed to meet the conditions. As the soul unfolds it feels its nearness to other souls—it is growing toward the conception of the Oneness of things—and while the feeling and action may be selfish, it is the act and feeling of an enlarged self. Man's sense of Justice grows not alone because his intelligence causes him to form a higher conception of abstract Justice, but also because his unfolding soul causes him to feel the relationship of others and to be made uncomfortable at their distress and wrongs. His conscience is enlarging, and his love and understanding is spreading out. At first man cares only for himself, all others being "outsiders." Then he feels a certain "oneness" with his wife and children and parents. Then to his whole family connections. Then to his tribe. Then to the confederation of tribes. Then to his nation. Then to other nations speaking the same language, or having the same religion. Then to all of his own color. Then to the whole human family. Then to all living things. Then to all things animate and inanimate. As man's sense of "oneness" enlarges and unfolds, he experiences growing conceptions of "justice" and right. It is not all a matter of the Intellect— the Spiritual Mind rays are becoming brighter and brighter, and the Intellect becomes more and more illumined. And as the illumination increases, man's sense of justice grows and broadens out, and new ideas of "right" and "wrong" present themselves.

So you see the Utilitarian idea is correct so far as it goes, but to understand it intelligently one must take into consideration the higher principles of the mind, as well as the Intellect. Man finds that it is not only "the happiness of the majority," but the happiness of all that is the ideal. He finds that until all are happy he cannot be perfectly happy. He realizes that until all get justice, none get it. And so he goes on, doing the best he can—blundering, stumbling, committing follies, impelled always by that growing thing in his mind, that he understands not (until his eyes are opened) but which makes him mighty uncomfortable and restless—that makes him press forward in search of he knows not what. Now that you, friends, begin to see what is the matter, you will feel less of the pain—the understanding is healing, and you will be able to stand a little aside and watch the trouble of the race in this matter of "right" and "wrong," and how they are suffering from the itch of ignorance. But, beware how you attempt to set them straight before they are ready for it—they will turn upon you and rend you, calling you "immoral," "atheistic," "anarchistic," and what not. Let them alone with the "infallible" codes of laws, morals, and ethics (which are changing over night)—let them go on making and unmaking their laws, for that is a good thing for them, and they need to do it to bring them out of their trouble. Let them tie themselves up with red-tape and chains, if they like it, and let them condemn their brother because he does not see things as they do—that is their nature and a part of their evolution. But do not let these things affect you—you know that all this constantly changing system of laws, ethics and morals is a part of the great plan of unfoldment, and that each is a step upward, and that no one step is absolute or infallible. You know that short of the full realization of the Fatherhood of God and the Brotherhood of Man—the conception and realization of the Oneness of All—there can be no real peace or rest. Stand aside and let the children play.

The evolving life of the soul—the unfoldment—gives you the key to all this system of change and unrest—this endeavor to square human needs with human laws—this endeavor to establish an absolute standard of right and wrong in the shape of human, relative, yard-stick and scales. The race is doing the best it can—each individual is doing the best he can—led ever upward by the light of the Spirit. Hold fast to the best you see, knowing that even that best is but a step toward the real best— and do not condemn him whose best is almost as your worst. Do not sneer at human law, even though you see its imperfection— it is a needed and important step in the evolution of the race. Finite, relative and imperfect as it may be, it is the best of which the race (the average) is capable and deserving of today. Remember, there is nothing Infinite, Absolute and Perfect, but the Whole—The One—The Absolute. Remember, also, that the race is slowly unfolding in an understanding of; a consciousness of; an identity with That One. And you, who are growing into that understanding, consciousness and perception—you who are beginning to feel the meaning of the I Am—be you as the rock against which dashes and beats the waves of the sea. Let the relative things dash themselves upon you, but be undisturbed, for they cannot harm you. They can but refresh and cleanse you, and as they roll back into the sea you will still stand there strong and undisturbed. Or, as one gazing from his window upon the groups of little children playing, quarreling, disputing, "making up," playing their games, making rules, imposing forfeits, awarding prizes—so view the world of men and women around you who are taking it all so much in earnest. And in both cases, send them forth your Love and Understanding, though they know not what you mean—though they cannot understand your view-point. We trust that we have made plain to you that the three generally recognized theories of ethics—revelation, conscience or intuition, and utility, are not antagonistic, but are complementary. Each presents its own phase of the truth— each teaches its own lesson. And the three pillars support Dharma. Let us now consider Dharma as a whole. As we stated in our last lesson, Dharma may be defined as "Right Action" or, to be more definite, we might say that "Dharma is the rule of action and Life best adapted to the requirements of the individual soul, and best calculated to aid that particular soul in its next highest step of development." And, as we said in the same lesson: "When we speak of a man's 'Dharma,' we mean the highest course of action for him, considering his development and the immediate needs of his soul." The student will have gathered, by this time, the idea that the philosophy of Dharma holds that "right" and "wrong" are relative terms, and that the only absolute "right" there is must rest in the Absolute itself. And that there is no such thing as absolute "wrong," the relative wrong that we see when we use the term, being merely an action resulting from either a low conception of "right," or else an action falling short of complying with the highest conception of "right" on the part of the actor. In short no action is absolutely "wrong" or "bad" in itself, and is only "wrong" or "bad" inasmuch as fails to come up to the highest conception of "right" on the part of the actor or observer. This may seem like dangerous doctrine, but let us consider it a moment. You will notice by studying history and the story of the evolution of Man, that man's highest ideals in his savage state were but little removed above those of the lower animals. It was not thought wrong to kill, steal, or lie; in fact, some races esteemed a man if he did these things, providing he confined his operations to those outside of his immediate family or tribe, in fact the principal objection to his killing his fellow tribesman seems to have arisen from a recognition of the fact that this course weakened the fighting and resisting power of the tribe, and the idea gradually obtained force that killing was "wrong" if the murdered man was a member of the tribe, but right and even commendable if he be of an outside tribe. (This seems very barbarous to us now, but the traces of it are seen even to this day when so-called "civilized people" still consider it right to kill men of another nation or people, and to "capture" their goods, providing "war" has been declared. The savage carried the matter to its logical conclusion, and did not wait for a declaration of war, that is the principal difference,) We find primitive man committing all the things we now call crimes, without being blamed for them, and, providing the crime were committed upon a person sufficiently removed from the tribesman, according to the customs and ethics of the time, the greater the crime the greater the "good" or "right" was it considered.

As the race evolved many of these "right" things began to be considered "wrong" and "bad," according to the "revelations" made by the priests and prophets; according to the awakening "conscience" in the people arising from an unconsciousness recognition of their relationship to one another; and according to the working of the idea of "utility" and "public policy" in the developing intellect of the race. And as the race evolved and unfolded, the ideals enlarged and grew higher. Things that were considered perfectly "right" and justifiable a few hundred years ago, even to the "best people" of the times, are now regarded as very "wrong" and base. And many of the things that seem perfectly right to us today, will be regarded by our descendants as barbarous, "wrong" and almost incredible. Read a chapter of life in the Middle Ages, for instance, and see how ideals and ethics have changed. Then come near home, and see how differently slavery is regarded now than fifty years ago, not to speak of one hundred years, Then read Bellamy's "Looking Backward" for instance, and see how it may be possible for public opinion to radically change. (We mention this book merely as an illustration—we do not claim that just those changes are to come to pass, although we know that changes just as marked and radical are before the race.)

And even in our own time we can see that different ideals are held by men and women in different stages of unfoldment, and that there is no fixed and arbitrary standard of "right" and "wrong" accepted by all. We may agree on the main points of ethics, but we, as people, differ materially upon the minor points. The average intelligence and "conscience" of the people are represented by their laws and "public opinion," although, as we have said, the laws are just a little behind even the average ideal, just as the average "conscience" is just a little ahead of the average rule of conduct. The average man is fairly well satisfied with the laws as they are at any particular time, although some of those upon whom the laws bear heavily consider them too strict and based upon a visionary idea of "good," while to men above the average the prevailing laws often seem based upon too low and undeveloped an ideal, and are often considered absurd, inadequate, more or less unjust, and not based upon an advanced ideal of ethics.

Not only do "good" things grow "bad" as time rolls on, but many "bad" things gradually lose their "badness" and are seen as perfectly good and proper when viewed from the point of advanced knowledge. Many things have been pronounced "taboo" or "bad" because they did not fit in with the fashionable religion, or social views of the times, and when custom changes, and religious ideas grow, the "taboo" is lifted. Many of these "tabooed" things were made "bad" by the priests of different times, for reasons satisfactory to themselves, their power often being increased in this way.

You will notice that as time passes, the average intelligence, and the average conscience, taking form in "public opinion" and law, demands of man a greater consideration for his fellows— insists that he "be kind" to a greater degree. This because of the dawning consciousness of the relationship of one man to another—the growing knowledge of the Oneness of All (often unconscious knowledge). And you also will notice this fact, that while a higher standard of "right" and "good" is required in the above stated matter, the "taboo" is gradually being lifted from man's action as regards his thoughts, life and actions affecting only himself. While man is expected to "be kind" to a greater degree each year, he is being accorded more freedom and is being given a better opportunity to "obtain a place, a free field, a harmonious expansion for his activities, his tastes, his feelings, his personality, his self," as Edward Carpenter has expressed it.

The blockade is being raised—the "taboo" is being taken off and man is to be given an opportunity to "fearlessly and gladly live his own life," provided only that he observe the highest degree of "being kind" to his brothers and sisters.

Now this idea of Dharma—this knowledge that "right" and "wrong" are relative and changeable, instead of absolute and fixed, does not give anyone an excuse for doing anything "bad" or "wrong" that he would not have done under the old idea. On the contrary, Dharma holds one up to his highest conception of "right," and expects him to do what seems "right" for right's sake, and not because the law compels him to do so—it expects right-action from him, even though the law has not as yet reached so high a stage. It teaches him that, if he sees a thing to be "wrong," it is wrong for him even though the law and public opinion have not yet reached so high a standard of ethics. The advanced man will always be a little ahead of the average conception—never behind it.

And Dharma does not teach that because an undeveloped and ignorant man may think it "right" to commit crimes against his neighbors, that he should be allowed to do so without hindrance or restraint. While no one would call a cat "bad" who would steal, or a fox "bad" who would kill chickens, still one is perfectly justified in restraining these animals from pursuing their natural instincts to the injury of man. And likewise with the "criminals" of society, while recognizing that their actions are the result of undeveloped minds and souls; ignorance, failure to live up to even the elementary ideals of ethics possible to them; we are justified in restraining them from preying upon us. But the idea should not be "punishment," but restraint and reform. Criminals are practically savages and barbarians, and their acts while entirely "wrong" when seen from our present viewpoint, were seen as "right" from the viewpoint of the savage. And these criminals should be treated as younger brethren of the race—undeveloped—ignorant—but still brothers.

The rule of Dharma is for each man to live up to the best in him—no matter whether that "best" has been impressed upon his soul by revelation, intuition or conscience, or by his intelligence in accordance with "utility." In fact all three of these influences have impressed him somewhat, and his "best" is a composite of the three influences. When in doubt, open yourself to the light of the Spirit, and your "best" will stand out clearly under the illuminating influence. That best will be your Dharma.

And another rule of Dharma is to refrain from criticising or condemning the Dharma of another man less developed than yourself. He is not looking through your eyes—he is not standing in your shoes. He may be living nearer to his highest ideal than you are to yours—how dare you judge him? Are you so near perfect that you set your standard up as the absolute? Will your highest ideal—and your best action—measure up creditably when laid next to the yard stick of the Absolute? Did you ever stop to consider that if you were in exactly the condition of that lowly brother or sister you would do exactly as does he or she. You cannot imagine yourself in exactly their condition, for you can think only of yourself as you are, and when you try to put yourself in their place you are able only to think of yourself (with all your past experiences and present attainments) clothed in the flesh and garments of the other. It is not the same at all—to be exactly like them you would have to cast aside all your past experiences and present attainments, and take the experience and attainment of the other instead. And, in that case, would you not be the other instead of yourself, and could you then (being that other) act differently from him?

The student who has followed us in our consideration of the schools of ethics—the three pillars of Dharma—very naturally asks us what crowns the structure—what ideal of conduct Dharma holds out to those who are ready to perceive it. When one has mounted into the temple supported by the three pillars, what does he find there? Let us see what answer Dharma gives to these questions.

The main point to remember in the consideration of "Right Action" as seen from the point of view of Dharma, is that the soul of Man is in a state of evolution or unfoldment. It is moving, stage by stage, from the lowest to the highest—from the idea of separation to the knowledge of Oneness. This unfoldment is the aim of life—the Divine plan. This being the case, can you not see that anything in the line of that unfoldment that aids it and tends to forward the work is "Good" or "Right?" And then, equally true must be the statement that anything that retards that unfoldment or tends to delay or frustrate it must be "Bad" or "Wrong," when measured by the same standard.

It is true that you may say "Not-Good," or "Not-Right," instead of "Bad" and "Wrong," or you may say "Less-Good," or "Less-Right," if you prefer the terms—but the meaning is the same, no matter what words are used. The "Right" or "Good" falls in with the plan of unfoldment, while the "Wrong" or "Bad" tends to retard it, or to frustrate its work. It is "right" for the tiger to be blood-thirsty and revengeful, for that is not contrary to his stage of development, but for a developed man to revert to that stage, or stages corresponding to it is "Wrong," because it is a going back, or retrogression. For an advanced soul to harbor feelings of hate, revenge, jealousy and the like, would be "wrong" for it would be a going back to stages long since past, and would be contrary to the knowledge and intuition of that man. In climbing the steps of the temple of Dharma one man may be on the third step, and a second man on the fifth. Now if the man on the fifth step descends to the fourth one it is a going back for him, which is "wrong;" while if the man on the third step advances to the fourth one it is a going ahead for him, which, consequently is "right" and desirable for him, for he is advancing. The law of evolution and unfoldment leads upward. Whatever falls in with that law is desirable and right—whatever goes contrary is undesirable and wrong. If a teacher has a dull or wilful scholar, and after working hard with him she finds that he is doing "just a little better," she praises him for the improvement and is greatly pleased. But that same teacher would be greatly distressed if one of her brightest and best behaved pupils would do just the same thing for which she had just praised the poor scholar! And yet both acts would be the same, when seen from one point of view, and yet how different from the broader outlook. Do you see what we mean?

Go on, dear friends and scholars, living up to your best. Read what we have written in Lesson i., of this series (pages 27, 28, 29, 30) and learn to "seek in the heart the source of evil and expunge it." Be a tamer of the wild beasts within you. Learn to cast out these relics of the past. Learn to keep in leash the lower animal parts of your nature—drive the beast to his corner of the cage, in spite of his teeth and claws. Learn to grow and develop and unfold until you are able to reach that step of the ladder of Attainment when you may look upon the past and realize that Dharma has become a part of the past with you, for then you will have entered into that consciousness of the Real Self, and will be able to see things as they are. Then will you receive the light of the Spirit without the dimness caused by the sheaths. Remember the words of "Light on the Path."

"Make the profound obeisance of the soul to the dim star that burns within—steadily as you watch and worship, its light will grow stronger. Then you may know that you have found the beginning of the way—and when you have found the end, its light will suddenly become the infinite light." Peace be to thee.

LESSON X. THE RIDDLE OF THE UNIVERSE.

In Lesson vi, of the present series, entitled "Gnani Yoga," we reminded the student that we had touched merely upon one phase of that branch of the Yogi Philosophy, and that we would take up some of its other features in subsequent lessons. The subject of Gnani Yoga is so large that many volumes could be written upon it, in fact, very many have been written in past ages, and thousands of volumes have been inspired by its teachings. In this lesson we shall touch upon some of the more important phases, and endeavor to present them in a plain simple style that the underlying principles may be grasped, at least partially, by many who have found other presentations of the subject too abstruse and technical. As we stated in Lesson vi:

All existence, conscious or unconscious, is an emanation of one Being.

This underlying "Being" has been called by many names by philosophers, the terms best adapted to it being "Spirit" or "The Absolute." The word "Absolute" is used in the sense

"Unconditioned; Free from limitation; Complete in itself; Depending upon nothing else; Actual; Real." In other words, it is "The Real Thing." We wish you to understand how we use the word, as much misunderstanding arises from a confusion of terms, and their meanings.

In our consideration of the subject we shall use the word "Relative" quite frequently. This word is opposed in meaning to "Absolute," to the extent that it implies that it arises from the Absolute—it is incomplete; conditioned; limited; depending upon something else; partial (not in the sense of a separate part, but in the sense of an incomplete view or conception.) In our consideration of "Things as They Are" we may cast aside one after another relative feature or quality—that which remains at the last, incapable of further analysis, exclusion, or division, is "the thing in itself;" the "absolute" thing. The Yogis often speak of the Absolute as "the Thing as it Is"—the Relative being "The Thing as it Seems." A simple plan of keeping the idea clearly before the mind, is to think of the Absolute as "The Whole Thing, as it is," and of the Relative as "An incomplete and imperfect view of one phase, aspect or quality of the Whole Thing." It is quite difficult to give an intelligent idea of the exact meaning of the two terms, for the reason that if we could understand the exact meaning of the word "Absolute," we would understand the Absolute itself. The word is the feeble effort of man's mind to express an inexpressible idea. Man's mind, in its present state of unfoldment, is "relative," and therefore is unable to grasp within itself the full meaning of the term "Absolute." So all it can do is to form an idea of its own limitations and boundaries, and then, realizing the relativeness of its own conceptions, it calls that which is without the boundary "Absolute." Man's mind cannot grasp the full sense of Absolute Space (Infinity); Absolute Time (Eternity); Absolute Intelligence; although it may be able to understand the general meanings of the terms by reason of its understanding of the relative phases of the things. For instance, man is able to draw a circle on a piece of paper, the circle enclosing a measure of Space—by thus expressing Relative Space he forms a conception of Absolute Space (Infinity), as "all the space lying outside of the circle, in all directions, to infinity."

In the same way he knows Time—he measures off a second, a minute, an hour, or a year—all relative terms. Having done this, he is able to think and say that all that lies on either side of the measured time—back of it, or ahead of it—is Absolute Time, Infinite Time, or Eternity. In the above illustrations, the Absolute Time, and Absolute Space, of course include the relative thing that man has measured off or set aside, the separation or setting aside existing wholly within the mental conception of the man, and having no actuality or reality in truth. One may form a mental conception of a "part" of the Absolute, in the sense that his attention is limited to that particular presentation of the thing apparent to his immediate consciousness, just as one may see a "part" of the ocean, by looking through a telescope pointed at it, but that "part" is not a part in the sense of a "separate" or "divided" thing—the "separateness" or "division" being wholly a matter of his consciousness, due to his inability to see the whole. Likewise, one cannot separate a portion of Space or Time from the whole—all that he can do is to form a relative conception of Time or Space and give it a name—he cannot detach either from the whole, in reality. In fact, both Time and Space are purely relative terms, used by man to help him to form a finite idea of Eternity and Infinity. Both words presuppose, of necessity, a measuring, or setting apart, while Infinity and Eternity having no limits, cannot be measured at either end, and are Absolute terms.

This Being—Reality—Spirit—Absolute—the Thing that is— The Real Thing—the Whole Thing—of course is inconceivable to the finite human intellect. Man's higher states of consciousness, as they unfold, help him to understand the matter more fully, but none may understand the Absolute fully, unless he be the Absolute himself. The Final Secret is insoluble to our ordinary consciousness, or any consciousness outside of the Absolute Consciousness. But as our consciousness unfolds, we may obtain (and do obtain), further and fuller knowledge—as sheath after sheath is thrown off, and the rays of the Spiritual Mind beat upon our consciousness, we are able to know many things formerly thought to be unknowable. And, we may make good use of the intellect in this matter. We have been told, so often, that we must take certain things "on faith," and that it was "no use bothering our minds concerning them," but this is only a partial statement of truth, for the Intellect does give us a reliable report concerning the real nature of things, and which reports, although only partial and incomplete, are worthy of respect. This is particularly true when the Intellect has received the beneficent light from the Spiritual Mind resulting from the recognition of the higher principle and the willingness to accept light from it. Although our first realization of God does come in the way of a blind faith, caused by a feeble ray of the Spirit breaking through even the dense material sheaths of the soul, and although much of the following "knowledge" of the Supreme Something that is back of and under it all is "intuitive" and "not from the Intellect," still the Intellect is able to give us valuable information, and is a proper instrument for such inquiry into truth. The higher teaching—the Spiritual Knowing—is not contrary to Intellect, but simply goes further along the line—it does not contradict Intellect, but simply transcends it. And Intellect will bear it out from its own store of knowledge, if properly asked. The Intellect is not a mocker—a liar—although many metaphysicians would have us to so consider it. It gives us accurate reports of matters coming before it, although often our undeveloped powers of judgment and discrimination cause us to misinterpret its message. When the Intellect is held to a clear answer, it will show us that it is forced to admit certain things from certain premises—that it is unable to conceive the opposite conclusion. Let us not fear the conclusions of the Intellect—let us not fear to apply its tests to our Faith. The Intellect has its limitations, but it is true so far as it goes, although our imperfect and mistaken judgment of its messages often leads us astray. In our search for knowledge we must call on all planes of the mind. Let us not, with many denominational teachers, consider the Intellect foreign and antagonistic to religious knowledge. Let us not, with many of the material teachers, consider Intellect everything and the higher states of consciousness mere illusions, and false witnesses. Each phase of the mind has its province—they are sisters—let them walk hand in hand, helping, explaining, agreeing—instead of declaring themselves sworn enemies. Let us see what the relative Intellect can tell us regarding the Absolute—what the finite Intellect can inform us regarding the Infinite. It is true that we cannot see "the Thing in Itself" by the Intellect, but inasmuch as the Intellect is a partial manifestation of that "Thing," and, inasmuch as unless we use the Intellect, we, in our present state of unfoldment, cannot think of the "Thing" at all, we may feel fully justified in asking the Intellect the question: "What can you tell us concerning this thing?" And in the following pages we will endeavor to tell what is the answer of the Intellect. Later on, we will offer the evidence of the higher plane of the mind—the message of the Spiritual Mind, so far as it has been shown us.

The mind of Man when it unfolds sufficiently to reason at all about the Universe—Life—Existence; when it forms even the elementary idea of Cause and Effect—when it reaches the stage of consciousness known as Self-Consciousness, that is, the stage at which it forms an idea of the "I" and the "Not I"— invariably conceives the idea of "something back of it all." The man's first ideas are crude, but he grows in understanding and constantly improves upon his idea of the underlying cause of Life and the Universe. In addition to his intellectual conception, he is impressed by a "feeling" of a

Higher Power, which feeling he afterward called "faith," and the manifestation of it "religion." He evolves fanciful theories, according to the direction of his religious thought and teaching, and invents gods without number (not to speak of devils), to explain that which the mind and "feeling" insisted upon.

After a bit the thought on the subject split into two forms— the thought of the priests, and the thought of the philosophers. The priests contented themselves with assertions that their particular god or gods "created" everything, and invented fanciful tales to illustrate the same, as time went along. The philosophers generally discarded the theory of the priests, and attempted to explain the thing by theories of their own, although as a matter of safety and prudence, they generally took care to fall in with the prevailing religious ideas, at least so far as words were concerned. After a time, the priests, inoculated with the reasoning of the philosophers, invented "Theology," a system of philosophy attempting to explain "why" and "how" a preconceived personal god did certain things, and what was the logical conclusion of certain theories starting from a certain premise. Then metaphysics sprang into existence in response to the needs of men's minds. Metaphysics is the name given to the science of the inquiry into the "reality" of things—the reality as compared with the "seeming"—the seen, as compared with the unseen—the subjective as distinguished from the objective— an inquiry into the Absolute, in fact. Metaphysics tried to find "the thing in itself," while Theology contented itself with assuming a Deity (usually a personal God), and attempting to reason out the attributes, nature, etc., of that Deity, and the relation of the Universe to that Deity, who was assumed to be its Creator. Later on, came the material or physical scientists, who attempted to explain the Riddle of the Universe upon a purely physical or material basis. The theologians, metaphysicians, and physical scientists of the Western world have fought each other's theories vigorously, and for a time were very far from each other. The Oriental thinkers, however, saw in theology, metaphysics, and science only varying phases of the same subject, and so the friction was avoided. In passing, however, let us say that the advanced theologians are fast coming to an understanding with the advanced metaphysicians, and the advanced scientists are meeting the other two on many points.

They eventually will agree in the main, the principal points of difference now being mere words—they are searching after the same Thing, and must eventually meet.

The theologian; the metaphysician; the philosopher; the scientist; each assumed the necessity of there being "something underneath" Life and the Universe. Their minds could not get away from that idea—they found it a logical necessity— something forced upon them by their Intellect. Some thought that this "something" was an extra-universal thing—a something outside of Life and the Universe, and which "created" it. Others thought that the "something" was the "Reality" of Life and the Universe, as distinguished from the appearance or partial-reality, but which was not apart from the Universe, but the soul or moving spirit within and of it. The theologians called it God; the metaphysicians called it Mind, Reality, Actuality, Truth, and similar names; the scientists called it Matter, or Force, or even Force-Matter; the philosophers called it Substance, Life, etc. But by each name, these thinkers meant "The Thing in Itself"—the Thing after all its "appearances" had been drawn into it—The Ultimate—The Absolute.

We do not think it necessary to devote more space to the statement that the human mind is compelled to think of an "underlying something"—the "Thing in Itself." All thinkers (no matter what their schools or theories) admit this conclusion, and every man will surely find this conclusion in his own mind, if he will search for it. Therefore we may assume as an axiom ("a self-evident and necessary truth; a proposition which it is necessary to take for granted"—Webster), the following statement:

First—The Absolute is.

We are then led to a consideration of what our Intellect informs us regarding this thing that is—we must see whether the mind contains any more "self-evident truths;" "propositions necessary to take for granted;" things which the mind cannot help believing.

The conception of the fact that the Absolute "is," carries with it the corollary, or consequent conviction, that:

Second—Whatever really "is" must be the Absolute.

There cannot be two or more Absolute Beings or Final Things. There can be only One Absolute or Final Thing. All else that "appears" to be must be relative—things relating to, or arising in connection with the Absolute—"of" it. The Absolute is what really is; and everything that really is must be the Absolute. The two statements of truth are necessary to each other, and cannot be divorced. When we say "is" we of course mean really is, in its entirety and completeness—not that which is incomplete and unable to stand by itself—not "appearances" of reality. Or, perhaps this may appear plainer to you: There cannot be two Whole Things, or two Totalities, or two Alls. One Whole Thing; Totality; All; is the necessity of the Intellect. These terms, of necessity, all are more or less imperfect, and fail to carry the full meaning. Some words will mean more to one student—others more to other students—therefore we have used several. The one term, in place of "The Absolute," that seems to be more readily grasped by beginners, is the one used in the first part of this lesson, i. e., "The Whole Thing, as it Is." This second statement leads us to a third, which is akin to it, namely:

Third—The Absolute comprises all that there really is; all that ever really has been; all that really ever can be.

The All must comprise All. And it must always have comprised All. And it must always comprise All. This from the very nature of things, as conceived by the Intellect. All must always be All. There can be nothing outside of the All. And whatever is must be in the All. There is no outside of the All—nothing can exist outside of it. To say that a thing exists outside of the All, is to state an absurdity. The Absolute never had a beginning, therefore there could have been nothing before it. And there can be nothing come from anything but it. And as it has no ending there can be nothing to come after it. So it must comprise all there is, has been, or will be. With this idea in mind, let us consider the fourth statement:

Fourth—The Absolute is Omnipresent—present everywhere at the same time. This statement is self-evident. There can be no place outside of the All. There can be no existence or presence except in the All. The All must be Everywhere. There cannot be a place with nothing in it. The Intellect is unable to grasp a conception of Nothing as an actuality; a reality; an absolute fact. An absolute Nothing is unthinkable, for an absolute thing is something, and "something" is opposed to "nothing." "Nothing" is a negative term, and is used to denote the absence, or apparent absence, or of some relative thing. The Absolute being All, it must include everything (see Statement iii). That which we call space; time; matter; mind; energy; etc., are but relative manifestations of the Absolute. Therefore it must be present everywhere, at the same time. Any other idea is unthinkable.

Fifth. The Absolute is Omnipotent—All-powerful—Possessing Unlimited Power—Possessing All the Power there is. This statement must be self-evident, if we admit the statements that the Absolute is All; is everywhere; is universal, and providing that we admit that there is such a thing as Power or Strength. Of course, it may be argued that Power and Strength are relative terms, being things relative to or incidental to the Absolute, rather than absolute things in themselves. This reasoning is correct, at the last, but we are conscious of something that we call Power or Strength, which we are justified in considering a relative manifestation of the Absolute. If there is Power (even relative) it must be "of" the Absolute. There can be no other Power. The Absolute must be given credit for All Power—not partial Power—not simply more Power than something else possesses—but all Power; All the Power there is—Unlimited Power—Power enough to accomplish anything. Later on, we shall speak of Power as an Appearance or Manifestation of the Absolute, and as relative in that sense. This axiom conveys the self-evident truth that all of that which we call Power, is a manifestation of the Absolute, and that there is no Power possible from any other source, for there is no other source from which it can come. Some metaphysicians make the statement: "The Absolute is All-Power—God is Power," but we regard Power as a relative manifestation of God or the Absolute, instead of a name for "the Thing in Itself." We regard Matter and

Mind in the same way, as shall more fully and at large appear, in this and following lessons.

Sixth. The Absolute is Omniscient—All-wise—All-knowing—Possessing All Knowledge—Knowing Everything—Having Infinite Knowledge. This means that there is nothing not known by the Absolute; nothing not absolutely understood. If there is a single thing that is not fully known by, and understood by, the Absolute then the words "Absolute" and "Omniscient" are meaningless and absurd. This, of course, applies to all knowledge appertaining to and concerning the past; present; and future, if we may be permitted to use these relative terms. The Knowing must be complete to be Omniscience—complete down to the smallest detail—to the final point. The Being possessing Omniscience cannot make mistakes; change its mind by reason of improved knowledge; cannot err in judgment, discrimination, or any process of what we call "mind." Such Knowledge and Wisdom must indeed be absolute, to fit the term. When the Absolute knows everything, it simply knows itself, for it is everything in everything. We must admit the existence of "Knowledge," for we know it, relatively, in an incomplete and unfolding degree in ourselves. We not only "know," but "know that we know." And admitting the existence of "knowledge" or "intelligence," we of necessity must admit that such "knowledge" or "intelligence" must pertain to the Absolute, and be possessed by it or within it, or at least be "of" it. Whatever Is must be of the Absolute. And the Absolute must possess all that there is of anything, or everything. In our consideration of that manifestation of the Absolute which is called "Mind," we shall speak of the universality of intelligence.

Seventh. The Absolute is Infinite. This statement is almost superfluous, as the term "Absolute" carries the term "Infinite" with it, and yet there is a shade of difference between the two, and so, "Infinity" may be spoken of as a quality of the Absolute. Infinity means: "Unlimited or boundless, in time or space; without limit in power, capacity, intensity or excellence; perfect; boundless; immeasurable; illimitable; interminable; limitless; unlimited; unbounded."—Webster. "Without Limit" gives the idea. The Absolute is without limit or bounds, because it is everywhere in space and time (if we must use the words); because there is nothing with which to limit or bound it, and a thing cannot limit or bound itself; because there is nothing outside of; beyond; or back of it; because there is nothing else but itself. Infinity is an absolute term, and the mind cannot fully conceive it, although it intuitively perceives it.

Eighth. The Absolute is Eternal. Webster defines the word "Eternal" as: "Without beginning or end of existence; always existing; underived and indestructible; everlasting; endless; infinite; ceaseless; perpetual; interminable." We cannot conceive of the Absolute as having had a beginning, neither can we conceive it as ever having an ending. If we try to think of it as having had a beginning, we must think of it as proceeding from something else, and in thus thinking we make the Absolute a relative, and set up a new Absolute a little farther back, and so on ad infinitum. The mind is unable to think of the Absolute as having a beginning, for a beginning presupposes a cause, and that cause another cause, and so on. The mind cannot admit such an idea, and so must be forced to admit that back of all the effects arising from causes there must be a something without a cause—a something that always existed—a "Causeless Cause"—The Absolute. It is true that in the world of relativity we have never seen a thing without a cause, because the law of cause and effect is in operation in that relative world, but all these so-called causes and effects are within and "of" the Absolute. There is no cause outside of the Absolute to affect it—there is nothing outside—there is no outside. This is hard for the untrained mind to grasp, but every mind must be forced to this conclusion, for there is no escape for it—the mind cannot help itself, and must admit the truth, although not able to understand it. The Intellect likes to cling to the idea of Cause and Effect, and is loath to part with it, even in considering the Absolute. But abandon it it must, for it is compelled to admit an exception, and a single exception breaks the law, and shows its relativity. For instance, if one admits that there is a "First Cause," the chain of cause and effect is broken, for then the "First Cause" is something without a cause, and therefore the law cannot be an absolute one—the exception breaks it. Or, on the other hand, if one claims that the law of cause and effect is infinite, the answer comes that an infinite thing can have no beginning; and a thing without a beginning—a beginningless thing—can have no cause. And so in this case, also, the chain is broken, and the mind must admit that there must be something without a cause. In the last case, the Intellect in using an absolute term, "Infinite," which it cannot understand, has knocked the bottom out of its own argument, and is forced to assume that there is a "Causeless Cause," although it is unable to illustrate that thing by anything in its own experience. It does the best it can, and so, at least, is frank to admit the existence of something which it cannot understand—in fact, it is compelled to do so if it is honest with itself. Cause and effect are relative things, not a necessity to the Absolute. Eternity is an absolute term, and the Intellect cannot fully conceive it, although the mind intuitively perceives it. "Time" is a relative term used by man because of his inability to grasp the absolute truth. Man is never able to grasp a moment of time, for before the mind can fasten upon it it has passed into the past. Time is relative and the greatest period of time that the human mind is capable of imagining or thinking about, when compared to Eternity or Absolute Time, is but as a strand of spider-web when stretched before the lens of a telescope the field of which embraces Infinite Space—in fact the spider-web would have to be reduced an infinity of infinity of degrees, before it would begin to answer for the purpose of comparison. An aeon of countless millions of years, when compared with Eternity, or Absolute Time, comes so near being absolutely (?) nothing, that only the Absolute Mind could distinguish it. Advanced minds in their teachings inform us that they often lose their sense of relative time entirely, in their consideration of Eternity or Absolute Time, and a million years seem as but a moment, in the thought. The same thing happens when the advanced mind explores the mental regions pertaining to Space—the relative is lost in the Absolute, and relative Space melts into Infinity. Time and Space are relative terms, belonging to the finite mind of Man of today—when the Absolute thinks, it thinks in terms of Infinity and Eternity— its own terms. From the Absolute (even our puny intellect can grasp this) everywhere is Here—every time is Now.

Ninth. The Absolute is indivisible. The Absolute is the All—the Whole Thing. It cannot be divided into parts, because there is nothing to divide it—nothing to divide it with—and nothing to "fill in the cracks." There can be no real partition, division, or separation of the Absolute. It always has been the Whole— always will be the Whole—is the Whole now. It is an Ultimate thing—not capable of being separated, divided, or parted. The mind is incapable of conceiving of the Absolute as being broken into bits; separated; divided, etc., for the reasons given above. The mind refuses to form the picture, and is forced to acknowledge the truth of the above statement. It is true that in our finite conception of things we may use the relative terms: "part of," or "portion of" the Whole Thing, or Absolute, meaning the particular presentation of the Whole coming within the field of our consciousness. We are unable to see the thing in its entirety, and consequently speak of that which we see as "a part," or "a portion" of the Absolute or Whole. But the limitation is within ourselves, and our mind makes the relative distinction because its field is too limited to take in a view of the whole. The mind breaks up the Whole into these limited and partial views, and calls each "a part," although in the absolute and true sense there is no partition, division or separation of these so-called "parts," and, in reality and truth the Whole remains unchanged and unseparated, although the little finite, relative, field of consciousness breaks it into imaginary "parts" for its own convenience and accommodation. The matter may be illustrated, crudely, by the following example. From the window by the side of which this lesson is written, there may be seen a great mountain range. As far as the eye reaches, it extends. Our eye takes it in as a whole, or rather recognizes it as a whole as it sweeps along its stretch, notwithstanding that at no time does the field of vision cover the whole range. Still the sense of continuity or wholeness is there, and if the eye were to be placed at a sufficient distance, it would take in the whole picture as one. But suppose that we wished to photograph this range, from this window. We would be compelled to first point the camera at one "part," and then after snapping it, point it at another "part," and so on until we had secured pictures of the whole. The several pictures would show no connection with each other, and the whole range would appear as if broken up or separated into "parts" or "portions," and yet in reality there has been no partition, separation or division in the mountain itself. The mountain itself remains unchanged—whole, and undivided. Distribute the pictures, and each person looking at his particular one would see only a "part," each looking different, and having no connection with any other, unless the two be placed together. One wishing to get a correct view of the range, would have to piece together the "parts," before he could see a representation of the whole without division or separateness. And yet, whether the pictures be viewed separately or together, the mountain itself remains the same, undisturbed and unaffected by the "appearances" of the pictures. The illustration is quite crude and imperfect, but may help to show you how, even on the physical plane, a partial view may give one the impression of "parts" and "separateness," which impression has no basis in reality or truth. Every so-called "part" of the Absolute is in touch with every other "part" and the Whole—all is One, undivided, indivisible, incapable of partition or separation. Remember this, students, you will need this truth to solve problems as we proceed. Tenth. The Absolute is unchangeable, constant, and permanent. Intellect is compelled to admit this statement as self-evident. The Absolute cannot change, because there is nothing into which it can change without losing itself, and it is inconceivable that the Absolute could lose itself or its identity. All outside of the Absolute—the All—is "nothing," and something cannot be nothing, much less can the "Whole Thing" become "No-Thing." The Absolute, of necessity, must be the same thing always, yesterday, to-day, and tomorrow. It is perfect, therefore cannot be improved upon. It is all wise, therefore cannot commit the folly of making mistakes or of losing its Perfectness. It is all Powerful, therefore it cannot lose or suffer to be taken away from it anything that it has, even if there were anything outside of itself to take it away. There is nothing outside—there is no outside—there is nothing that can affect it in any way. Being Everything that really is there cannot be anything into which it can change. There is an unvarying stability and constancy about the Absolute. There can be no evolution, development, or growth on its part for it is already Perfect, and there is no field for growth. These things being the case, we must realize that all that we call change; growth; improvement; progression; retrogression; life and death (as commonly understood) are relative terms, and are but incomplete appearances of the Absolute, and are not absolute facts. They are only "appearances" of Reality, the trouble being with our finite minds which see only a small and often distorted part of the Whole, and, not understanding, mistake that imperfect part for the Whole— mistake the appearance for the reality. We turn our telescope on the star, and when, shortly after, it passes out of the field of vision, we say: "it is gone," when, in reality, the star is still in its place, but we have moved and see it not. The shifting and changing that we think are real, are but the waves, foam and bubbles on the bosom of the ocean, mere surface appearances— the ocean is unchanged. The Absolute is outside of the law of cause and effect. Cause and effect cannot touch it, because they are but relative things, dealing with other relative things, and touching not the Reality or Absolute at all. The Absolute has no beginning, can have no ending; has no cause, and is not the effect of anything. From the position of the Absolute, there is no such thing as the law of cause and effect, such law being a relative thing having only the world of relativity for its field of operation. Cause and effect are relative appearances within the Absolute, and having no control over it—they are creations, mere instruments or tools of the Absolute, serving some Divine purpose of the moment, but possessing no reality to the Absolute. The Absolute is Free.

Eleventh. That which is not Absolute must be Relative to the Absolute, or else Nothing at all. That which is not the Absolute Being ("the Thing in Itself") must be "of" it, or else must be nothing at all. This statement is a corollary of Statements i, ii, and iii. All reality—and all relativity—must be either The Absolute itself, or else "of" the Absolute. In other words it must be either the Absolute (the Whole Thing as it Is), or else the Relative ("an imperfect and incomplete view or aspect of the Whole Thing"). If it is neither of these two things (which are really one thing, you must remember), then it is nothing—a Lie—an Illusion of an Illusion—a mistaken judgment of a Relative thing (or a series of such mistaken judgments), or a positive lie having no foundation either in the Absolute or the Relative.

The Three Great Manifestations, or Relativities.

The ordinary Intellect is unable to see plainly, or comprehend fully, the Absolute in Itself. But the relative aspects of the Absolute are apparent to the ordinary consciousness, and a glimpse of the "thing in itself" (Spirit) may be had through the Spiritual Mind as the consciousness unfolds so as to admit its rays. Although a little ahead of that part of our subject, we think it better to make the following statement in order that the student's mind may rest for a moment in the asking of the question that must inevitably come after a consideration of the above eleven statements. The question we mean is this, coming from Man: "And where am I in this Absolute and Relative?" Or, as an American recently asked: "Where do I come in?" The question will be taken up in our final lesson, but we have this to say here: Man, as he seems to himself to-day, has within him both the Absolute; the Relative. This is what we mean, he has within him, his Real Self, Spirit, which is Absolute. This Spirit is surrounded with a mass of the Relative, viz.: (1) Matter; (2) Energy or Force; (3) Mind. The Sanscrit terms for the above are: Atman, meaning Spirit, or the Eternal Self; Akasa, meaning Matter, or the all pervading material of the universe; Prana, meaning Force, Energy, etc., and

Chitta, meaning "Mind-substance." The Yogi Philosophy teaches that these four things are found in all things in the Universe of Universes. The Atman or Spirit being the Reality, is present everywhere, in everything. But not in the way of being shut off, or separate, or a piece allotted to every particular object. It may be described as "brooding" over the Universe and being in, under, around, and all about everything. We may speak (and we have in these lessons), as Man having within him (or else, as "being"), a "drop from the Ocean of Spirit; a Spark from the Divine Flame," "a Ray from the Sun of Spirit," etc., but these are mere figures of speech, for there is no separation of Spirit—there cannot be (see Statement viii). Instead of individual men being like pearls having a bit of gold in their center, they are like pearls strung upon a gold chain, the same chain being in and through each. This is a most clumsy illustration, but may give a faint idea of the essential difference between the two conceptions.

Each relative entity, or center of consciousness, or atom, or thing (call it what you will), rests upon this golden chain of Spirit, is a point on that chain, in fact. The pearls passing along the chain are composed of Matter (Akasa); possess Force or Energy (Prana); and Mind substance (Chitta), all of which three substances, or things are relative manifestations of the Absolute, the Spirit being the only "thing in itself" apparent— the only "real thing" about man, for the other three are changeable, temporary, incomplete, etc., and lacking in the qualities that belong to the Absolute as we have mentioned them in the above statements. We shall take up this matter of the constitution of Man, in our next lesson, and merely mention the above in this place, as an aid to the student, and partially to answer the inevitable question that comes up at this part of the instruction. We must now go on to a consideration of the Three Great Manifestations or Relativities. We will then speak of The Spirit, Atman, or Absolute, and Man's Relation to God, which is the heart of "The Riddle of the Universe." The Spirit is the Unmanifest—Matter, Energy and Mind are Manifestations (relative, of course) of the Absolute. Remember this, always, in order to prevent confusion.

The Three Great Manifestations of the Absolute, which may be sensed, studied, and comparatively well understood by the Intellect of even Man of to-day, are as follows:

(1.) Matter, or Substance (Akasa).

(2.) Energy, or Force (Prana).

(3.) "Mind-Substance" (Chitta).

These three divisions are recognized by the modern advanced Western physical scientists, although some of them try to "dodge" the last mentioned form. In our consideration of the subject, we shall give you the views of the best Western thinkers, or rather the result of their speculations and investigations, so that you may see how closely they are approaching the Yogi Philosophy, at least so far as the relative "world of form" is concerned. The

Yogis know that the three above mentioned manifestations are really not three, but are three phases of one manifestation, their teachings being that Matter is a grosser form of Energy or Force, gradually shading and melting into the latter; also that Force or Energy is a grosser form of "Mind Substance," gradually shading and melting into this last mentioned manifestation. And the Mind-substance in its highest phases and operations almost reaches the plane of Spirit, from which it has emerged, in fact, it becomes so fine at the point of its emergence, that the human mind (even the mind of the most advanced souls), cannot point to the exact line of difference. These things we shall consider later. Our first concern is a consideration of the Manifestation of Matter.

(1) Matter. (Akasa) "Matter," is a word or term used by scientists to designate that substance of which the material and physical Universe is composed, which substance is claimed to have extension in space which it occupies, and to be perceptible to the senses— the "body" of things—the "substance" of things. It is usually divided into three classes, or phases, i. e., Solid, Liquid and Aeriform. Solid Matter is matter whose parts firmly cohere and resist impression, such as stone, metal, wood, etc. Liquid Matter is matter having free motion among its parts and easily yielding to impression, such as melted metals, tar, treacle, oil, water, etc., in short, matter that "flows." Aeriform Matter is matter that may be called "elastic fluids," such as vapor, gas, air, etc. Of course, these three forms of matter are really variations of one form, for all matter may be placed into either and all of the three classes by a change of temperature, for instance, Ice is a kind of matter in Solid form; Water the same kind of matter in Liquid form; Steam the same kind of matter in Aeriform. The degrees of temperature, producing any of the three mentioned forms vary, but any and all forms of matter are capable of changing their form, as above, upon being subjected to the proper temperature. For instance, Air, which is generally thought of as being Aeriform, has been liquidified and changed into Liquid Air by the application of a very low degree of temperature, and science knows that if a sufficiently low temperature be produced, the Liquid Air would "freeze" and become solid. Likewise, take Lead, which appears as a solid in our ordinary temperature, and subject it to sufficient heat, and it "melts" and becomes a liquid, and if a still higher temperature be applied it will pass off into a "gas" and become Aeriform. This is true of all the elements of Matter, the degree of heat regulating the form. Heat is known to science as a form of force, the degree depending on the rate of its vibrations, so that the change in the apparent form of matter is the result of the playing upon it of Energy or Force (the Second Manifestation). Certain gases combining in certain proportions produce liquids, for instance, Water is composed of two parts of Hydrogen gas, combined with one part of Oxygen gas. And certain other Aeriform substances are composed of other "gases," for instance Air is

composed of Oxygen and Nitrogen, combined in certain proportions. Of course, both Water and Air may, and do, hold other substances in solution, but the elements named are the only ones necessary, and the matter held in solution may be subtracted without impairing the virtue and nature of the solvent. The same form of matter may assume apparently different phases, for instance, the rocks composing the earth's surface crumble, disintegrate and are resolved into "earth," "dust," "dirt," etc. Then the plant-seed, sprouting and sending forth roots and shoots, draws upon this "dirt," taking from it certain elements needed for its welfare and life, transmuting these elements into its own substance, cells, etc., and so thus that that was once a part of a rock, is now a part of a plant. Then comes along Man, who eats the plant, and its matter is transformed into bone, muscle, blood, and even brain of the man. If an ox eats the plant, and man eats the ox, the result is the same. The element in the rock is now the element in the man. And throughout all this change, although the form, shape, and character of the matter has changed, not a single atom of the original matter has been destroyed. Constant change and infinite combinations, but eternal existence is what physical science claims for the atom of matter. That which was once an atom of the rock, and is now an atom of matter in your body, will, in time, be a part of the plant or animal life of some other form of creature, and will always be so, and has always been so, according to science. Science seeing this apparent eternity of Matter, naturally jumps to the conclusion that Matter is the Absolute thing, ignoring the fact that it is but the relative manifestation of something behind it—the Absolute Being. Physical Science has analyzed matter until it has been able to classify it into about seventy classes, called "elements," which it has assumed to be ultimate, that is, incapable of further analysis or division. The Yogi Philosophy teaches that all these so-called elements are but forms of one element—that there is but one form of matter, as may be found when chemistry reaches a higher stage of development. Modern science is reaching the same conclusion, although it has not been able to positively demonstrate it by experiment.

Then science has assumed that Matter is composed of minute atoms, not visible to the sight, and that the Ultimate Atom is incapable of further division, and is therefore the "real thing" in matter. Some have held that this Ultimate Atom is the Absolute, from which all the elements, and then all the forms of matter have sprung, and also all that we call Energy and Mind are incidents and qualities of this Atom. They would have made this Atom their God, but alas! still more recent discoveries have shown them that their Ultimate Atom is not ultimate at all, and they are now hunting for another Ultimate Something in Matter. They will find, as did the Yogis thousands of years before, that when they reach their "Ultimate" in Matter it will dissolve and melt into Force and Energy, and then they must hunt for their Ultimate atom of Force. Advanced science has hinted at this very fact within the last few years, and we may expect the fact to be accepted generally before very long. When the scientists then probe Force or Energy until they find its "Ultimate," they will come to a melting point when the elusive Force will dissolve into Mind-substance, and that back of "Mind-substance" is the Absolute. But that is a long way off for the physical scientist, although an old fact for the Yogis.

We have reached the end of our space, and must postpone the further consideration of Matter until the next lesson.

LESSON XI. MATTER AND FORCE.

Our last lesson closed in the midst of an inquiry into the manifestation known as Matter. As we stated there, Science has assumed that Matter is composed of atoms, and that these atoms may be divided and re-divided until, finally, there will appear an atom incapable of further division—an Ultimate Atom, in fact—something in the nature of Absolute Matter. Various theories have been advanced by scientists to account for the atom—you must remember that this Ultimate Atom is a purely theoretical and hypothetical thing—no one has ever found it, and it could not be seen even with the strongest microscope, even if it were found. Recent discoveries, notably that of the "X Rays," and "Radium," have disturbed these theories, and scientists just now are very much at sea regarding this question of "the atom." They generally had accepted the idea that the atom of hydrogen was the "Ultimate Atom," or at least so near to it that the difference was infinitesimal, when these recent discoveries upset their theories, and the experiments showing the so-called "radiant energy" and "radioactivity" caused them to agree that that which had been considered the final thing in atoms was capable of still further analysis. Science at the present time is on the verge of admitting the Yogi teachings that the finer forms of Matter shade or melt into Energy or Force, and that Matter is but a less refined, or a grosser form of Energy or Force. "The last thing in Matter," as the newspapers and magazines somewhat flippantly style it, is what have been called "electrons," which are in the nature of minute charges of electricity. It has been stated by an eminent scientist that one may get a feeble idea of the relations between these electrons and the atom by imagining a room 200 feet long, 80 feet wide, and 50 feet high, and having scattered within this space 1,000 little electric charges, each the size of an ordinary full-stop or "period" of newspaper type—this (.) is the size. The space and room enjoyed by the "full-stop" in the aforesaid room, corresponds to the space and room enjoyed by the "electrons" in an atom. When it is considered that the atom itself, containing these electrons, is invisible to the human sight, we may form an idea of the size of this thing called an "electron" by modern science. These "electrons" are stated to be violently energetic and to be in constant motion, revolving around each other like planets in a minute universe. It must be remembered that this theory has been evolved and accepted as a necessity by the scientists, although both the atom and "electron" are invisible—they became necessary to account for certain other things, and so were invented, and will serve their purpose until something better offers itself. We mention the matter, not as accepting it as final, but merely to point out how near modern science is to accepting the Yogi theory of the identity of Matter with Energy or Force. Students will notice, from time to time, that each new scientific discovery will point further to this idea, and how, later on, Force and Energy will be recognized as shading and melting into "Mind." Some reader of this lesson, fifty years or more from now, will smile when he reads this prediction (?) and sees how nearly it has been fulfilled. We extend our hand across the half-century to such future reader, who is very likely unborn at this moment. And even in that day, there will be no understanding of "Mind," unless it be considered as a manifestation of the Absolute, instead of being itself absolute, for Spirit is as much higher than Mind as we know it, as Mind is higher than Force or Energy, and as Force or Energy is higher than Matter. Mind, Force and Matter are three forms of one manifestation, and the Absolute underlies all—it is the Manifestor of Manifestations.

Let us rapidly run over the accepted theories of modern science, regarding Matter, so that we may see how closely it is touching the Yogi teachings. Modern science regards Matter as occupying infinite space continuously, and being everywhere in some form. It also holds that the sum of matter is eternal and unchangeable, that is, that there neither can be an addition to, or subtraction from, the sum total of matter—that there never can be more matter, or less matter, than there is at the present time, and that the total quantity now has always been the total quantity. This theory, of course, holds that Matter must have always existed, as it could not have been made out of "nothing"; and must always exist because it cannot be destroyed, for "something" can never become "nothing." It is held by science that although Matter may change its form, and work into countless combinations (as it does constantly), still Matter (in itself) never really changes; loses anything, or gains anything; and that it is the same yesterday, today and to-morrow. That it is, in fact, Infinite and Eternal. You see that science has been making a God of Matter—has been attributing to it qualities of the Absolute, instead of qualities belonging to a manifestation of the Absolute, such qualities being merely loaned it instead of being the "property" of Matter. The Yogis hold that Matter (in itself) does not exist, but is a form of Energy, which Energy is a form of Mind, which Mind is a manifestation of the Absolute. For the purpose of teaching, however, it speaks of the three, Mind, Force, and Matter, as the Three Manifestations, shading into each other, and we will so speak of them in our lessons. Some scientists have held that Matter was "The Whole Thing," and that Force and Mind were but qualities and incidents of Matter. Others have held that Energy and Force was the "Real Thing," and that Matter was but a manifestation of Force, and that Mind was a quality or kind of Force. So far, none of the physical scientists treat Mind as being the "Real Thing," with Force and Matter as qualities or attributes, although some of the metaphysicians and philosophers have held that "Mind is All, and All is Mind," and that Matter and Force were "illusions," or, non-existent. This view has been followed by certain schools of metaphysicians of religio-metaphysical cults. The student will see that the Yogi Philosophy accepts each and all of these views as partly correct, either viewed separately or collectively, but teaches that underlying all three of the so-called "absolutes," "ultimates," or "real things," lies the only Reality—the Absolute, from which the three Manifestations emanate. The Yogi Philosophy antagonizes none of the schools of thought, but harmonizes and explains each set of theories, under one grand system. Even among the various schools of Oriental thought are found the above mentioned three forms of thought or theory, but those who search among the head-waters of the stream of the Ancient Teachings will find that all emerge from the true Yogi teachings of the One—the Absolute—the Manifestor of All Manifestations, transcending Matter, Force and even Mind.

Before leaving the physical scientists' theories of Matter, we must not neglect to mention that science has been forced to accept the theory of an "ether," or very fine form of Matter, which is stated to fill all space—the space between the stars and solar systems—the spaces between the atoms, molecules, "electrons," etc., in so-called "solid" bodies. This "ether" is stated to be quite thin, tenuous, rare, fine, etc., far more so, in fact, than any of the finest gases or vapors known to us. No one ever has seen, heard, tasted, smelt, or felt, this "ether," but its existence is found necessary to account for certain physical phenomena, the transmission of light and heat, etc. Science has found it imperative to hold that Matter is infinite, and that it exists in some form everywhere, and so it is compelled to formulate and accept the existence of a very tenuous form of Matter to "fill in the spaces," and so the theory of "ether" arose.

The Yogi Philosophy has no quarrel with Western physical science over this question of the "Ether." In fact, it holds that this "ether" exists, in seven different grades of thinness or tenuity, the Sanscrit term (in use for centuries) being "Akasa." Akasa is the Sanscrit term for the principle of the Manifestation of Matter. The teachings are that it pervades and penetrates infinite space—that it is everywhere; omnipresent. It is taught that every and all forms of Matter evolve from this Akasa—first the six lower forms of "ether" in succession; then the gases and vapors, in their order of fineness; then the air; then the liquids; then the solids. The Akasa is the substance composing the finest gases, and the densest solids—the sun; the moon; the stars; the air; the water; the human body; the body of the animals; the body of the plants; the earth; the rocks— everything having form; every shape; everything that can be sensed by the ordinary senses. Besides this, the higher forms of Akasa are finer and more tenuous and subtle than any form of matter perceptible to the senses of the ordinary man. The "souls" of the disembodied, both those that have passed out at death, as well as those which are traveling in the astral body, have a "body" of fine matter, imperceptible to the ordinary senses. And beings on higher planes than ours are encased in some of its subtle forms, such a vehicle being necessary for the holding together of the several elements in the constitution of man and the higher beings. Matter in some form is necessary for Force and Energy to play upon, and Mind must always have a body of Matter (oftener of the most refined kind) in order to manifest itself at all. The Absolute uses its finest form of Manifestation (Mind is its highest form) for certain expression, and Mind in turn, uses the lower vehicles, Force and Matter as its tools; instruments; conveniences; and vehicles of expression. We mention this at this place that the student may remember that there are grades of matter very much higher than that which are perceptible to our ordinary senses. So clearly is this fact known to advanced occultists, that some of the old writers, using Oriental imagery, have used the term "The Body of God" in referring to Matter. And this expression may help the student to appreciate the importance and dignity of Matter, although seeing its comparative lowness in the scale. We should avoid the folly of the physical scientists who make of Matter a God; and the twin folly of many metaphysicians and idealists, who would make of Matter a base thing, a Devil, or even "Nothing."

We did not intend to take you into the details regarding Akasa in this lesson, but we may mention this much at this point. The essence or finest principle of Akasa is of so fine a form of Matter that it cannot be sensed by any except the highest form of intelligences—it is unknown to all except the highly evolved souls who use this form of Akasa as a vehicle or body. It is the thin veil of substance separating those advanced minds from the Universal Mind, but there is no real separation, and such Minds are in the closest contact with the Universal Mind. This form of Akasa is the highest form of Matter—some Yogi writers call it "Matter Itself." At the beginning of the several great periods of life in the various parts of the Universe—or in the various Universes, if you prefer the term—the only form of Matter manifested is Akasa in its finest form. Then the Absolute, using its manifestation of the Universal Mind, sets into operation Force, Energy or Prana which plays upon, or acts upon, this Akasa, and causes it to become each of the lower six forms of "ether" in succession. That is, causes it to send forth a part of itself in those forms. Then, in succession it becomes manifested in the shape of the finer vapors; gases; air; liquids; solids, etc., until there is a manifestation of each form of Akasa from the highest (or Akasic Essence) to the densest solid. At the end of a world cycle, or as it progresses toward its end, there is a gradual "drawing in" of the forms of Akasa, the densest forms disappearing, and being followed (after ages) by the next in line, until solids disappear; then liquids; then gases and vapors; and so on until all Akasa is drawn into itself, and only its essence, the principle of Akasa, remains, until it is again set into motion at the beginning of a new cycle.

The attentive and thoughtful student may ask himself whether, by analogy, he may not suppose that in some great Cosmic Cycle, there might not come a time when the Akasa would be drawn into the Prana and the Prana into the Chitta, and the Chitta into the Absolute itself. And whether the statement that these things are manifestations of the Absolute manifestor, does not imply that they had a "beginning"—a time when the manifestation began. And whether this conclusion might not lead to another that there are a series of great Cosmic Cycles, and so on until the mind can think no further. To this expected question we would say that there are Cosmic processes so stupendous and magnificent that even souls so far advanced that they may be considered archangels and gods are unable to grasp the thought of them. The highest teachers have handed down to us this word, but as they do so they confess to having had glimpses of things so far transcending even their capacity for understanding and comprehension, that their god-like minds reeled and swam. This being the case, we may be justified in not asking the student to consider anything higher than a World Cycle, of which we may speak in a future lesson, or a future series of lessons. But remember this, brothers on the Path, that though this contemplation of the workings of the Divine Cosmos and its parts may seem to carry God afar off from this earth—from us—the Truth is that notwithstanding these stupendous operations and workings God—the Absolute—is here with you always; here around you; here in you. Closer than a brother is He—closer than a mother to her babe—closer than a lover to the loved one—nearer to You than is your heart; your blood; your brain. The Spirit is always with you—do not lose courage. And this is true of the humblest; the lowliest; the vilest—as truly as of the most exalted; the highest; the purest. The difference is only in the degree of recognition of the Spirit on the part of the man. Let not these scientific statements and teachings distress you, if you fail to understand them, or have no taste for them. It is not necessary for you even to believe them, much less understand them, much less like the study. This is all that is necessary: Learn to know that God is within you and all others—that you are as necessary to Him as he is to you, for you are a part of His plan—learn to realize the One Life in All—and open yourself to the inflow of the Divine Love and Wisdom, and be willing to grow, develop and unfold. In your studies you will find that the same law applies to the great things and the small, in this world of forms. The same law governs the evolution of Universes that regulates the life of the atom. "As above, so below," says the old occult proverb, and the more you study the more will you perceive its truth. Study the things that lie nearest to you, and you will have the key to the things beyond you. "There is no great; there is no small" in God's World of Forms. Have Faith— have Courage—have Hope—and above all have Love, and Charity. We shall now consider the Second Great Manifestation or Relativity. (2) Energy or Force. (Prana.) Energy or Force is a principle of Nature which may be defined as "the power of resisting or overcoming resistance," or "that which produces Motion." A bent spring possesses Energy, for it is capable of doing work in returning to its former form; a charge of gunpowder possesses Energy, for it is capable of doing work in exploding; a Leyden jar charged with electricity possesses Energy, for it is capable of doing work in being discharged. All particles of Matter that fill infinite space are in constant and perpetual motion. This Motion is considered by science to be infinite and eternal, that is, existing everywhere and forever. Every physical change and every chemical process is associated with a change in the atoms composing Matter—a readjustment and changing of combinations. All forms of motion; gravitation; all forms of force; electricity; magnetism; light; heat; cohesion; nerve-force; in fact all forms of motion, or force, that manifest in the change in the position of the particles of matter, are forms of Energy, or manifestations of its principle. To those unfamiliar with the subject, the idea of Energy perhaps may be best carried in the mind by the idea of "the Principle causing Motion and Change in Matter."

The theories of modern science regarding Energy, resemble those regarding Matter. That is, it is held that although Energy may manifest in numberless forms, and may be transformed and changed from one form to another, yet the sum total of Energy in the Universe is fixed and unchangeable, and that not a single particle of Energy may be created, nor destroyed— that no matter how it may change form and transform itself into varying forms, that such changes are like the changing forms and combinations of Matter, and are merely relative and not actual, inasmuch as Energy as a whole is not affected and remains the same in principle and amount. This theory or principle of physical science is known as "The Principle of the Conservation of Energy."

It will be seen from a consideration of the above that science holds that no material power can bring into existence a single particle of Matter, or a single particle of Energy. Nor can any material power take out of existence a single particle of either Matter or Energy. Both are regarded as fixed and unchangeable. We may change the form of Matter, or rather the combinations of its atoms, and we may transform one form of Energy into another, and so on, but neither may be created nor destroyed. Energy is the principle that works change in Matter, and many scientists speak of it as a "property or quality of Matter," while others regard it as a separate principle, working in connection with Matter. An example of the transformation of one form of Energy into another, and so on, is as follows:

An electric lamp shows a light, which light is produced by the passage of electricity through the little thread of carbon, the latter offering a resistance to the electricity—resistance causing the energy of the electricity to be transformed into heat and light. The electricity is produced from a dynamo, the power of which is imparted by a steam engine. The steam engine takes up motion from the Energy of steam, which steam is produced by the expansion of water by the Energy of heat. The heat is a form of Energy transformed from the Energy in the coal, which energy is released by combustion. The coal obtains its chemical energy from the sun which imparted it to the trees from which the coal originated, or else, perhaps, from the Energy inherent in its atoms. The sun or atoms obtained their Energy from the Universal Energy. So you see, the whole process is a chain of transformation. It might be carried much further; for instance, the electricity might have been used to run a belt, and the belt to impart its motion to certain machinery, and so on. But the principle is the same in all cases. The student is advised to read some elementary work on Natural Philosophy, or Physics, in order to get a more detailed idea of Energy, Force, Motion, etc. Examples of the transforming of Energy from one form of motion to another may be seen in every act. We pick up a ball, and sending a nerve-current from the brain, cause certain muscles of the arm to contract and expand, which process imparts motion to the ball and throws it from the hand. The ball strikes another object, and throws it down, and so on. A row of bricks extending around the world could be toppled over, one after the other, by imparting a slight motion to the first one, which would pass it on to the next, and so on. The Energy in gunpowder, when released in a close chamber, is imparted to the bullet in the shape of motion, and the bullet travels through space, until the Energy in the earth, known as the Attraction of Gravitation, overcomes the imparted motion of the powder, and eventually imparts to the ball a new motion which causes it to be drawn toward the earth.

Science (both physical and occult) teaches that all Matter is in constant motion—that is, the atoms are in constant vibration. This motion or vibration of course is imparted by the principle of Energy. We cannot perceive this motion, but it is known to exist, and Life as it is would be impossible without it. Each form of Matter has its own rate of vibration. We cannot spare the space for a consideration of this part of the subject, and must refer the student who wishes to investigate the theories and facts of material science to the many text books on the subject which may be found at any book store or public library. We have stated the principal theory, and will now pass on to the Yogi teaching of Prana, which corresponds very closely with the teachings of physical science regarding Energy. In fact there is very little ground for difference on general principles possible to investigators of the subject.

The Yogi Philosophy teaches that in the world of forms, or relativity, all Matter, or forms of Akasa, is in perpetual motion— there is no rest in the world of Matter. The apparent rest of material objects is only relative and not a fact. Heat and Light are merely forms of motion, a manifestation of Energy. Suns and worlds rush through space—their particles are constantly changing and moving—chemical composition and decomposition is constant and unceasing—building up and breaking down are invariable incidents of cell-life; atom-life; and molecular being. There is no rest in Nature at any point. Work is constantly being done, and something is always being produced (in the sense of new combinations being formed, for there is no creation of something from nothing).

This Energy or Force, the cause of Motion, Change and Action, is known by the Sanscrit word, "Prana." Prana, like Matter or Akasa, is present everywhere. Modern physical science holds that both are "eternal" in themselves, but the Yogi Philosophy teaches that they are both emanations or Manifestations of the Absolute, and are eternal only through the Absolute, and not in themselves—in themselves they are relative and not eternal.

They were expressed, manifested or "projected" from the Absolute, and again may be withdrawn within the Unmanifest, but with this explanation, they are what physical science supposes them to be, when it speaks of them as "infinite and eternal." Modern science, as a rule, considers them as separate principles, but the Yogi Philosophy teaches that Matter or Akasa is a grosser form of Energy or Prana, and was projected from the latter. But to all intents and purposes, they may be regarded as two separate principles, in our consideration of the Universe.

Prana manifests in all forms of action, energy, motion, and force, as we have explained in our consideration of Energy. It has many grades, forms and degrees, but the principle underlying each is the same. These different forms may be transformed from one to another, as we have seen in our consideration of Energy, the Eastern and Western teaching agreeing perfectly in this respect. They also agree, in the main, in the theory of the "Conservation of Energy," inasmuch as the Yogi teachings are that the sum-total of the Prana in the Universe cannot be added to or taken away from; but here, note the difference, the Yogis teach that Prana is a grosser form of Mind, and is expressed by the Absolute through Mind, and may be withdrawn eventually in the same way. But in the general consideration of the subject, the Western theory may be accepted as a reasonable "working hypothesis."

Western science teaches that "there can be no Matter without Energy—and no Energy without Matter." The Yogi Philosophy agrees that Matter without Energy is inconceivable, but that there is such a thing as Energy without Matter, for there was Energy or Prana before there was Matter or Akasa, although in that case there was merely the real principle of Energy, latent and not manifested in Motion, which is far from being the same as that something caused by the play of Energy upon Matter, which we call Motion or Force. One was non-acting, while the other is manifest action. As we sense the Universe, however, there is no matter without Energy, and no Energy not manifested in and through Matter. So, in this case also, the Western theory may be accepted by the student as a "working hypothesis," although he must not lose sight of the real teaching.

We have spoken of Prana, or rather, of that form of Prana known as Vital Energy, etc., in our little manual "Science of Breath," and in some of our "Fourteen Lessons," and in "Hatha Yoga." In our next series of lessons, which will be on the subject of "Raja Yoga," we will take up many important questions regarding Prana in its other forms (that is, apart from Vital Force, etc.) and its control by the Mind and Will. The student may see, from what we have said, that Prana being a grosser manifestation than Chitta or Mind-substance, and, in fact, a projection or form of same, that one who understands the laws and principles of the matter may exercise a great control over Prana through the Mind, under the direction of the Will.

This subject comes under the head of "Raja Yoga" and will be considered in our treatment of that subject in our next lessons as above stated. We cannot dwell upon the matter at this point, but in order that you may form a general idea of it, we may say that the positive can always control the negative. Chitta stands to Prana in the relation of the positive to the negative—and the control is possible, with knowledge, under the direction of the Will. What the Yogis know as Pranayama is the science or art of controlling the Prana by the Mind, or Will. This is a feature of the science of "Raja Yoga," and in its highest form, as possessed and exercised by the advanced spiritual men of the East and West, constitutes the basis of the power of the "Adepts," and "Masters," as they are known to the world. The greater teachings on the subject are carefully kept within the knowledge of the few, lest mankind would basely misuse the power were it to be made known generally. But, still, there is quite a portion of the teachings that are now allowed to be made public to those ready for it, and anyone possessed of sufficient application and determination, in connection with spiritual development, may put into practice a greater or less degree of the science of Pranayama. There are other features of "Raja Yoga," besides this one, such as the control of the Mind or Chitta, etc., etc., but Pranayama forms one of the leading teachings.

Before leaving the subject of Energy or Prana, we wish to call the attention of our students to the fact that occasional glimpses of the truth of the Yogi teachings that Energy is a grosser manifestation of Mind, and shades or melts into the latter, are afforded to close scientific observers of the phenomena of Energy or Force. Observers and investigators have been struck by the occasional conviction that Force or Energy, in some of its forms, displayed a something akin to intelligent action, instead of acting like "blind" force. When the attention of the scientific investigators is directed to this fact (and it will be before long) they will notice, classify and investigate the same, and new theories will be evolved and taught to account for the same. Science must eventually come to accept facts bearing out the truth of the Yogi teachings—for they exist.

Leaving the subject of Prana or Energy, we pass on to a consideration of the Third Great Manifestation or Relativity:

(3) Mind; Mind-substance (Chitta). Let us first see what physical science has to say regarding what is known as "Mind." Western material science has hazarded many theories regarding the nature of Mind. As a rule they have

discarded the theories of the metaphysicians and philosophers of the past, and have sought to find a material basis for mental phenomena. They have tried to find a satisfactory theory along the lines that Mind is simply a manifestation of Matter—a chemical effect—a mechanical effect, etc.—something growing out of; emanating from; or manifesting from Matter. One leading scientist has hazarded the idea that the brain secreted Mind, just as the liver secreted bile. Just think of it—Mind a secretion of Matter! The materialists have made the mistake of commencing at the wrong end. They would make Matter the Ultimate and Absolute, and Energy and Mind something springing from it, when the reverse of that process would be far nearer correct according to the Yogi teachings. However, advanced science is beginning to see its error, and is inclining to the idea that Mind, Energy, and Matter are one thing—different forms of something that they are calling "Substance," and similar names. They are drawing much nearer to the "dreams" of the occultists, whom they formerly despised.

Webster defines "Mind" as follows: "The intellectual or rational faculty in man; the understanding; the power that conceives, judges or reasons," which definition entirely overlooks the fact that Mind is manifest in the lower animals, and in plant life, and even in minerals. However, those holding the idea that Mind belongs to man alone, call the Mind of animals, instinct, appetency, etc., and the Mind in minerals, "chemical affinity," etc.

"Instinct" is the term generally applied to the mental operations of the lower animals, and" Appetency" is defined as follows by the authority above mentioned: "Appetency is the tendency of organized bodies to select and imbibe such portions of matter as serve to support and nourish them, or such particles as are designed through their agency, to carry on the animal or vegetable economy." So that those holding the theory of man's monopoly of Mind, nevertheless have to admit the possession of "something like Mind" in the lower animal and vegetable kingdoms. Recent scientific observers regard the chemical or molecular action of minerals as a form of mind, which view, of course, is that of the Yogis who hold that Mind is an invariable accompaniment of Matter and Energy, this being true of every atom as well as the combinations of atoms. The Yogis hold that all forms of consciousness from mere sensation to the highest forms of spiritual consciousness, are all manifestations and forms of Mind.

In this lesson we shall not have space to consider questions of psychology, in fact, such a course would be foreign to the purpose of the lesson. But in order to convey to the student our idea of the meaning of "Mind" we must say that by "a manifestation of Mind" we mean any act of consciousness, and by "consciousness" we mean any evidence or manifestation of "awareness," from mere "sensation" to the highest forms of consciousness. The student presently will see why we make this explanation.

"Sensation," the lowest form of consciousness known to us, is defined by Webster as: "An impression made upon the mind through the medium of the organs of sense; feeling awakened by external objects, or by some change in the internal state of the body." Sensation is that form of "awareness" or consciousness, known as a "feeling." It is not exactly the same as "perception," for "sensation" is a "feeling," while "perception" is a "knowing" of the "sensation"—the "perception" interprets the "sensation." For instance, we may "feel" the presence of a fly on our hand— that is "sensation." When our mind realizes that something is on the hand causing a sensation, that is "perception." One's sense of smell may make him aware of an odor, then his mind turns its attention to the odor, in response to the stimulus of the sensation, and realizes that he is smelling a rose—do you note the distinction? However, this is not a lesson in psychology— we merely want you to realize what "sensation" is, when we speak of it as an evidence of mind. There can be no sensation without some bit of Mind-substance to accept it. Just as there can be no sensation unless there is something to "cause" it—so there can be no sensation unless there is something to "receive" it—and that receiving-thing is Mind-substance in some degree, or form. This is the point we wish you to remember. Simple Consciousness and Self-Consciousness are higher forms of "awareness" than Sensation, but the difference is only in degree, not in kind. The Sensation of the most undeveloped form of life differs only in degree from the highest form of consciousness or mental effort on the part of Man, or even beings much higher in the scale than Man (for such beings exist—they are as much more advanced than man, as man is than the beetle—but they were once men, and men will be like them some day). Outside of the Absolute, all degrees of "knowing" are acts of the Mind, and the forms are mere matters of degree. Mind is a universal principle, just as is Matter or Energy, and it resembles them very closely regarding its manifestations and combinations.

Let us return to the views of modern physical science. We will take Ernest Haekel as representing the front rank of advanced science of to-day. His works are regarded as extreme and radical, and he embodies in them the advanced theories of the materialistic thought of the age. Haekel does not recognize anything higher than "Substance," and believes the Universe to be self-existing, and without any preceding cause. His works show, however, that modern science has gotten away from the old materialist idea of "dead" matter, and "raw" matter, and that he, himself has reached the highest materialistic conception known to the mind of Man. In fact, the school of thought that he has founded, advancing along the lines laid down by him, will soon be separated by only the thinnest partition from the school of advanced "spiritual" thought. One is reminded of the creation of the great tunnel through the Alps, in which the work was begun from each of the two sides, the two sets of workers meeting exactly in the middle, and the two halves of the tunnel being found to fit exactly to each other's lines. Each set of these mental workers will meet the other, and will find the Absolute in the centre—although they may call it by different names.

Haekel in his great work "The Wonders of Life," lays down the doctrine of a Monism composed of a "trinity of Substance." He formulates it in the following three propositions: "(1) No matter without force and without sensation; (2) No force without matter and without sensation; (3) No sensation without matter and without force." He goes on to say of the above: "These three fundamental attributes are found inseparably united throughout the whole universe, in every atom and every molecule." This is a most wonderful admission coming from one of the leaders—if not the leader of modern materialistic thought. Its significance will be appreciated by those of our students who are familiar with the old materialistic point of view, as contrasted with that of the Yogi teachings. Haekel in his consideration of the three-fold aspect of Substance, holds that Matter is an extended substance, occupying infinite space, and being eternal and unchangeable; that Energy or Force is also infinite, in eternal motion, and unchangeable in its sum-total, according to the law of the "conservation of energy"; that sensation being joined to matter and energy as the third attribute of substance, the universal law of the permanence of substance must be extended to it, therefore, sensation must be eternal and unchangeable in its quantity or sum-total. He holds that the "changes" in sensation, like those in matter and energy, mean only the conversion of one form of itself into another form of itself. It will be seen that by "sensation," Haekel means that which we call Mind, for he explains that "the whole mental life of humanity ... has its roots in the sensations of each individual," and he approvingly quotes Nageli's remark that: "The mind of man is only the highest development of the spiritual processes that animate the whole of nature." Consider this as coming from the centre of advanced materialistic thought. Is not the trend of events made plain?

The student will note the differences between the Yogi Philosophy and Scientific Monism as expounded by Haekel and other leading scientists representing the school of "The New Materialism." The Yogi Philosophy teaches the existence and being of the only Reality—the Absolute, which reality manifests in the shape of Three Great Relativities, Matter or Akasa; Energy, Force or Prana; and Mind, Mind-substance, or Chitta (the latter being in the nature of "a refined and subtle principle," rather than of a "substance" akin to matter.) These three manifestations, are really but three forms of one great manifestation, and proceed from the finest, Mind, to the next finest, Energy or Force, on to the grossest, Matter—the three shading into each other, as explained in this lesson. The manifestations emanate from the Absolute, and may again be withdrawn into it—they are relative to it, and in the absolute sense of words have no real existence, that is, no existence apart from the Absolute. The Absolute is all that really is—that is, that exists of itself—is self-existent—depends upon nothing else— has no cause—has nothing into which it may be withdrawn or absorbed. The school of Scientific Monism holds that all that there is is a physical something which they call "Substance," which possesses three "attributes or properties," which are called Matter, Energy, and Sensation. Matter is regarded as the space-occupying property or attribute; Energy as the moving or motor property or attribute; and Sensation as the feeling (and consequently "thinking") attribute or quality. "Substance" is held to be self-existent; infinite; eternal; and unchangeable in quantity or sum-total, although apparently changeable in the forms of its attributes or qualities.

The Yogi Philosophy teaches the existence of the Spirit, that presence of the Absolute outside of its manifestations— Scientific Monism has nothing to say of Spirit (it does not recognize it) and "Substance" seems to be the sum or combination of Matter, Energy, and Sensation, rather than as a "thing in itself" from which all relativities flow. So far as we are able to see and understand the philosophy of Scientific Monism, it does not speak of or teach of anything akin to the "Spirit" or "Essence" of "Substance," but, instead, treats Substance as a purely physical thing, the spiritual nature of things being denied, or ignored as unnecessary and non-existent. We trust that we have correctly reported the ideas of this Monistic school of materialistic, scientific thought, at least such has been our intention. It seems to us as if that school holds to the idea of a self-existent Universe—a universe without a cause, or God, or Absolute Being—in other words, its teaching seems to be that the Universe is its own God. It, of course, denies the survival of consciousness after death, or the immortality of the soul, and teaches that the "soul" is a purely material and physical thing, a development of "Sensation." We call our students' attention to the differences between the two philosophies, as well as to their points of resemblance. Both teach the "Oneness of All," but how different is the understanding of that one! We think that the Spiritual Mind of the student will so illuminate his Intellect that it will see the truth in the midst of these conflicting teachings, which still show in their resemblance, that instinctive and intuitive leaning of the human mind toward the idea of "Oneness." To those to whom have come the spiritual awakening of consciousness, will be apparent the point at which the Monistic Philosophy leaves the right Path for the illusive side track from which it will be compelled to return in the future.

In our next lesson we will endeavor to explain the nature and qualities of Chitta or Mind-substance, as well as to give you the teachings regarding Atman or Spirit, and Man's relation to the Absolute.

Peace be with thee.

LESSON XII. MIND AND SPIRIT.

In this lesson we shall take up the subject at the point at which it was dropped at the close of the last lesson, i. e., the consideration of the nature and qualities of Chitta— Mind-substance, which is the First Great Manifestation or Relativity.

While we speak of this Manifestation as Mind, we have thought it better to give you the Sanscrit word used by the Yogi teachers, which is "Chitta," which word when freely translated means "Mind-substance," rather than "Mind," the difference being that the English word "Mind" has a rather metaphysical meaning, signifying a vague something—a condition or state rather than a "thing," while "Chitta," the Sanscrit word, means Mind as a "substance," a "thing," hence our definition of it as "Mind-substance." In order to fix the idea more firmly in your mind, let us see just what the word "Substance" means. Webster defines it as "that which underlies all outward manifestations; nature; essence." The word is derived from the Latin words "sub," meaning "under," and "stare," meaning "to stand," the two words combined meaning "to stand under," or "to underlie." (When we realize that "substare" may be defined also as "to understand," we may see new light in the meaning of "substance," and realize that its use as the "underlying principle of Mind" is proper.) So you see Chitta means "Mind-substance," or that which underlies the outward manifestations that we know as Mind—it is "Mind in itself," the Universal Mind (not the Absolute, however, as you must remember).

The Yogis teach that this Chitta or Mind-substance, is universal and omnipresent—that is, exists everywhere, and is found at every place in the Universe. Its sum-total is fixed and cannot be added to or taken away from, and therefore it is unchangeable in its sum-total, although like Matter and Energy many apparent changes may occur within itself, resulting from the forming of new combinations.

Mind-substance may be considered as a higher phase of Energy or Matter, just as Matter may be considered as a grosser form of Mind-substance or Energy. You will remember that Mind-substance was the First Manifestation, and from it emanated Energy, and from Energy emanated Matter, so you see that all form parts of one real substance, varying in degrees—all are parts of the great three-fold manifestation of or emanation of the Absolute.

Mind-substance somewhat resembles Energy, but still it is "more so." It bears the same relation to Energy that Energy does to Matter. Let us see if we cannot describe it better. In some of the higher forms of Matter one sees that the characteristics of Matter melt into those belonging to Energy. Take Electricity or Magnetism for example—you may see there a combination of Energy and Matter that is most interesting, and are enabled to see Energy appearing as a "thing" that can "almost be cut with a knife." And in the same way, in some of the higher forms of Electrical Energy, one may be compelled to feel that "the thing almost thinks," so near does it come to the blending line between Energy and Mind-substance. In a few years physical science will discover forms of Energy which will give a still more striking evidence of "thinking" or "rational action," than any now known. The discoveries that will follow that of Radium, will cause a most startling revolution of scientific thought. Science is almost on the border line separating Mind and Matter—they will soon be seen as one in the final analysis, with Energy forming the centre.

We are unable to exhibit to the physical senses of students a "piece" of Mind-substance as proof of its existence, and although the student of advanced psychology or occultism may have seen many manifestations of it as a force, still this evidence is not as yet accepted by material science. And yet everyone is conscious of that activity of Mind-substance that we call "thought." Mind-substance, as well as Energy and Matter, must be accepted by the student in somewhat of an abstract way, for all these three manifestations may be known only by their forms of outward expression. Thus, the Ether, the highest form of Matter, cannot be sensed by Man, and only when its atoms combine in the shape of solids, liquids or aeriform matter do the senses take cognizance of it. In the same way Energy itself is not in evidence to the human mind, and only is sensed when it manifests through matter in what we know as forms of Force or Motion. And the Mind-substance is known to us only as thoughts; thought-force; etc. Matter is the thing the soul uses to clothe itself in; Energy is the thing the soul uses to act; Mind-substance is the thing the soul uses to think with.

Mind-substance is the thing by which is set into operation the Energy that causes Matter to be in Motion. The theory of the material scientists which they call the "vortex-ring" theory, is very close to the facts as taught by the Yogi Philosophy, and the latter carries the theory into the region of Mind as well as in that of Matter. The Yogi teaching is that the "ultimate atom" of Matter is really a "little whirlpool" of ether, in the ether, formed by the action of Energy upon the Ether. The ether itself, being frictionless, the "ring" loses none of its motion, and becomes "permanent" (in the relative sense of course, when the Absolute is considered) and possesses all the properties generally ascribed to matter, i. e., dimension, volume, elasticity, attraction, extension, etc., and also possesses motion in itself. These "rings" are of various sizes and rates of vibration, which fact accounts for the different "kinds" of atoms that have been puzzling science, which explanation of "kinds" may throw some light on the question of the seventy odd "ultimate (?) elements" of Matter, that have confronted science. (It may be seen that if the rate of vibration or motion of these "rings" be changed, the dream of the alchemists may be realized, and one "element" be transmuted into another, and gold produced from lead. Woe unto "High Finance" if some dreamer stumbles upon this secret, which is fully known to the "Adepts" and

"Masters," but for which they have no need or use, unless, indeed, they may see fit to use it as a means of upsetting prevailing economic conditions, and bringing mankind back to "first principles" of living.)

Science, in its consideration of the vortex-ring theory of Helmholtz and others, has run up against the stone wall regarding the cause of the original motion imparted to these "rings" which lie at the bottom of the question of Matter as it is known to science. They could not imagine the Ether as having sufficient intelligence to move of its own accord, even if it had the power to do so. Here is where the Yogis come to the rescue of their Western brethren, and "lend a hand" in the hour of need. (It is questionable whether the Western brother will be so willing to accept the extended hand just now, though.) The Yogi Philosophy teaches that Mind-substance, of course "knowing" itself, manifests itself in "Thought." This "thought" is really a motion in the Chitta or Mind-substance caused by its calling to its aid Energy, which energy remember has originally been manifested from it. This "Thought-force" thus called into play, communicates itself to the Ether, and the "vortex-ring" results, and the "Ether-whirlpool" becomes an "element" or "atom" in matter, possessing form, dimensions, etc., as well as having within itself Energy and Mind, thus forming the trinity of Matter, Energy and Sensation spoken of in our last lesson as being taught by Haekel and the physical scientists. Some of the Yogi teachers prefer to describe the process as follows (merely a different manner of presentation). They say: The Ether having proceeded from Mind-substance, through Energy, has in itself the elements of its "grandparent and parent" (Mind-substance and Energy, or Chitta and Prana), its inheritance, which it is capable of using. So it merely thinks the Energy into motion and forms the "atom-ring" in itself, for the purpose of further manifestation. This view gives the impression of Matter being possessed of Mind and power of Motion, which, to a certain extent is correct, although the three manifestations are somewhat different, and all proceed from one original source— the Absolute.

So you see the Yogis teach that all Matter (as known to our senses) is the result of a Thought; and that Thought is "Mind in Action" ; and that Action is the outcome of Energy; and that Energy is the product of Mind-substance—therefore indeed Matter is Mind—All is Mind—not only in a metaphysical or mystic sense, but in reality. The teaching conveys the remarkable truth that everything in the material world has been thought into existence. In this teaching may be found the practical explanation of the theories of the metaphysical schools and cults which claim that "All is Mind," and that "Matter is Nothing," and then build up a structure of metaphysical and religious theory upon that foundation. But such thinkers often ignore that great underlying Truth, that both Mind and Matter—Mind as well as Matter—are but relativities and do not exist in themselves, but are manifestations and emanations of the Absolute, which is the only Real Being;

which is All there Is. Beware of making a God of Mind, or of Matter—both are false gods. The Absolute is the One—the only One.

We have taken Western physical science into consideration in our explanation of the Yogi teachings of the Three Great Manifestations, in order to show the points of agreement and difference; and that the Western mind might be able to more readily absorb the Oriental thought by associating the same with the thought more familiar to the Western world; and also that the student might perceive that the mind of man, as it unfolds, travels toward the same intellectual conclusions and seeks to make truth axiomatic and self-evident. But we wish to add, at this point, that although using the Intellect just as the Western scientists are now doing, the Yogi Fathers or ancient teachers (as well as their advanced modern followers) verify their conclusions by the use of the unfolded higher faculties of the mind—the region of the Spiritual Mind. In some of these higher mental states, made possible by Yogi development, the Yogi realizes that he simply "knows" certain things to be true, without reference to the familiar intellectual processes. This "knowing" cannot be understood by those familiar only to the operation of that part of the mind known as Intellect, but those who have experienced it know it to be a higher form of reason than is the Intellect, which it transcends and surpasses but does not necessarily contradict. Many things that the Intellect is beginning to see as truth, are at once recognized and understood by the Higher Consciousness, and the conclusions of the Intellect are thus verified. But many results are reached in a different way, viz., the Higher Consciousness sees and "knows" certain things to be so, and the man, relapsing into his ordinary consciousness carries with him the impression, knowledge and certainty of the truth of some thing, but is not able to express it or explain it (even to himself) in the terms and by the processes of the Intellect. Consequently, a sage may "know" a thing quite surely, having received his information through the higher channels of the mind (often in the form of symbols), but may find it very hard to explain its details to others, or even himself. He may know that a thing is, but cannot tell the why and how of it, or explain its relations to other things and ideas. The Yogis teach that all truth regarding the Universe, from the point when it began to be manifested from the Absolute, are locked up in some part of the Mind-substance, and as all parts of the Mind-substance are identical in nature and principle (just as are the drops of a body of water) so does every man's mind "know" all truth of the manifested Universe, and the bringing of such knowledge into the field of consciousness is a matter of unfoldment—in the end we shall know all. The consciousness is the relative "I," which is always growing and enlarging its field of consciousness, or rather, moving its field of consciousness toward higher regions of the mind. But the Mind of Man cannot know the secrets and mysteries of the Absolute itself—none but the Absolute may know itself—and the Mind can know only itself, that is, all that emerged from the Absolute in manifestation or emanation. There is a difference and distinction here—do you see it? But the Atman—the Divine Principle in Man—that something above even Mind—which is the real Self—that real presence of the Absolute—knows the knowledge of the Absolute—itself—and when Man at length throws off all the confining sheaths—even that of the highest forms of the Spiritual Mind, and becomes merged with his Real Self, then shall he know all, for he will have found himself in the Absolute, and his consciousness and knowledge shall include the All—then will he cease to be Man.

Those of our students who are interested in the scientific side of the subject, may be interested in the statement that those of the Yogis who impart the scientific side of the philosophy, teach that neither Matter, Akasa, in its highest form of Ether— Prana in its essence or highest form—nor Mind-substance in itself—are atomic. None of these manifestations, in their essence, are atomic, but what are called the atoms of each are really "vortex-rings" in the thing itself, which form atoms, such atoms forming combinations which become apparent to the senses.

For instance, Mind-substance, when combining with action, forms atoms called Thought; Energy when in action manifests atoms called Motion or Force. Energy in itself is passive, if the paradox may be voiced; and the essence of Matter which we called the highest Ether, when acted upon by Energy under the direction of Mind, is formed into vortex-rings called atoms, which form into the grosser forms of Matter, i. e., solid; liquid, and aeriform.

Lest we be accused of fitting a new Western scientific theory to the old Yogi philosophy, we refer the student to the Sanscrit word "Vritta" (found in the Vedas or ancient Yogi writings) which means waves or vibrations of Mind, forming "thought," the literal translation of the word "Vritta" being "whirlpool." As "vortex" (the word used in Western science) also means "whirlpool," and as both refer to a movement in "substance," presumably causing the formation of "atoms," it will be seen that the Yogi is merely voicing his ancient teachings when his theories crowd the "vortex-ring" theory very close. In this lesson we cannot attempt to go into the subject of the workings of the mind; the principles underlying the same, or the physical effects producible by thought. These things, the psychology of the Yogis, as well as the teachings regarding the Dynamics of Thought, belong to that part of the philosophy known as "Raja Yoga," which will be taken up in our next course of lessons.

We wish to say here, however, that students must not mistake the brain or the brain-matter for Mind-substance. The brain-matter is merely the material or matter through which Mind-substance manifests itself. The student will find it better to think of Mind-substance as a force, rather than as a form of Matter. The word "substance" when used in connection with Mind, seems to give the idea of a "material" substance or form of matter, which is far from being a true idea of its nature. And yet, we cannot very well say "Mind-Force," for that would indicate either a combination of Mind and Force, or that form of Force used by the Mind when in activity. Mind-substance is a higher form of Energy, and remains, like Energy itself, in a quiet or passive state in its essence. Only when aroused into Thought does it form a union with active Force. Remember these points please.

Concluding this consideration of Mind-substance, we would say that it is omnipresent, that is present everywhere, and like Energy and Matter (its progeny) it cannot be changed, added to, or taken away from. Moreover, it cannot be really divided or separated, although in appearance it may be. That is, although the mind of each Ego or Soul represents so much Mind-substance, apparently separated from other Mind-substance by a thin wall of the finest kind of matter, yet, in reality, each mind is in touch with other separated minds, and with the Universal Mind, of which it forms a part. All Mind-substance is not separated or expressed in the shape of individual minds any more than is all Ether manifested in gross Matter, or all Energy converted into Force or Motion.

We would also have you remember that there is no such thing as "dead" matter, for all the Universe is alive. And every particle of Matter contains Energy and Mind-substance. The Universe is a great big vibrating, thinking thing, from atom to sun, although its "thinking" may vary from the faintest form of mere sensation or feeling (even chemical attraction and repulsion being a form of sensation) up to the highest form of mental effort known to man or beings much higher than man.

The Atman, or Spirit.

We now pass on to a consideration of the Atman, the Real Self, the Spirit, and its expression in Man. In the consideration of it, we shall drop the Sanscrit term Atman, and will use the word "Spirit," to convey the same meaning. We mention the Sanscrit term only that you may recognize and understand it when you see it in other writings on the subject.

To grasp the idea of Spirit, we must turn the mind upon the subject of the Absolute. In a previous lesson we have tried to give you the report of the Intellect upon its consideration of the Absolute. In that report we have tried to tell you what the Intellect finds itself compelled to believe or acknowledge. We may say here that this testimony of the Intellect is confirmed by the testimony of the higher faculties of the mind, and the advanced souls of all ages, who have acquired spiritual insight, corroborate the report of the Intellect regarding its conceptions of the Absolute. The highest reports are along the same lines. But, student, remember this fact which is lost sight of by many investigators—the Mind, even the Mind of the most advanced souls, can report only that which it finds within itself. And even the Universal Mind, the sum-total of all the Mind that has been projected by the Absolute—and this includes such part of the Mind as is now manifested in conscious intelligence as well as Mind not so manifested—is not able to go outside of itself for knowledge. It is conditioned and limited, the limitations and conditions having been placed upon it by the Absolute. So, you see that even the Universal Mind—the sum-total of all the mind there is—can report only what it knows in itself, and can give no report concerning the nature of the Absolute, other than that which the Absolute allows it to have and has deposited in it. The Universal Mind is not the Absolute, remember, but merely an emanation of it. The Mind—the Intellect and the higher phases—gives us a report of what it finds within itself regarding the Absolute, and we are able to say that according to the testimony of the Mind we must believe that the Absolute is certain things, and has certain qualities and attributes. But, the advanced student will see readily that even this conception and testimony is relative and not absolute. It is only truth as we see it, and not Truth Absolute, for the latter belongs to the Absolute itself, and is not capable of being thought of by finite mind—even the Universal Mind. The Universal Mind is not Omniscient—it does not know everything. It knows every particle of knowledge (down to the finest detail) of itself, and of the Universe. It must do this, for it is the Mind of the Universe, and knows itself and all through which it works—itself and its tools. But it cannot transcend or go beyond its own limits and it is confined on all sides by the "dead line" separating it from the Absolute. This separation is only relative and not real—that is, it is real to the Universal Mind, but not real to the Absolute. The Universal Mind, however, knows positively the existence of the Absolute, for it recognizes its presence at the point of apparent separation, and thus has every evidence of the reality of the Absolute. It is able also to "know that it does not know," because it knows that it knows all within its own province, and, of course, sees that that which it sees but cannot understand is the Unknowable to it. So that there are some things that the Universal Mind does not know, not in the sense of not having as yet found out, but in the sense of their being "beyond knowledge," as the Mind understands knowledge, but which, of course, are fully understood and known to the Absolute itself. The Absolute must know itself, and all things; for it is Omniscient or All-Knowing. Omniscience is vested in the Absolute, and all other knowledge is relative, imperfect, and incomplete. The student is again reminded that what we call the Universal Mind, is not something through which the Absolute thinks, but something through which the Universe thinks—the Universe being the sum-total of the emanations of the Absolute, and not the Absolute itself. The soul of Man is capable of drawing upon the Universal Mind for a knowledge of everything it knows, and the advanced souls avail themselves of this privilege according to their degree of unfoldment. Such souls report the fact of the existence of the Absolute, which had been predicated by the Intellect, but they also report that they are unable to pass over the border.

So you see that the Absolute in itself is Unknowable—all that we can know of it, is what the Universal Mind knows of it, and that knowledge, of necessity, must come from "the outside," the "inside" knowledge being found within the Absolute itself. We may be able to solve the Riddle of the Universe, as we unfold, but we can never hope to know the real nature of the Absolute until we pass beyond the limits of even the highest manifestation of Mind, and pass into a consciousness and realization of our Real Self—Spirit. For this is the Truth, that in each and all of us is to be found a particle of the Absolute itself, unconditioned and unlimited, and that the Real Self of each of us is the Real Self of All—the Spirit, Atman, the drop from the ocean of the Absolute—the ray of the sun of the Absolute— the particle of the Sacred Flame. This Spirit, being the Absolute, of course knows the Absolute and its mysteries and secrets, and when we finally enter into a consciousness of that Spirit we shall then know all, for we shall be at One with the Absolute— at Union with God. This is one of the highest teachings of the Yogi Philosophy.

The teaching is that this tiny bit of the Absolute—which is apparently separated, but is not really separated, from the One—is the highest principle within each soul. Even the lowest form of soul contains it. It is always there, and we may perceive its light to a greater and still greater degree as we unfold and our consciousness moves up a degree toward it. The Spirit is ever there—changeless. But the consciousness of the Ego is constantly moving upward toward the Spirit, and will in time merge in it. This is the end of Spiritual evolution, and all the effort of the soul is toward this goal. Life is the effort of the soul to free itself from its confining sheaths—a desire to avail itself of its inheritance.

We come now to the great Mystery. The student who has followed our teachings closely will now find himself asking the question—that question which has been asked by the souls of all ages when they reached this stage of their unfoldment, or investigation. The question may be expressed in this way: "Why did the Absolute separate itself, or a portion of itself, into parts; or apparent parts; or apparently so separate itself—what was the use—what does it all mean—what was the sense of it? There could have been no necessity for it, for the Absolute is beyond necessity—there could have been no object, for the Absolute possesses all there is, and is perfect—it could not have been the result of any desire, for the Absolute must be desireless.

Therefore why did it emanate into the Universe at all; and why did it cause that which we call 'souls' to exist; and why did it place a portion (or apparent portion) of itself within each soul? As everything must have emanated from the Absolute, and as everything must return to it, what is the use of it all, what does it all mean?"

We have expressed this question as clearly as we can conceive it, and we cheerfully admit that we are unable to answer it, and have seen no answer or explanation worthy of serious consideration. The answer is locked up in the Absolute, and Mind, being a manifestation, cannot grasp that which is beyond the plane of manifestation.

Many thinkers have attempted to answer this question, and the schools of thought of the East and West have indulged in various speculations regarding it. Some say that the separation has not even a shadow of truth in reality, and that Maya, or ignorance and illusion, causes us to see the One as Many. But this does not answer the question—it merely puts it back another stage—for whence comes the illusion, and how could the Absolute be made a subject of illusion? And if we, the projection of the Absolute, fail to see our identity or relationship, then the Absolute must be the cause of the non-seeing. Some would say that we are self-hypnotized into seeing ourselves as separated, but this is no real answer, for if we are hypnotized then the Absolute must be the cause of it, unless we assume that the Absolute is self-hypnotized, which thought is ridiculous. Similar to this is the explanation that this world— the Universe—is but the "dream" of the Absolute. How could the Absolute "dream"? Akin to these so-called explanations is that which holds that the phenomenal world, including Man, is the result of the "play" or "pastime" of the Absolute. Such an explanation is absurd, as it reduces the Absolute to the condition of a child or adult man seeking diversion and "fun." Besides this, such a being would be a Devil rather than a God. Others would have it that the Universe has no existence at all, but is merely a "thought" of the Absolute. This explanation will not answer, for while the emanation probably was occasioned by a process something akin to "thought" as we know it, there is a sense of reality in every human soul that will not admit of its being a "thought" or "daydream." This consciousness of the reality of "I," possessed by each of us, is caused by the sense of the presence of the Spirit, and is a reflection upon our Mind of the knowledge of the real "I" of the Spirit, which is the sense of "I" of the Absolute. The presence of this "I" sense in each is a proof that we are all of the "I" of the Absolute, and are not foreign to the Real Being. This idea of "Brahma's play with the Universe," and his reabsorption of the objects of play into himself, after the sport is over, is the result of a childish mythology that even some of the learned Hindus have allowed to become fastened upon them by the fairy-tales of their ancestors. It is but another form of anthropomorphism—the tendency to make of God an exaggerated Man. We are forced to admit the "illusion" arising from an imperfect conception of the true nature of things, and the Yogi student fully realizes that many things that seem very real to the soul still in the bondage of ignorance—still in the illusion of name and form—are in reality far from being what they seem. He sees self-hypnotization on the part of many, and realizes what it means to be awakened from this world of delusion and to be emancipated, freed, delivered from it all. Nearly every student who reads this lesson has had a greater or less experience of this awakening, or he would not be able to take enough interest in the lesson to read it. But this sense of perception of the illusion, and the comparative "game-tasks" and play of the world, does not carry with it the explanation or reason for it all as it must appear to the Absolute. It may tell us many things about the "How" side of things, but is absolutely silent regarding the "Why" of it. The "How" belongs to the plane of manifestation, and the Universal Mind finds that plane within its jurisdiction. But the "Why" plane belongs to the Absolute itself, and the doors are closed to the Mind. We may actually know—and many of us do—that the Absolute is.

Not only because our Intellect makes necessary the acceptance of the fact, but because the higher regions of the mind give us a positive knowledge of His presence. The soul, when sufficiently unfolded, finds within itself that wonderful something, the Spirit, and knows it to be higher than any phase of Mind. And the Universal Mind (which may be explored by the Adept or Master) finds itself confronted with the Absolute, and cannot doubt its existence. But the soul may not understand the "whyness" of the Spirit, nor the Universal Mind the "Whyness" of the Absolute.

Minds in all ages have endeavored to solve this Mystery of the Absolute and its Manifestations. And equally futile have been their attempts to find the answer. Plotinus, the Greek philosopher, thought that the One could not dwell alone, but must forever bring forth souls from himself. Some of the Hindu writers have thought that love or even desire were the moving reasons for the manifestations; the longing to go out from self; the desire for companionship; the craving for something to love; these and similar reasons were given. Some have even spoken of the Absolute "sacrificing" itself in becoming "many" instead of one. One Hindu writer assumes that the Absolute "causes his life to be divided, not content to be alone." But, in closing this consideration of the "Why," we must remind the student that each of these "explanations" is based upon a mental conception that the Absolute is like a Man, and acts from similar motives, and through a similar mind. It seems that anthropomorphism (the representation of Deity with human attributes) dies hard, and raises its head even in philosophies which claim to have long since performed funeral services over it. The student is cautioned against falling into any of these pitfalls of thought, his safety lying in the recollection that all these so-called "causes" and "explanations" and "theories" arise from an imputation to the Absolute—the Unconditioned—the Unmanifest—the attributes, thoughts, motives, and actions of the Relative, Conditioned, Manifested. The answer to this "Why" can come only from the Absolute, and will be ours only when we reach the consciousness of the Spirit—in the meantime let us be Men, and acknowledge that: "I (in my present state) do not know."

But though we may not know the "Why," we have the whole field of the Universe at our disposal in investigating the "How." And every detail of the working of the Universe is possible to the knowledge of the human mind. In fact, it is already known to the Universal Mind, and to those who are able to explore that vast region to its limits. And every human soul contains, potentially, the knowledge of the Universal Mind. In solution, in every mind, is all the knowledge of the Universe, and the exploration of the whole ocean is but the exploration of the drop. The adept is able to ascertain every bit of "knowledge" possessed by the Universal Mind by the exploration of his own drop of Mind-substance. And he is able to come in contact with all "thought" vibration or waves in the great ocean of Mind, because each drop has relation to every other drop and with the Whole. Knowledge does not come from without, nor is it manufactured by brains. It comes from within, and is simply the ability to grasp that which already exists. All knowledge is known to the Universal Mind, and to our drop of the same, and the "new" knowledge that comes to us is not created, but is drawn from that which already is, the Realization coming from our ability to sense it—our unfoldment. And so, while even the highest developed soul must take "on faith" certain questions regarding the Absolute, still it may assure itself of the existence of that Absolute, and acquaint itself with the "how" of the machinery of the Universe, and even may be able to take a conscious part in the operation of things. The Mind may be used to mould Matter by Energy, and to do things which to the ordinary man might seem miraculous, but which are quite within the realm of the Universal cause and effect. And the developed soul may, by its knowledge, raise itself to a position where it is immune from the operation of cause and effect on the lower planes of manifestation. The Yogis do not ask their students to take everything "on faith," as the riddles of the Universe may be solved by the Mind, and each step verified by actual experiment and experience. There is a Faith that

"Knows"—and the advanced Yogi possesses it. But beware of the teacher who claims to be able to explain by his manifested Mind—by means of manifested thought and expression—to your manifested Mind, the secret and mystery of the "Why" of the Absolute, which is beyond manifestation and knowledge by means of the Mind. When in sore doubt and mental distress over the questions that inevitably arise, from time to time, regarding this last question—this Great Mystery—calm the mind, and open it to the influence of the Spirit, and you will find Peace and Bliss—that "Peace which passeth Understanding."

The Soul is a "Centre of Consciousness" (for want of a better name we call it this). It contains the Divine Spark surrounded by confining sheaths of Mind-substance (in several forms and degrees); Energy, and Matter. Even when it leaves the body upon the occasion of physical death, it does not depart from Matter, for it has several vehicles or bodies of Matter of varying degrees of fineness, the several forms of Mind-substance itself being provided with a very fine "coat" of Matter which separates it from the

Universal Mind in a measure, making it an "entity" while yet in communication with the Universal Mind and other individual minds. It may be called an Ego—or a Spiritual Monad, as some have termed it—names explaining but little. It is projected into Matter of the grossest kind, and from thence works its way by stages of evolution to higher and higher forms until, in the end, after passing through stages when it becomes as a god, it is again taken into the Absolute, not in the form of being "thrown in a melting pot" but in the sense of having a consciousness of the Absolute and realizing its oneness with it. This last fact is known from the testimony of those souls which have reached the last stage preparatory to the attainment of Oneness—Nirvana. There is a stage just before this final attainment, when the soul pauses for a moment which sometimes extends over millions of years, and during which time the soul often temporarily renounces its immediate attainment and returns to the active Universe in order to help other souls on their upward journey. The reason for all of this journey on the Path, from gross Matter unto the highest stages, is known only to the Absolute, as we have explained, but we are fully able to see the progressive steps on the journey, and to feel the attraction of the Absolute as well as the Divine urge within us, causing us to mount step after step of the ladder of Attainment. And we are able to deduce therefrom, both through our Intellects and our higher mental faculties, that that which leads the soul upward is "Right" and "Good," and that which retards its progress, or causes it to linger at some low stage of the journey, is "Wrong" or "Bad," and we are therefore able to deduce rules of conduct and ethics therefrom, although ethics, and the idea of "right and wrong," "good and bad," etc., are all relative as we have explained in our lessons on Dharma. Any step in which is recognized the Oneness of All, is always higher than the step just below it in which the recognition is not so plain. Upon these conceptions depend all that we know as Right and Wrong—"Good and Bad."

The "How" of the projection of the Spirit into Matter—the birth of the Soul, we may call it—is said by those advanced souls who have risen to planes wherein they may witness many of the processes of the Universe, to be caused by an action of Divine Will somewhat akin to the expression of an earnest Desire on the part of Man. God "thinks" and the manifestation occurs. (Of course the act is not "thinking" just as we know the word, but we cannot describe it better.) If we may be pardoned for using an illustration taken from human experience, and if you will remember that we realize the absurdity of comparing any act of the Absolute to any act of Man, we would say that this act of the establishing of the Centre of Consciousness—the birth of a Soul—the projection of Spirit into the confining sheaths of Mind, Energy, and Matter—is in the nature of the pro-creation and birth of a child. The Absolute may be compared to the Father-Mother elements in One—the Spirit may be compared to the child begotten of those elements. The child, in such a case, must be begotten of the nature, character and quality of the parents. The Spirit must be of God, and be the soul of the soul—the sheaths of Matter, Mind and Energy must be the body of the child. And both the soul and body of the child must have been begotten of and composed of the substance of which the parents were composed, for there is nothing else from which it could have been produced. A Western writer named Calthrop hath truly said: "Of the very substance of God (in perfect accordance with the law of all parenthood) we, his children, body as well as soul, come. Verily we are begotten, not made; being of one substance, and children because we are so in very deed and truth."

Like the human child that is plunged into low material form at the beginning, only to grow by degrees into consciousness, self-consciousness, manhood, until it is one with its father in power, form and intelligence, so is this Divine child projected into the lowest form of Matter (which may be called "the body of God") and as it unfolds it rises from lower to higher form, and then on to still higher and higher and higher, until the mind reels at the thought. And at the end when maturity is reached, the soul finds itself before the mansion of the Father, and the doors are opened for it, and it enters and flings itself upon the breast of the Father that is waiting to receive it—and then the doors are closed and we may not see what follows. Safe in the bosom of its father the Soul, now grown to maturity, is resting— it has come home after many weary years of wandering—it has come Home.

Another illustration, that has a meaning that will be apparent to the more advanced of our students, is as follows: As the Sun is reflected in the Ocean, and in every tiny drop of the ocean if they be separated, so is the Absolute (God) reflected in the bosom of the Great Universal Mind and in each individual manifestation of that Mind as a "Soul." The Sun when reflected in the Ocean of the Universal Mind is called The Absolute (God)—when it is reflected in the centre of the drop called the "individual soul" it is called the Spirit. The Reflection is not the Sun itself, and yet it is not an illusion or a false thing—for the Sun has sent forth a part of itself; its energy; its heat; its light; its substance; and so, both the ocean and the drop really partake of the Self of the Absolute—the Spirit of the drop is Real. And this is the miracle and the Mystery, that while the Presence is in the drop, still the Sun itself (as a Whole) is not there, except in appearance. One seeing the reflection in the drop, sees the shape and light of the Sun, and yet the Sun is in the heavens. So that while the Sun is in the drop it is in the heavens—and while it is in the heavens it is in the drop. This is the Divine Paradox—that contains within it the explanation of the Many which is One, and the One which is Many, each being real—each being apparently separated, and yet really not separated. And the Sun may shine on millions of drops, and the drops may reflect millions of Suns in that way. Yet while each drop contains the Sun, still there is only One Sun, and it still remains in the heavens. He who can grasp this parable has grasped the secret of the relation of the Spirit to the Absolute—of the Many to the One. This is our message to our students as we close this series of lessons. Hark ye to it!

May each drop understand that it has within it the Sun of Life, and learn to grow into an actual realization of its Presence. Peace be with You.

41148240R00103

Printed in Poland
by Amazon Fulfillment
Poland Sp. z o.o., Wrocław